Praise for Richard D. Jensen

Reviews for *Tristeza*—

"*Tristeza* is one of those rare novels that live on in the heart of a reader long after the last page. It is a tender love story set in Mexico, and it brims with joy and anguish, with mystery and beauty, with wisdom and miracles. I found myself utterly absorbed in the story of the young gringo cowboy who finds his heart's desire in Mexico. He is no usual cowboy, nor is Mexico of the late 1930s a usual place, and on these remarkable pages we meet Leon Trotsky and Diego Rivera and other charismatic figures of the times, each with a prescription about how life should be lived. This novel should be garlanded with honors."

—Richard S. Wheeler, five-time Spur Award winning author of *Trouble in Tombstone*

"…an interesting mix of old and new, a western set during the Depression, but with a two fisted cowboy hero who packs a six gun. The book has a touch of science fiction to it, too, and somewhat reminds me of the terrific novel, *100 Years of Solitude*…in that the reader is best off to just go with the flow, to just get into the story and let it take you where it will. A romantic story, this one is about true love, about love at first sight, but it is far more than a mere romance…it is a wonderful piece of historical fiction, captures perfectly the flavor or the place and time, and wraps up the reader in a web of unusual action. If you like westerns and like to read something different, do check out *Tristeza*. Richard D. Jensen writes very well, and this is a marvelously good book. I highly recommend it!"

—Tom Ogren, author of *Allergy-Free Gardening*

Reviews for *The Amazing Tom Mix—The Most Famous Cowboy of the Movies*—

"Here is Tom Mix as he really was. Richard D. Jensen has written a captivating biography of the Hollywood actor who enchanted the whole world in the 1920s and '30s. This book is destined to become the standard work on Tom Mix. Drawing on new material, the author brilliantly depicts the flamboyant actor who won and lost it all. This delightful book will enchant anyone, young or old, who has ever wondered what it was like to be on top of the world in early Hollywood. This is one of those special books that will leave a glow in readers. It is a splendid book."

—Richard S. Wheeler, five-time Spur Award winning author of "Trouble In Tombstone."

"…the most complete biography of Mix's life of trials, tribulations and victories."

—John Duncklee, author of "Bull By The Tale.'"

Reviews for *When Curly Won A Cathouse*—

"A funny book about life changing and what to do about it."

—Roundup Magazine

"Helluva good story. Great characters!!!!!"

—John Duncklee, author of *Graciella of the Border*

"The reader will find it fun a'plenty."

—True West Magazine

Reviews for *Ride the Wild Trail*—

"When Tom Mix, Wyatt Earp and Hoot Gibson set out on an adventure just to cure what ails them, you can count on some fun. Richard Jensen's *Ride the Wild Trail* is a richly wrought, comic and nostalgic novel about Hollywood and the

Old West. The flashy Tom Mix, the stern Wyatt Earp, and the cowboy comic Hoot Gibson, all spring to life here in Jensen's engaging story. Jensen had a very good time writing this, and you will have a very good time reading it.

—Richard S. Wheeler, four-time Spur Award winning author

"…Totally fascinating! I really enjoyed 'Ride the Wild Trail'

"…an interesting glimpse into the end of one era and the beginning of another…a fun book!"

—Randi Platt, author of *Honor Bright* and *A Forest Clearing*

"…a fun book!"

—Frank Turner Hollon, author of *The Pains of April* and *The God File*

"…A towering achievement!"

—BarnesandNoble.com

"The perfect Christmas includes giving and receiving *Ride the Wild Trail* and *When Curly Won A Cathouse*, two celebrated western novels by Richard D. Jensen. These enormously funny and bittersweet westerns are both exciting and historically accurate, and are a hit with readers and critics alike."

—True West Magazine

"If you love westerns, or have someone on your holiday list that does, order one today!"

—Shoot Straight Newsletter

Reviews for *Trespass In Hazzard County: My Life As An Insider on the Dukes of Hazzard*—

"The most interesting Hollywood memoir in years."

—booksaholics.com

The Amazing
Tom Mix

The Amazing Tom Mix

◆

The Most Famous Cowboy of the Movies

Richard D. Jensen

iUniverse, Inc.
New York Lincoln Shanghai

The Amazing Tom Mix
The Most Famous Cowboy of the Movies

Copyright © 2005 by Richard D. Jensen

All rights reserved. No part of this book may be used or reproduced by any means, graphic, electronic, or mechanical, including photocopying, recording, taping or by any information storage retrieval system without the written permission of the publisher except in the case of brief quotations embodied in critical articles and reviews.

iUniverse books may be ordered through booksellers or by contacting:

iUniverse
2021 Pine Lake Road, Suite 100
Lincoln, NE 68512
www.iuniverse.com
1-800-Authors (1-800-288-4677)

ISBN-13: 978-0-595-35949-3 (pbk)
ISBN-13: 978-0-595-80402-3 (ebk)
ISBN-10: 0-595-35949-3 (pbk)
ISBN-10: 0-595-80402-0 (ebk)

Printed in the United States of America

For Tom, with the hope that I got it right.

Foreword

I have been intrigued with Tom Mix since 1973, when I watched *Riders of the Purple Sage* (1925) on WTCG, Ted Turner's original cable superstation, in Atlanta, Ga. I was 13 years old at the time and I was immediately struck by this amazing man who seemed—unlike many movie stars—to be the real deal. I began reading and collecting books and articles about Tom, in hopes of one day piecing together the pieces of his life and times for a book. Little did I know that I would not begin writing that book for 32 years.

In the late 1990s I located VHS copies of Tom's films—many of them thought lost. Through collectors, I purchased and watched a great many of Tom's Fox Studios and Selig Polyscope Studios films. Thanks to two other collectors, I now have all of Tom's sound westerns.

These films did much to educate me about Tom's real persona, his mannerisms and his way with guns and horses. For those of us who grow up raising and tending horses and other livestock, it is a way that cowboys judge each other's character.

From 2000 to 2002 I wrote a novel called *Ride the Wild Trail*, a fictional account of Tom on a last hurrah across the west with Wyatt Earp and Hoot Gibson. That book only served to increase my desire to write as true and correct an account of Tom's life, and also to capture his spirit in a biography.

I hope I have done that.

Acknowledgments

Thanks to Richard S. Wheeler, for his mentoring and friendship in the past year. Having the encouragement and wisdom of such a respected novelist and generous human being is a gift upon which one cannot place a value.

Thanks also to John Duncklee, for his sage advice and good humor. In addition to being a gifted writer and raconteur, John is also a wise sage whose wit and sarcasm have helped me appreciate all that I have in the world.

Thanks to Ted Turner, who had thousands of hours of programming to fill on his cable channel and decided one day to run a Tom Mix silent movie, which changed the life of a young boy.

—And to my mother, who sat with me recently and watched *My Pal the King*, and relived a golden moment from her childhood.

A Word of Thanks

Thanks to the University of Oklahoma Library, Western History Collection, for providing me with considerable assistance in the research of this book, especially for providing three invaluable research assistants, Jaymie Long, Brittany McCain, and Camilla Walker, who dug through dusty rooms filled with boxes to find the tiniest extra bit of information for this book. Without their help, this book would be markedly different.

Thanks also to Chad Williams of the Oklahoma Historical Society for his tremendous assistance in providing boxes and boxes of Tom Mix materials and documents which made this book possible.

Thanks to Michelle Parvinrouh for her research help, enthusiasm, insight and friendship.

PREFACE

Tom Mix was killed in a high speed car crash in the Arizona desert. When he died he was one of the most famous men in the world, known to millions of movie fans around the globe as the greatest cowboy star of his generation.

Tom was an action star beyond compare. No other movie star before or since, with the possible exception of martial arts star Jackie Chan, ever risked life and limb as much to bring jaw-dropping stunts to the screen.

By 1940, Tom hadn't made a movie in five years, but his circus and wild west show appearances continued to promote his popularity. Still fit and trim at 60, Mix was rumored to be planning a film comeback, more than 35 years after his first turn before the cameras.

His death made headlines the world over, prompting public expressions of grief as far away as Europe, where he was hailed a hero, and South America, where his machismo was highly praised.

Tom's body was flown home to Hollywood in a sleek, red airplane piloted by famous Hollywood stunt pilot Paul Mantz, who himself would die in a plane crash while making a movie 20 years later. Tom's death met with widespread mourning in Hollywood. His funeral was attended by the luminaries of Tinseltown, many of whom had labored behind the scenes of Tom's films before their own stars rose.

Once a multimillionaire, Tom died nearly broke by the standards of his Hollywood heyday, but his net worth was still well ahead of the average American in 1940.

Sixty five years later, Tom Mix's name and his image linger, mostly because he was the archetype for every "B western" hero that followed him. Dressed in bright, gaudy shirts, form-fitting embroidered pants, brightly-colored custom boots and an enormous high-crowned, wide-brimmed Stetson, Tom was the model of the modern cowboy hero.

With each generation, Tom's fame dims, mostly due to the sheer passage of time and the fact that the bulk of his film work is lost to time—and the films that do exist are in the archaic silent film format.

This book is designed to prevent any further fading of the memory of Thomas Hezekiah Mix, a man who rose from poverty to become the highest paid movie star in the world at a time when movies were silent and tickets cost a penny.

1

Thomas Hezekiah Mix was born on January 6, 1880 in Drift Run, also known as Mix Run, near Cameron, Pennsylvania. He was not born in El Paso, Texas as his Hollywood publicists insisted when Tom was a full-fledged movie star. Various records conflict, but Tom was most likely born in a small, rural, two-story wood frame house near Driftwood, a small town near the Bennett Branch of the Susquehanna River in Cameron County.[1]

Tom was the third child and second son of the marriage of Elias Edwin Mix, an English-Irish lumberjack and horse teamster who was born in 1855 in Mix Run and Elizabeth Mix nè Hiestand, a petite woman of Pennsylvania Dutch blood who was born in 1859 in Lancaster, Pennsylvania.[2]

Elias Mix, who was usually called Ed, had married Elizabeth in 1875, a year after he met her.[3] He was a tall, gaunt man with a hard jaw and steely eyes and a prominent hook nose. Tom Mix's looks would favor his father throughout his life, though his height would not match his father's, no doubt the result of his mother's genes. Elizabeth Mix was an industrious woman who had been raised by her grandparents Samuel and Mary Feltenberger Smith, who ran a tavern called Halfway House because it was located halfway between the towns of Mt. Joy and Marietta, Pennsylvania.[4]

The elder Mix worked as a lumberjack and teamster hauling logs with draft horses in the dense Allegheny Mountains.[5] As was the custom of the time, Ed Mix wanted a big family, and he was delighted to have a second son. He and Elizabeth would celebrate the birth of their second daughter, Esther in 1881.[6]

In 1884 the Mix family moved into Driftwood. Ed Mix had been working for John E. DuBois, a timber magnate who owned a large estate nearby. In 1888, DuBois needed a coachman and stable manager and, aware Ed Mix's skill with horses, decided to make him manager of his stable. DuBois was under pressure from his wife who was distressed that the family's current coachman was unable to properly back a team of horses without running the heavy, wooden wagon wheels onto the manicured lawns around the DuBois' enormous English Tudor mansion. When Ed Mix arrived at the DuBois estate, he was asked to back a wagon and team down the long driveway without running the wagon onto the lawns. Ed Mix was said to have a magic touch with horses and he completed the task with such skill that he was immediately hired.[7]

Ed Mix returned home and told his wife and family and they moved expeditiously to DuBois.

The coachman's job was perfect for Ed because DuBois was an avid horseman and breeder of fine harness racing stock. The men developed a close relationship, within the parameters of the master-servant relationship. For Tom, living in DuBois was idyllic. He had inherited his love of horses from his father and each day he hung around the stables, playing in the hay lofts, watching and learning by example the proper way to handle horses.[8] He once said that his father "could do about anything with a horse, except make him speak."[9]

Tom hated attending school at the one room schoolhouse and was always chomping at the bit to get out of doors.

Tragedy struck when Tom's older brother, Harry, died at age 15 from a heart attack caused by a freak incident. Harry had sat down on the overstuffed chair where Elizabeth often did her sewing and a tiny sewing needle penetrated the skin on his arm. Efforts to remove it caused a small piece to break off, which ended up in Harry's vein. The rush of blood returning to the heart took the needle tip with it and, when it reached the Harry's heart, he had a massive coronary.[10]

The family was grief-stricken. Tom, four years younger than his brother, no doubt felt profound grief at the death of his older brother. Ed and Elizabeth buried their eldest son and stoically went on about the business of raising a family.

Elizabeth insisted that Tom return to school, which he did until the fifth grade, when he quit and refused to return. By then he had undergone a life changing experience—he had seen Buffalo Bill's Wild West Show.[11]

Colonel William F. "Buffalo Bill" Cody was the most famous frontiersman in American history, due in part to his heroic deeds during the westward expansion of the nation into the Great Plains and in part to his skill at self-promotion. Indeed Cody became the first world-famous celebrity in modern history, touring with his wild west show and "Congress of Rough Riders" throughout the United States and Europe for decades.[12]

The Buffalo Bill show was the first major traveling show to bill itself as a "wild west show." The concept was simple. Audiences would be treated to a panorama of the western experience, from stagecoach robberies and Indian attacks to exhibitions of mounted shooting and trick shooting. The hero in the center of it all was Buffalo Bill, who rode to the rescue in the stagecoach robbery and the Indian attack on the frontier cabin. Hundreds of authentic cowboys and Indians were employed by Cody, who mixed reality with dime novel fantasy. Indeed, Cody mixed the reality and fantasy of the American west so convincingly that he cemented the iconography of the American west in the consciousness of the entire world.[13] When Tom became famous, he put his own stamp on that western iconography for decades to come.

The best estimate is that Tom Mix went to see Cody's show in 1890. From that moment on he made it plain that he wanted to be a cowboy or a frontier sheriff.

"My first boyhood dreams were when I was learning to ride a horse," Tom said years later. "My desire at that time was to be a topnotch sheriff in the West where a man had to be a man."[14]

Such was the effect that Cody had on boys of that time. When Cody's show played in Saginaw, Michigan on July 16, 1898, the police chief's son was inspired to become a cowboy. That youth moved to Wyoming, became a top cowhand and later an officer in the U.S. Cavalry and still later one of the most popular movie cowboys of all time—Tim McCoy.[15]

Along with his boyhood friends, Tom borrowed his mother's rope clothesline and the boys went into the DuBois pastures to try to rope the cows. It became such a favorite pastime that the boys became a nuisance and Elizabeth heard constant complaints about the boys roping and tying cows belonging to neighbors.[16]

Inspired by Cody and influenced by Ed's magic with horses, Tom went about learning how to handle horses with great enthusiasm. He practiced on any horse, donkey or mule he could get his hands on, and taught himself flying mounts, where a rider grabs a running horse and vaults onto its back. Tom even taught himself to "roman ride," where the rider stands on the horses back while it runs.[17]

While Ed and Elizabeth had little quarrel with Tom's infatuation with wild feats of horsemanship, they were horrified by such antics as the boy's youthful attempts at trick shooting and knife throwing, usually with his sister, Esther, as his assistant.[18] It was during one of these forays into self-taught trick shooting that Tom was nearly killed. When a bullet lodged in the chamber of Tom's single-shot pistol, he and friend Denny Dwyer attempted to dislodge the bullet with Denny's pocket knife. The gun went off as the barrel was pointed at Tom's left knee. The bullet hit Tom above the kneecap, barely missing the joint.[19] Had it struck Tom's kneecap, he would have never ridden a horse again and history would have been changed drastically.

Tom and Denny, frantic that Tom's parents would find out, began digging clumsily for the bullet with a pocket knife. The bloody wound became worse. Denny helped Tom bandage the wound with a rag and Tom raced home to get help from his mother. Elizabeth dug for the bullet but could not find it. She gave up and cleaned and bandaged the leg, which healed without complication.[20]

It wasn't long before Tom was back to his usual antics, undeterred. Indeed, Tom carried the bullet in his leg for more than 16 years before it was removed.[21]

Tom's infatuation with living the cowboy life was encouraged when Elizabeth made Tom his first cowboy outfit. An expert seamstress, she cut and sewed a short, charro jacket with fancy embroidery and some leather chaps with conchas down the out seams. She also sewed a matching band along the brim of a wide-brimmed hat Tom had acquired. The results are still available in a photo dated 1892, in which Tom stands as proudly as any 12-year-old cowboy could, posing for a photographer with his rifle and single-shot pistol in front of a painted forest panorama.[22] The photo bears witness to Tom's vibrant youth. He is athletically built, with long straight legs and arms. His face is handsome, his dark eyes penetrating. His mouth is straight and firm and his nose is prominent, much like his father's.

Elizabeth Mix remembered that it was Tom who sewed his first cowboy outfit in a 1935 newspaper interview. "When he was 12 years old, he made his own first cowboy suit. He sewed some old rick-rack lace along the leg of his trousers. Then he cut off his coat and made a jacket which he trimmed with fringe from a red broadcloth table cover.[23]

With some money he earned from tending some cows, Tom bought himself an old revolver and a rifle."[24]

Tom grew into adolescence ever more aware of his family's social status. It wasn't hard to see. Each day his father went to work on the estate of one of the richest men in Pennsylvania, who lived in an enormous Tudor mansion with ceiling-to-floor cut-glass windows and owned prized race horses.[25]

He entered his teens as a rambunctious youth, athletic and agile, prone to fistfights and rowdy behavior.[26]

Despite his lack of scholastic effort, Tom was permitted to play on the DuBois High School football team. When he could no longer play football at the school, he continued to play games for amateur leagues and for civic leagues. He also played baseball and took up bicycle racing.[27]

All of this athleticism would follow Tom for the rest of his life. Whether he worked as a bartender, town sheriff, cowboy, movie star or circus performer, Tom kept in shape in the gymnasium, boxing and lifting weights. He also watched what he ate. An examination of photos of Tom throughout his life reveal that his physique rivaled those of modern triathletes.

By the time he was 18, Tom was also working for the DuBois estate, helping his father with the horses and doing farm labor. That would change when the United States battleship *Maine* was sunk in the harbor of Cuba's capital city, Havana. The ship had been sent there by President McKinley on the pretext of protecting American lives in Cuba, a Spanish colony, from the totalitarian Spanish colonial government. When the ship exploded and sank on February 15, 1898, yellow journalists loyal to pro-war elements in the halls of power stoked American sentiment into an all-out nationalistic war fever. Five days before the U.S. declared war on Spain, Tom quit his job at the DuBois estate and took a train to Washington, D.C. to enlist.[28]

It was a time when war still held an image of valor and honor among the general public. Cynicism about war and national policy would not become prevalent until the 1960s, when the military action in Vietnam would fuel antiwar sentiments and change public attitudes about the goals of warfare.

Tom was caught up in the promise of battlefield glory and adventure and he took his pre-enlistment physical on April 28, 1898, the day the U.S. government declared war on Spain. Tom enlisted into the U.S. Army at Washington Barracks, D.C. and was assigned to Battery M, Fourth Regiment, U.S. Army Artillery. The records of Tom's pre-enlistment medical exam and interview have survived. Tom's physique was described by First Lt. A.N. Stack, assistant surgeon, U.S. Army, as a man of good health. He was five feet, eight inches tall, and weighed 148 pounds. He had a 36-inch chest and 33-inch waist. His hair and eyes were listed as dark brown. Tom had signs of numerous scars from various injuries as a youth, including the bullet wound scar over his left knee, which, amazingly, Dr. Stack did not recognize as a bullet wound.

When Tom was interviewed by Second Lt. C. C. Williams of the Sixth Artillery, he found Tom to be a well-spoken and intelligent young man.[29]

What is telling about Tom's interview record is that it contains false and misleading information. Indeed, during the rest of his life, including much of his entertainment career, Tom would fabricate his exploits, or allow others to do it for him. To begin with, he lists his name as Thomas E. Mix rather than Thomas H. Mix, and he lies on the form when asked if his name is an assumed one. He would claim his middle name was Edwin for the rest of his life, no doubt in honor of his beloved father.

Tom lied and said he was 21 when he was only 18. This issue was relevant because, for Tom to enlist at 18, he needed his parents' signatures. By changing his age, Tom could enlist without his parents' permission. It is unknown if Ed and Elizabeth objected to Tom entering the military. No doubt they worried that

Tom, their only surviving son, would die on a mosquito-infested tropical island, or return with malaria or some other tropical ailment.

When asked on the recruitment form if he had ever had a brother or sister die, Tom wrote "none." One must wonder why Tom didn't mention his brother Harry's untimely demise. When asked if he'd ever suffered any injury, he doesn't mention his bullet wound.

What is most intriguing in hindsight is Tom's answer to question number 13, which asked if Tom understood the meaning of General Order No. 68 and its definition of "desertion." Tom wrote "yes." He would desert from the army four years later to become a cowboy.[31]

2

A wise person once described military service as months of unendurable boredom punctuated by moments of sheer terror. Tom learned about the boredom almost immediately. For a restless, rambunctious 18-year-old, the Army was not what it was cracked up to be.

Tom enlisted, full of dreams of war glory and adventure, and accepted his assignment to Battery M with great excitement. He was then shipped to the wilds of Delaware, where he would encounter abject boredom almost immediately. Battery M had been assigned the task of guarding an enormous supply of brown prismatic gunpowder. The DuPont plant in Montchanin, Delaware was producing 25,000 pounds of the gunpowder per day. The plant was located on Brandywine Creek, which drained into the Delaware River. The plants were fort-like structures which utilized water power to turn the stone wheels which ground the powder.[1]

Tom underwent artillery training on 50-ton big guns which fired 10, 11 and 12-inch shells. He was promoted to corporal on July 1, 1898, but the Spanish-American War ended before the end of the month and Tom realized he had little chance to see combat.

When his unit was transferred to Fort Constitution, New Hampshire on November 24, 1898, Tom was in line for a promotion to sergeant, which he received on New Years Eve, 1898.[2]

Try as he might, Tom was bored as a soldier in a heavy artillery unit charged with defending the United States coastline from invading Spanish forces. It was like watching paint dry. Not much changed for Tom until he was transferred to Battery O in Fort Monroe, Virginia in April 1899.[3]

Fort Monroe, in addition to being an artillery battery, was also home to the National Soldier's Home, which served as a hospital set up to treat soldiers returning from the war. Tom spent his time doing construction and remodeling labor as part of an upgrade of the facilities. He also visited the old soldiers in the nursing home and listened to their tales of battlefield valor.[4] Some of the tales Tom heard from these old soldiers likely became part of Tom's public relations years later.

Tom served out his enlistment in Fort Hancock, New Jersey and at age 21 reenlisted for a second tour of duty on April 26, 1901.[5] By the time he had signed up for his second tour Tom had grown two inches and put on 27 pounds of muscle.[6]

He was given a two-week re-enlistment furlough and headed to Fort Monroe to see friends. While there, he met a strikingly beautiful school teacher name Grace Allen, the daughter of a Louisville, Kentucky furniture dealer. Tom was instantly attracted to her and fell head-over-heels in love. Whatever experience Tom had with women prior to meeting Grace is unknown. What is known is that Tom wanted to marry Grace almost immediately. He returned reluctantly to Fort Hancock and it wasn't until 14 months later that he was able to take another furlough on July 12, 1902. He went straight to Fort Monroe to see Grace.[7]

Six days later Tom and Grace were married in Louisville by Justice of the Peace Ed Meglemry. Grace's father did not attend the wedding, but her mother and two sisters did. After a 12 day honeymoon, Tom returned to his post in Fort Hancock and Grace returned to Fort Monroe.[8]

There was trouble from the beginning. Grace did not like living apart from Tom and began to pressure him to return to civilian life so that they could be a normal couple. It wasn't long before she gave him an ultimatum. He had to choose between the Army or her.[9]

Tom's choice would forever alter his life.

On October 25, 1902, First Sergeant Thomas E. Mix went "AWOL"—absent without leave. It had started with a furlough which began five days earlier.[10] Tom had told his superiors that he was traveling to Pittsburgh, Pennsylvania, but it is likely he went to Fort Monroe to reunite with Grace.

Tom's AWOL status was changed on November 4, 1902 when he was officially listed as a deserter.[11]

Now that he was a wanted man, Tom had to put some distance between himself and his old stomping grounds, so he rounded up Grace and they headed west to the Oklahoma Territory.[12] Oklahoma had only been opened up for settlement by whites on April 22, 1889 in the Great Oklahoma Land Rush.[13] Prior to that the massive territory was called Indian Territory and was a haven for outlaws and renegades. Such a wild outpost was perfect for Tom for two reasons—firstly he still harbored a strong desire to be a cowboy and frontier marshal and secondly the chances of anyone discovering that he was a deserter were slim and none.[14]

Tom didn't know at the time that the U.S. Army did little to pursue deserters in 1902. There was no policy in place to hunt them down and army records indicate that Tom's commanding officer did not pursue his arrest and did not sign a federal arrest warrant for him.[15]

Tom and Grace settled in the town of Guthrie, Oklahoma Territory. Grace found a job teaching school and Tom found two jobs—teaching physical fitness in the basement of the Carnegie Library and tending bar at the Blue Belle Saloon on West Harrison Avenue. The bar was the preeminent watering hole for cattleman and territorial legislators, who often belied up to the bar and then sauntered upstairs to the brothel. From there these men of high position could discreetly take the wrought iron catwalk from the second floor brothel across the alley to the next door Elks Hotel.[16]

Tom also earned extra money breaking horses for local ranchers. Without a ranch of his own, Tom used a corral adjacent to the railroad depot owned by the Santa Fe Railroad.[17] Before long the townspeople began to take notice of this energetic, vibrant man with the flashing brown eyes and quick smile.

Ranchers who stopped into the Blue Belle soon learned that Tom the friendly bartender was also Tom the local wrangler and bronco buster. Zack Mulhall, owner of the Mulhall Ranch,[18] and the notorious George and Zack Miller, owners of the Miller Brothers 101 Ranch,[19] encountered Tom both at the corral and in the saloon and took an instant liking to the young, athletic man. Newspaper editor Thomas B. Ferguson, the Oklahoma territorial governor appointed by President Theodore Roosevelt, also thought highly of Tom.[20] Their friendship would make Tom a lifelong Republican.

About a year after arriving in Guthrie, Tom could see Grace was unhappy. Soon after that, she packed her things and returned to Kentucky, where her father instituted annulment proceedings.[21] What lead to the dissolution of the marriage is unknown, but it is likely that Grace, who was used to a comfortable life, found the wild and wooly Oklahoma Territory a little too wild and wooly for her. Tom spent most of his day away from home, breaking horses while Grace worked all day as a school teacher only to spend her nights alone while Tom tended bar in the saloon. In the era when men showed little sensitivity to women's emotions, Tom spent his time hanging out around other men in a perpetual state of "boy's night out."

Indeed Tom's drinking had picked up since he'd joined the army. When he first enlisted in 1898 at age 18, he told the army he only drank "slightly."[22] By the time he reenlisted he classified his drinking as "in moderation."[23] It is not unlikely that his drinking increased working in a saloon. He would turn to alcohol with increasing frequency as his fame grew and his fortunes waned.

Throughout Tom's life and his five marriages, one pattern emerges—that the women were married to Tom and not the other way around. His restless energy and pursuit of good times often kept him far from home and hearth. Such was the army way. Such was the cowboy way. Such was the way of traveling wild west and circus performers, and such was the way of cowboy action movie stars. In his entire life, Tom never once lived a 9 to 5 existence. Tom's path took him to far-flung places as he sought to escape the boredom of the everyday existence.

Zack Mulhall, in addition to being a rancher, was also a livestock agent for the St. Louis and San Francisco railroad. He also dabbled in wild west shows.[24] When Grace left Tom, Mulhall felt sorry for the normally cheerful young man. To ease Tom's depression, Mulhall and Ferguson suggested that Tom join the Oklahoma Cavalry Band as a drum major. Tom had no musical training and was a deserter from the U.S. Army, and he was not a member of the Oklahoma militia, but he applied for the job and was accepted. The drum major's job was to dress up in a uniform resplendent with epaulets and fine embroidery and march at the head of the band carrying a large staff. He was responsible for raising and lowering the staff as he marched in time to the music, in essence conducting the music the way a conductor guides a symphony with his tiny baton.[25]

When the World's Fair was opened in St. Louis, Missouri in 1904, Tom and the Oklahoma Cavalry Band attended the dedication of the Oklahoma building.[26] The concept of World's Fairs was a unique one for its time. Prior to mass media and televised images, most people got their news and information from newspapers and books. Photography was still primitive at the time and few people had the opportunity to see much of life and culture beyond their nuclear communities. A World's Fair was a giant exposition, filled with exhibits from around the world. It was at these fairs that most Americans of the day saw their first exotic animals and their first indigenous people from far off countries in the Middle and Far East. The St. Louis World's Fair was an enormous undertaking and attracted tens of thousands of people from all over the nation and the world.

At the opening of the Oklahoma Building, Tom lead the band and was described by a St. Louis newspaper as "a gallant figure who attracted a great deal of attention, especially from the ladies."[27] Tom took notice of the attention he was getting in his fancy, gold-embroidered uniform. It was the first time he realized that gaudy dress would get him noticed and it would become a habit for him. Throughout the rest of his life, Tom was always a flashy dresser. When he became the highest paid movie star in the world, his clothing was the topic of much conversation, especially when he wore jewelry and belt buckles imbedded with platinum and precious jewels.

During this time Tom also learned the value of self-promotion. He learned the art of the tall tale, spun as only cowboys can spin them. He would use this tale-telling for two reasons—to create a persona that would intrigue his fans and to distract them from the truth that he was a man who had deserted from the U.S. Army.

Zack Mulhall brought his "Colonel Zack Mulhall Wild West Show" to St. Louis and in doing so changed history. It was at the World's Fair that Tom Mix met the Cherokee Kid, a part-Indian cowboy and trick roper named Will Rogers.[28] Tom took an instant liking to Will, who was everything in life that Tom wanted to be. Indeed, Tom would later adopt many of Will's mannerisms and much of his background to embellish his own life story, and to prevent anyone from discovering that he was a deserter. Surprisingly, Will Rogers was such an affable man, and he had such warm feelings for Tom, that he never bridled at Tom's antics.

Will Rogers had grown up in the Indian Territory. As a kid he'd become a master with the lariat, and with each passing year learned more and more complex tricks. Soon he could swing multiple lassos at a time and catch three and four horses at once.[29] Tom would learn this trick and utilize it in his wild west show for years. The trick is captured on film in the 1932 Tom Mix film, *My Pal the King*.

During the St. Louis World's Fair, Tom and Will spent considerable time together. Tom and Will were about the same age and had similar interests.[30] Will told Tom tales of training horses in South Africa during the Boer War and of wrangling horses for the U.S. Army in China during the Boxer Rebellion. Tom thereafter would claim the same résumé. Tom watched as Will took part in the daily rodeo as a rodeo clown.[31] He would entertain the crowd with jokes and antics and act as a lifeguard for cowboys who got into trouble during the events, much the same as rodeo clowns do today.

During one performance, an incident occurred which brought Will his first brush with fame. A steer went berserk and leapt over the fence rail and into the stands. It charged into the crowd, it's enormous horns slashing at the panicked, fleeing bystanders. Will leapt the fence, ran into the stands and roped and hogtied the steer in short order. The crowd cheered as Will dragged the steer out of the stands and back into the arena.

The announcer asked Will why he'd dragged the steer out of the stands and Will quipped, "He didn't have a ticket." The legend of Will Rogers, the Cherokee Kid, was born. The incident made newspapers worldwide and overnight Will Rogers was a household name.[32]

Broadway beckoned and famed impresario Flo Ziegfeld booked Will as a featured act in his enormously popular show, the Ziegfeld Follies.[33] From that point on Will became as famous for his wit and wisdom as for his roping and from there he went on to star in vaudeville, Broadway, then radio and newspapers and then the movies.[34]

One afternoon, during a break between afternoon performances, Tom and Will were hanging around the fairgrounds when a dark-haired part Cherokee girl named Olive Stokes walked up to Will to say hello. Will was happy to see her and introduced Tom to the lovely 17-year-old.[35] Olive was born on April 10, 1887 on the Stokes Ranch near the town of Dewey in the Oklahoma Territory. She was dark, athletic and beautiful and carried herself with a striking confidence.

In her often wildly inaccurate memoir entitled *The Fabulous Tom Mix*, Olive Stokes recalled that meeting. She had come to St. Louis because a painting she had painted was being exhibited in the Indian Territory's pavilion at the fair. Her father had only recently passed away and she was in a deep depression which she called an "awful period of sorrow" and "an abyss of grief."[36]

Olive remembered that she blushed when she was introduced to Tom because she felt "an immediate attraction" to him.[37] While she was only 17, girls grew up quickly on the frontier and Olive recalled that she approached Tom as "a sober girl reaching for maturity."[38]

Will offered to take Olive to dinner but Tom butted in, clearly as attracted to Olive as she was to him. As they chatted for a half an hour Olive learned two things about Tom—he barely spoke unless spoken to and he was a bundle of energy, constantly fidgeting with his hands, usually twirling a rope.[39]

Tom and Will bid Olive goodbye because they had to perform with Zack Mulhall's show. Olive said that Tom and Will gave a performance equal to that given by Buffalo Bill Cody.[40]

After the show, Tom asked Olive if he could escort her to the Fair the next day. She accepted his invitation only after Will assured her that Tom was a man to be trusted. The next morning Tom arrived at the Jefferson Hotel, where Olive was staying under the watchful eye of owner Lyman T. Hay, a friend of her late father. Will would later tell Olive that Tom had sheepishly admitted to the Cherokee cowboy that he'd waited in the lobby all night for morning to come so he could see Olive.[41]

Tom and Olive had breakfast together and then headed for the Fair, where Olive admitted she gabbed all day long about herself. It wasn't until their date was about over before she realized that Tom hadn't said a word. When she apologized, Tom flashed a "wonderful, meaningful smile" and said, "I think you're going to learn all about me some day."

They parted later that day when Olive took a train back to the Oklahoma Territory.[42] They would not see each other again for four years, and thereafter their lives—for better and worse—would be intertwined until Tom's death.

It was at the World's Fair that Zack Mulhall got into a shootout with three men. There is no indication that Tom was present at the time of the shooting, but one can surmise that Tom's estimation of Mulhall grew when he learned that his benefactor has shot it out with three men and lived to tell about it.[43] He would later go to work for Mulhall's ranch and wild west show, but the men would have a rocky relationship in years to come.

Tom left the Oklahoma Cavalry Band when it traveled through Oklahoma City and fell immediately on hard times. He managed to survive by tending bar in a saloon on Robinson Avenue.[44]

When Teddy Roosevelt was elected president in 1904, Seth Bullock, a famous South Dakota lawman and businessman, formed a contingent of cowboys to travel to the nation's capital to herald the new president's inauguration. Dubbed Seth Bullock's Cowboy Brigade, or simply the Cowboy Brigade, the cowboys took their horses and boarded a Union Pacific train and headed for Washington, D.C.[45]

Tom learned about the herd of cowboys headed east to salute the famous soldier and Republican politician from some cowboys who rode with the Zack Mulhall's show. When the train stopped in Omaha, Tom loaded his horse and joined the Cowboy Brigade. To his surprise, many of the cowboys he'd met at the World's Fair were there, including a large contingent from the Mulhall Wild West Show.[46]

The train filled with cowboys arrived in Washington, D.C. on a brisk spring day, March 4, 1905.[47] The 20th Century was only five years old, but the sight of real cowboys riding en masse down Pennsylvania Avenue caused a stir. Everywhere the cowboys went people stopped and pointed and stared and waved.[48] To Tom's great joy, Zack Mulhall's troupe of cowboys was enlisted to entertain the new president at the inauguration.[49] Tom performed for President Roosevelt along with the brigade.[50]

In the photo of the event, Tom—dressed in a bright white shirt and hand-tooled chaps—stands out from the crowd of drab cowboys.

By the time the Cowboy Brigade disbanded, Tom had settled nicely into the lifestyle of a footloose Oklahoma cowboy. Tom no longer wore shoes and wore only cowboy boots and a cowboy hat. He had begun to remake himself in the image of his friend, mentor—and some would say idol—Will Rogers.

3

Tom Mix became a cowboy and frontier lawman—and a husband again—because he was in the right place at the right time.

Tom had been tending bar and was generally disgusted with the life of a barkeep.[1] The only good thing he had going for him was that he was living in the Perrine Hotel, located at the corner of Robinson Street and Park Avenue, not far from the saloon, and that he was courting the owner's daughter Jewell, who was known as "Kitty."[2]

Tom had asked Kitty to marry him but by early 1905 he was virtually broke and had little prospects.[3]

Fate had stepped in again when Tom met Zack and Joe Miller, two of the co-owners of the Miller Brothers 101 Ranch, when they came into the Blue Belle Saloon for a drink.[4]

Tom knew well who the Miller Brothers were. They owned or leased a total of 110,000 acres of Indian Territory land that swallowed up three entire towns—Bliss (called Marland today), Red Rock and White Eagle—and covered most of four counties, including Kay, Noble, Osage and Pawnee counties.[5]

The ranch was so huge it cost $50,000 just to fence it and used more than 300 miles of wire just to accomplish the task. The ranch was such a large cattle producing operation that the Santa Fe Railroad built a special line of track to reach its stock yards.[6]

The Miller Brothers were the sons of family patriarch Colonel George Washington Miller, who founded the 101 Ranch in 1871 by making peace with the Ponca Indians and leasing their land from them. By 1905, the 101 was modernized, with its own electrical generation plant, self-run telephone system, daily intraranch mail service. In short, the 101 Ranch was largely self-sufficient. The ranch operated its own schools and churches, grocery stores, creamery, a modern dairy, meat-packing plant, cannery, tannery, cider mill, alfalfa mill, and after oil was discovered on the ranch, even its own oil refinery. The 101 ran a herd of some 25,000 cattle, 10,000 hogs, and hundreds of horses and employed hundreds of cowhands to keep up with the herds. Additionally, Joe Miller was a zealous horticulturist who created many hybrid strains of fruits and vegetables, which he planted on hundreds of acres to provide grain for the livestock and to sell as seed stock.[7]

The Miller family was rich beyond anyone's imagination, even before oil was discovered on their land. And Joe Miller liked Tom Mix.[8]

All three of the Miller brothers liked Tom so much that they gave Tom his first job as a cowboy and later featured him in their immensely successful wild west show.[9] The Millers would become the first of many entrepreneurs who would expand their entertainment enterprises from their dude ranch to the sawdust trail to the newfangled flickers, and Tom would have his first experiences on camera working in the primitive short films made by the 101 Ranch company.[10]

At the time, though, the Miller brothers were enormously successful cattle ranchers who had operated for years in the Indian Territory that became Oklahoma. Their ranch house, a grand white structure which many felt outclassed the White House in Washington, D.C., was a testament to their wealth and power. They would grow richer still when oil was discovered and their investments would become part of a giant conglomerate that would later become Conoco.[11]

Tom happened to mention to Joe, Zack and George Miller that he was sick of bartending and wanted to work outside breaking horses and punching cattle in the open air.[12]

Tom left his bartender job and rode to the 101 Ranch where the Millers put him to work wrangling dudes and doing odd jobs as a cowboy.[13]

Zack sent Tom to New York City to ride bucking horses for the show the Millers were putting on at Madison Square Garden.[14] During the performance, Tom recreated the berserk steer incident that had made Will Rogers famous in St. Louis with less than spectacular results. This time, Tom stepped into Will Rogers' boots. Somehow a steer got loose in the crowd—though it is completely likely that it was allowed to get into the audience—and Tom chased it into the stands.[15] Will Rogers recalled years later that this event took place in 1903 and remembered that both he and Mix performed in the show with Zack Mulhall's show.

The April 28, 1905 New York Herald recounted the incident, noting that a "celebrated rope thrower" named "Tom Mixico" tried to rope the steer but missed and the steer got away.[16] There is no indication if the reporter got Tom's name wrong or if Tom gave an alias to avoid detection by authorities as a deserter. Tom would use the name on and off for several years. It is possible he used it to make his stage name more exotic as Mixico is similar to the word "Mexico." Tom was dark eyed and dark haired and often wore large cowboy hats. Perhaps the idea was to make audiences assume he was from south of the border. Another story is that the name was Will Rogers' nickname for Tom.[17]

"Tom Mix was with us," Rogers said. "That was his first start on his wild west career. We didn't have much money; in fact, our salary was supposed to be $20 a week. That was one time we were not overpaid actors, because we didn't even get the twenty."[18]

A funny story from that time period involved a night when Will and Tom had $5 between them. Tom offered to keep the money in his pants pocket. Having no money for a hotel, they opted to sleep that night in the barn. Tom hung his pants from the wall of a horse stall and Will hung his hat next to Tom's pants. The story goes that a mule in the next stall ate Tom's pants, Will's hat and the $5. Supposedly, the next day's performance featured Will Rogers without his hat and Tom Mix with his chaps over his longjohns.[19]

The story is typical Will Rogers whimsy. Indeed, mules are herbivores and would not likely eat a beaver felt hat any more than cotton blue jeans. Had a mule eaten such things, it would likely have gotten colic and died in short order. Still, Will Rogers was fond of telling the story when he and Tom had both become famous.

In any event, Tom often used the name until he began to achieve fame, at which time he reverted back to the name Tom Mix and thereafter made no attempt to hide his identity.

After the New York show, Tom returned to the 101 Ranch and continued his daily employment as a cowboy.[20] Since coming west he had learned one thing—the west was an enormous place filled with surprisingly few people. In his short time in the region he had met numerous celebrated figures, including Seth Bullock, Will Rogers, Zack Mulhall and the Miller Brothers. Before the end of 1905 he would meet Geronimo, the famous Apache warrior.

Tom was delighted with the ranch job and performing in the wild west show, even if it only paid cowboys' wages of $15 per month plus room and board. To him, he was finally a real cowboy, a goal he'd set back in DuBois, Pennsylvania when he was only 10 years old. He was now 25 years old and happy to be working out of doors, living the romantic life of a footloose cowboy. Little did Tom know that his life would be changed forever.

Cowboys who worked for the 101 generally worked the spring, summer and fall and were let go in the winter until the next spring roundup. This was true of most ranch operations throughout the American West. Tom was no different. He soon discovered, however, that working for the Miller brothers was different from working for most ranches in other ways. The Millers ran their ranch as both a working ranch and as a tourist attraction. The highly successful dude ranch operation would evolve into a hugely successful wild west show and the Millers, ever mindful of the tenderfeet and their dollars, kept coming up with ways to relieve the greenhorns of their money.

4

When Tom Mix went to work at the 101 Ranch in early spring 1905, he discovered his destiny.

The ranch was more than just a working cattle ranch. The cattle industry suffered from severe market swings and ranchers who relied solely on traditional cattle raising often went bust. Joe, George and Zack Miller, as heirs to their father's throne, knew that if they did nothing but ranch they would like suffer the same fate as many big ranchers who went under.

When the ranch was founded in Indian Territory 25 years before, it survived because much of its land was leased from Ponca Indians at favorable prices.[1]

Additionally, the Millers were not above the use of force and other chicanery to survive in the wild and untamed Indian land. When cattle prices dipped, the Miller brothers knew that they had to find some way to diversify their business beyond agriculture.[2]

Their fortunes would take a turn for the better when the Miller brothers heard that a national convention of newspaper editors was due to be held in Oklahoma City. The Millers had an uncanny idea: They would shuttle the editors out to the ranch and put on a grand exposition of western culture that would make the headlines in newspapers nationwide.[3]

The idea caught fire and before long the Miller Brothers 101 Ranch was joined by Zack Mulhall and his wild west show and the Pawnee Bill Wild West. This combined wild west shows enlisted the aid of the Ponca Indians to add even more local grandeur.

The enormity of the undertaking is astounding even by today's standards. More than 65,000 people took 53 trainloads on the journey from Oklahoma City to Bliss. Each train to the 101 carried more than 1200 people.[4]

The trains were so packed that people had to ride atop the train cars.[5]

One of the most bizarre elements of the entire affair was the appearance of Geronimo, the famous Apache war chief who had terrorized Arizona territory until his capture in 1886. Geronimo had been sent, along with his family and followers, to be imprisoned at Fort Gaines in Pensacola, Florida.

Colonel Joe Miller had arranged for the U.S. Army to permit the war chief to attend the event, which was now being called the "Buffalo Chase."[6]

The idea was to have Geronimo hunt and kill a buffalo as part of the show. What the organizers didn't know—or didn't care to know—was that Geronimo was a Mescalero Apache. Apaches didn't hunt buffalo because they were a desert tribe, not a Plains Indian tribe. Buffalo didn't live in the desert. So it was that Geronimo was brought to Oklahoma to shoot and kill his first and only buffalo.[7]

The spectacle was surreal.

On June 11, 1905, at the height of the Buffalo Chase, Geronimo arrived in a sleek, black Locomobile, an open top automobile which was owned by a Chicago physician. The Apache warrior was wearing a brand-new top hat.[8]

Geronimo, never having shot a buffalo because he was a desert Indian and not a high plains Indian, was given a Winchester rifle. The old chief stood in the vehicle and fired, missing the buffalo. The buffalo was herded closer to Geronimo and his car. The Indian warrior fired again and shot the buffalo, but missed its vital organs. Stack Lee, the famed marksman and trick shot who was a featured performer with the 101 Ranch, finished off the buffalo with one shot.[9]

To the disgust of the assembled easterners, mostly big city newspaper editors and their guests, the Indians began gutting and eating the buffalo meat raw. Other Indians shot and killed other buffalo in the herd and the largest barbecue in Oklahoma to date began.[10]

The 1905 Buffalo Chase was an enormous event, and it is widely believed that Tom was present for the event as a performer.[11]

By the time Tom began working at the ranch, the three Miller brothers had made a conscious decision to promote their ranch with the wild west show and with the tourist traps they created at the ranch headquarters.[12]

Tom was caught up in the cowboy lifestyle at the 101 Ranch. It was good, hard work, and the atmosphere was congenial. Tom spent most of his time breaking horses for the ranch at first, but his sunny disposition and quick wit made him popular with the dudes who came to visit from the east. In his first full year at the ranch Tom spent as much time wrangling dudes as he did wrangling horses.[13]

But Tom still had a long way to go before his cowboying skills would impress the old-timers. He had to learn to rope better, which he did with the help of 101 cowboys, and he had to learn cow-ography, the "science" of predicting the erratic behavior of range cattle.

Some 101 Ranch cowboys—and even Zack Miller, interviewed years later after Tom had become an international celebrity, gave fuel to antihero revisionists when they derided Tom's skills as a cowboy. Zack Miller was still full of animosity toward Tom years later over a handful of legal disputes when he told his biographer that Tom was a green cowboy when he arrived at the ranch. Miller said that it wasn't long before Tom "could handle a horse or rope well enough to fool any dude." Such a condescending recollection fails in the face of facts. Tom grew up with horses and by all accounts was a master horseman before he left Pennsylvania to join the army. Other cowboy skills were likely learned while working at the 101 Ranch, but Tom's skill with horses far exceeded Zack Miller's jaded reflections.

Zack added that Tom's job was to tell "windies," long-winded tall tales about the wild and wooly west designed to raise the hair on the backs of the dudes' necks. Zack said Tom's skill as a liar and tall-tale teller were those of "an artist."[14]

These revisionist—and self-serving—remembrances fly in the face of a far larger number of recollections that said Tom was—at that time—actually a taciturn man who spoke little about himself and was not prone to speaking unless spoken to. Tom was good at telling tall tales to entertain audiences. In that day, telling "windies" for a crowd of paying spectators was commonplace.

Lew Stockdale, a 101 Ranch cowboy, disputed this anti-Tom Mix revisionism when, at age 100, he told an interviewer that Tom was "a little shaver…who came to work on the ranch and with the rodeo. I'll never forget the night that Tom came in with rain frozen all over him, and I had to take a hammer to break him loose from the stirrups. Boys were better in those days," Stockdale said.[15] Tom was so happy with his newfound job that he looked forward to the Christmas season with a sense of optimism about the future, so much so that he and Kitty Perrine were married five days before Christmas of 1905 at the Perrine Hotel at the corner of Park and Robinson. The ceremony was officiated by Rev. Thomas H. Harper of the Pilgrim Congregational Church. Tom and his 22-year-old bride began the new year as newlyweds.[16]

They had only one problem: Tom would not go back to work at the 101 until spring.

So Tom set out to find other winter employment. In doing so he fulfilled his other childhood dream of becoming a western lawman.

In early 1906 Tom was hired to be a peace officer in the company town of LeHunt, Kansas. LeHunt was formed as a labor camp for the Hunt Construction Company. The camp housed the Western States Cement Plant. Both were owned by Lee Hunt, a prominent businessman and industrialist. Hunt had hired a construction engineer by the name of Ellis Soper, but Soper was displeased with the rowdy behavior in the camp. The camp was described by one Kansas newspaper as a "woolie" boom town. The camp had all the evils of any frontier tent city. For each laborer that came to work in the camp, a card shark, gambler, prostitute, con man or thief came as well. Soon LeHunt had a scurrilous reputation. There were violent outbursts among the men as they gambled and drank, usually erupting into a fistfight or knife fight. Often guns were pulled and bullets flew, sometimes striking innocent bystanders. In short, LeHunt was out of control.[17]

Ellis Soper went looking for someone who could gain control of this madhouse of a town. One day when he stopped into the Blue Belle Saloon for a drink, he met Tom Mix, the bartender who kept the rowdies in line. He offered the job to Tom, who was by this time married and largely unemployed.[18]

Tom accepted the job of labor camp peace officer, a job akin to a town marshal or city policeman. When Tom arrived in LeHunt it had an enormous concrete plant, a 40-room hotel, two mercantile stores, a doctor's office and drug store, a saloon and pool hall, a two-room schoolhouse and approximately 75 homes.[19]

Tom went to work on the formidable task of taming the town. How could one 5'10, 173 pound man tame a town of several hundred rowdies with what was nothing more than the authority of a city policeman? Tom had no training as a law enforcement officer, but he did have military experience and he had been a first sergeant in the army. Tom undoubtedly knew from his military experience that the way to control men is to give them respect when due and to never threaten what you can't deliver. It is unclear why, but Lee Hunt gave Tom the title of "major." Indeed, there are accounts of Tom's exploits which refer to him as having that title. Another newspaper account referred to him as a deputy sheriff. There is one article published in an Independence, Kansas newspaper about Tom's exploits arresting some horse and buggy thieves. The article referred to Tom as "deputy sheriff Tom Mix" and called the outlaws he arrested as "woolies."[20]

Little more is known of LeHunt, Kansas because seven years after Tom quit working for the town it dried up and is now nothing but a faded dot on old maps.

When the spring roundup began, Tom left the job at LeHunt to return to Oklahoma and the 101 Ranch, where he broke horses and wrangled dudes for the Miller brothers. By early 1906, the Miller Brothers had decided to mount a moving wild west show and had obtained 50 Pullman train cars to transport 126 performers and 100 freight cars to transport the livestock and equipment for the show. It is undocumented if Tom went out with the 101 Ranch on its first tour. Some reports show that he remained at the ranch, but that cannot be ascertained with certainty.

Adding to the confusion, Tom once said that at this time he headed west to Lamar, Colorado where he took part in a roundup and after the roundup that he tended bar in George Yowell's saloon in that town.

The 1906 season shaped up to be a busy one at the 101 Ranch and Tom looked forward to returning to the footloose lifestyle of a 101 cowhand. A photo of Tom on the 101 Ranch, taken in 1906, shows none of the opulence and flash for which Tom would become famous. Tom is dressed in a battered cowboy hat, a stained white shirt with his sleeves rolled up his forearms, weathered batwing chaps and worn boots. He is rail thin and his face is like tanned leather. He sits astride a skinny sorrel horse with a star on its forehead. Clearly, by 1906 Tom was barely supporting himself, much less his wife.

The atmosphere at the ranch was in many ways typical of most big ranches on the western plains. The cowboys lived in bunkhouses or slept out on the open plains, depending on the task at hand. Married men and single men alike lived under the same conditions. The cowboys who were married or courting often spent the entire spring and summer without seeing their women. Many kept in touch by writing letters or on the occasional long weekend when they could ride home for a visit.

Tom was no different. He left Kitty back in town with her family. Little is known about the status of their relationship at the time, but it must have been bleak. Kitty was a town girl. She was used to the nuclear existence of living in the bosom of her family and working in the family business as well. It is highly probable that she did not understand what drove her tall, dark and dashing husband to saddle up and disappear for months at a time.

Kitty and Tom would divorce just over a year after they were married.

It really didn't matter to Tom, who had already set his sights on Zack Mulhall's daughter. Lucille Mulhall was a woman of the west—she could ride and rope and shoot like a man. Lost in the history of the westward experience is the story of tens of thousands of women who worked alongside their fathers, husbands and sons taming the west. Such women were exemplified by women like Lucille Mulhall. Lucille was a crack shot, a expert roper and a horsewoman of tremendous skill. Indeed, she went on to fame as a wild west show performer and for good reason. She was as good as anyone else performing in the wild west shows.

Tom liked her spirit and her gumption and thought her no-bullshit attitude was endearing.

Unfortunately, Lucille's father—as much as he liked Tom—didn't approve of Tom romancing his daughter. This was a result, no doubt, of Tom's reputation as a bartender in saloons and brothels. Zack had spent enough time around Tom to know that Tom had an easy way with women and was resolutely footloose and carefree.

Legend has it that Zack ran Tom off at the point of a gun.[21]

Tom and Lucille would remain close for many years, while Tom's relationship with Zack Mulhall would sour and curdle.

Tom's relationship with the Miller brothers veered between a cordiality to outright animosity. Tom was a good employee for the company because he was as good with tourists as he was with horses. On top of that, he looked the part. Tom had begun to follow the Miller brothers' dictate that their cowboys look as gaudy as possible. He began by buying himself a nice pair of chaps and boots. He would later splurge on a nice Stetson hat.

True cowboys are a vain lot, even today. They pride themselves on their style and spend large sums for the best cowboy hats and tailored leather boots. In Tom's day the hats were broad-brimmed. The shirts were brightly colored checks and prints decked out with flashy bandannas, often worn bib-style in front. Chaps were usually festooned with silver medallions called conchas and guns and gun belts were usually the best that the cowboys could afford.

When winter 1906 came and Tom was laid off for the winter months, he again found work from Lee Hunt. This time Hunt wanted Tom to keep the peace in a mining town in Marion County, Tennessee, which sits just west of Chattanooga, Tennessee on the Alabama border.[22]

Nestled in the rugged mountains at the foothills of the Great Smoky Mountains, the company town was called Richard City, in honor of Richard Hardy, the founder of Dixie Portland Cement Company. Hardy and Ellis Soper—who had hired Tom to keep the peace in LeHunt, Kansas—were brothers-in-law. When Hardy was looking for a lawman to keep the peace in the boom town, Soper recommended Tom.[23]

Tom accepted the job and arrived with Kitty in the early winter of 1907. Kitty's reaction to the move is unrecorded, but there are records of her attending a town picnic with Tom on Independence Day, 1907 at which Tom put on a show for the camp which included trick-shooting and roping.[24]

Tom's arrival created a considerable stir. The town of Richard City sat nestled deep in the mountainous rural south, thus when its new lawman arrived in town wearing a cowboy hat and chaps and carrying a pearl-handled six-gun, word spread quickly. There is some speculation that Tom was carrying a .45 single-action pistol, but Tom's preference for Smith & Wesson double-action Frontier pistols is well documented. Whether Tom was packing a Colt .45 single-action or a S&W double-action is not documented.

Throughout his life Tom often kept many guns, though he wore few outside of his work as a performer. He owned a .44 caliber Model 1892 Winchester rifle, serial # 925114, branded with his signature TM brand. He owned a pair of matching pearl-handled, .45 cal. Colt SAA revolvers with his TM brand. He owned a Smith and Wesson .357 magnum pistol that he often kept in a shoulder holster. He also owned a matching pair of Colt police revolvers with pearl grips and nickel plating, serial numbers 530719 and 542511.[25]

Tom was given other tasks besides keeping the peace. He also broke horses and helped the company deal with the influx of workers by acting as an employment agent.[26]

Tom's success at keeping the peace in Richard City was equal to his success in LeHunt, Kansas. In both towns Tom was known as an affable man who didn't tolerate rowdy behavior. He often settled problems with the old military method of talking to a man and showing him respect. Indeed, Tom quelled a near brawl in a movie theater by simply talking to the men and reasoning with them.[27]

By all known accounts, Tom did not return to the 101 Ranch in summer 1907. He stayed on at Richard City until winter, but when the cold rain and sleet hit the mountains in early November, Tom and Kitty left Tennessee and returned to Oklahoma and Kitty filed for divorce. She told a friend, "If this is what it's like to be married, I don't much care for it."[28]

Tom was so busy that he probably didn't know he was getting divorced until it was too late.[29]

He would keep in touch with Kitty, who went on to run the Browning Hotel at 221 West Grand St. in Oklahoma City for many years, and he often visited with her when he was in Oklahoma.[30]

Tom returned to the Oklahoma Territory and managed to get a winter job as night marshal for the small town of Dewey, Oklahoma. He got the job thanks to Joe Bartles, a prominent businessman, and the mayor, Earl Woodward. Both men were Republicans and they knew and liked Tom.[31]

When Tom accepted the job, he was sworn in as a deputy sheriff by Sheriff John Jordan. Jordan was a Cherokee Indian and a popular county sheriff. His son, Sid, became a close friend of Tom's.[32]

Sid would follow Tom to Hollywood and work on most of Tom's early films. Sid and Tom were both deputy sheriffs. Thus, they were equals.[33]

They had similar interests and could often be seen having impromptu shooting competitions. The men developed a trust in each other that was unshakeable.

In fact, when Tom became a movie star ten years later, there were no special effects experts. Thus, when the script called for the hero's hat to be shot off or his bandanna to be shot off, and the like, Tom always entrusted the sharpshooting to Sid.[34]

In *The Man From Texas*, Tom's hat is shot off of his head and in another scene a bullet ricochets along a wooden wall, tearing a path only a fraction of an inch from Tom's head. In both scenes live ammunition was used and in both scenes Sid Jordan was the man Tom entrusted with firing the shots. Tom nicknamed Sid "Big Chief Rifle Shot."[35]

Tom's career as a night marshal began shortly after Oklahoma became a state on November 16, 1907. The state was dry—meaning no liquor sales were allowed—and the bulk of Tom's duties included rounding up bootleggers who sold illegal whiskey in the town. Tom would later write an article dramatizing his exploits searching for liquor. He claimed that his efforts earned him the nickname "Pussyfoot Mix."[36]

Tom's career as a lawman was intermittent and largely uneventful. His skill at handling horses—and at handling tenderfoots who came to vacation at the 101 Ranch—was in higher demand.[37]

It wasn't long before Tom was back at the 101, and it would be years before he would leave again.

By 1905, Tom Mix had achieved both of his childhood goals. He was a real cowboy and he had also become a frontier lawman, an experience that he would use in his public relations as a movie star. Indeed, by the time he was at the height of his fame, Fox Studio publicists had overblown Tom's resume', calling him a former U.S. marshal and former Texas Ranger, neither of which was true.

5

Tom's cachè with the Miller brothers increased greatly in 1908 when Tom won the ranch's all-around cowboy championship.[1]

Such a rodeo title carried great prestige, and almost immediately Tom was featured on postcards put out by the Millers to promote their wild west show. The tourists arriving at the ranch began to ask for Tom by name and asked to meet him and spend time with him.

Tom loved the attention. The more attention he got, the more he liked it. Not only that, his added fame earned him a raise to a whopping $35 per month.[2]

While Tom was having a successful season wrangling dudes and performing with the wild west show, the Millers were beginning to expand their holdings.

That same summer, an oil speculator named E.W. Marland arrived from Pennsylvania and began snooping around the 101 Ranch. Marland had been boom and bust and was looking for his next big oil strike. He and the Millers went into business, mostly because Marland wanted access to the 101 Ranch lands and he also wanted to take advantage of George Miller's close relationship with the Ponca Indian Tribe.[3]

The Ponca granted an oil drilling lease to Marland and Millers' new company, Marland Oil Company, and Marland began drilling for oil and gas.[4]

Marland knew his stuff and the wells came in big. Eight wells were drilled of which seven produced natural gas and the eighth produced oil, pumping 100 to 600 barrels of oil per day.[5]

The Miller brothers and Marland became filthy rich. Their company survives today with the name Conoco.[6]

At the end of the 1908 season, Tom was restless. He was laid off in December, as was typical, and he had to find new winter employment.[7]

He decided to take a ride over to Dewey, not to resume his duties as night marshal, but to go courting Olive Stokes.

Tom had met the lovely Olive at the St. Louis World's Fair back in 1904. At the time she was 17 years old. Girls as young as 13 and 14 were often married during that era and Tom clearly felt a strong attraction for her.[8]

It is unknown if Tom waited until Olive was 21 years old on purpose or by happenstance. Olive recounts in her autobiography that Tom did not write to her in the four years between their first meeting in St. Louis and their reunion in Dewey four years later.[9] As it turned out, Olive was not in Dewey, but out of town.

In early December of 1908, Olive traveled by train to Medora, North Dakota to buy horses for her family's ranch. Olive stayed as a guest of rancher Nels Nichols and his wife, Katrine. After looking over the Nichols' horses, Olive sent for Luke Bells, the foreman on the Stokes Ranch, to come help her arrange the purchase. Luke was scheduled to arrive about a week before Christmas and at the appointed time Olive and the Nichols took a buggy ride to the train station. Olive recalled that she thought she'd worn enough clothing to contend with the North Dakota winter, but the weather was brutal.[10]

The train arrived in Medora as a harsh blizzard set in. Olive greeted Luke as he stepped off the train and was immediately stunned to see Tom standing behind him. She "blushed furiously" as Tom stepped down from the train and doffed his hat to her in a sweeping, chivalrous gesture.[11]

Luke told Olive that Tom had come to the ranch looking for her and when Luke told him that Olive was in North Dakota, Tom tagged along.

Tom and Luke got a room at the Cowboy Hotel in town because the Nichols did not have room for extra guests. The Nichols invited the two cowboys to join them and Olive at the ranch for dinner and stuffed them with Norwegian dishes such as lutefisk, a cod dish, Fattignand, a deep-fried pastry, and lefse, an unleavened potato bread. The next day Olive joined the cowboys on a ride into the badlands to look at horses. Olive recalled that Tom was impressed with her horsemanship.[12]

They arrived at a ranch in the badlands owned by a man named Sam Short, where they were treated to the traditional open hospitality of the west. Tom and Luke rode out each morning to look at Short's horses and Olive tagged along. She remembered that Luke always seemed to ride off alone, leaving her and Tom to have long talks as they rode. Olive recalled that Tom told her lengthy, hair-raising stories about his service as "one of the Rough Riders in the Philippines."[13]

This is the earliest record of Tom's growing penchant for tall tales. It is interesting that the story is that Tom claimed to have served with the Rough Riders in the Philippines, rather than Cuba. The Rough Riders did not serve in the Pacific, so one must wonder if Olive misremembered the story or if Tom told his tall tale without having his facts straight. Indeed, it is likely that Tom had adopted some stories he had heard at the 101 Ranch from fellow cowboy Chuck Gephardt, who would later become famous as Buck Jones, and from Will Rogers, and told these "windies" to Olive to impress her.

The Nichols arrived at the Short Ranch in time for a big Christmas Day celebration, which lasted until News Years Day. Olive remembered that ranchers and cowboys and their families arrived in groups of two to ten through an endless, terrifying blizzard that did not stop the hearty plains folk from coming. The Christmas Day square dance lasted 24 hours. Dancers would whoop it up for two or three hours and then rest while others danced, as if they were dancing in shifts.[14]

Olive said that Tom refused to allow her to dance with others and that he showered her with such affection and attention that the night was "joyous." She mentioned to Tom that one day she'd like to get married and recalled that Tom scowled at her playfully, remarking that "single life sure doesn't hurt a man much."[15]

After the New Year, Olive sent Luke back to the Nichols corrals with a herd of horses and accompanied Tom up the Little Missouri River to Bill McCarty's ranch to look at more horses. They spent a week there inspecting the remuda and getting to know each other better. One day Olive spotted a big black stallion that had a reputation as a man killer because it would rear up and fall back onto any cowboy trying to ride him. When Olive told McCarty that she liked the horse he demurred. He told Olive that the horse was a man-killer. Tom asked if he could try and ride the horse and McCarty said he was afraid the horse would kill Tom.[16]

Tom enlisted the help of two cowboys and they got the big black saddled. Tom began to lead the horse out of the corral and McCarty looked puzzled. Tom explained that it was better to buck out a bronc on the open plain than in a corral. With that he jumped aboard the horse and, before it could start bucking, slapped the horse in the face with his hat and sank his spurs in, letting out a bloodcurdling yell. The black was too startled to buck and bolted into a dead run. Tom disappeared over the horizon on the frightened horse. Thirty minutes later Tom returned riding a lathered, exhausted and completely obedient horse.[17]

Tom whiled away the hours practicing his trick shooting and at night participating in sing-alongs by the campfire. He favored the minstrel songs of Stephen Foster.[18]

On the eve of Olive's departure for home, the Nichols held a big dance at the Cowboy Hotel and Olive looked forward to spending the evening with Tom. Tom begged off, saying he had to escort the widow of a friend. Olive went to the dance but spent the evening fuming because Tom was nowhere to be seen.[19]

Olive began to doubt whether she really knew Tom, who, at 28, was seven years older than she was.[20]

Later that night, as the band played the traditional "Good Night Ladies" to signal the end of the dance, Olive went looking for Tom. Unable to find him, she allowed Luke to walk her back to the Nichols' house. She found Tom in the kitchen with Nels Nichols. The Nichols' housekeeper, Mattie, had set out a feast of cold cuts and had baked an enormous cake. Nichols beckoned Olive to stand next to Tom and began conducting a wedding ceremony. Thinking it was a joke, Olive recited her vows along with Tom.[21]

When Tom kissed Olive, she was stunned. Nichols then explained that he was a justice of the peace and that he'd just actually married the couple. Olive was shocked.

"You're married to Tom," she remembered someone saying and she looked at him questioningly. He nodded to her reassuringly and she replied, "The least thing you could have done was to say you loved me!"[22]

The date was January 19, 1909.[23]

It is unknown if Olive knew at the time that she married Tom that he'd been married twice before. It is unlikely Tom told her about Grace Allen or Kitty Perrine. She was a young and impressionable 21-year-old and Tom was seven years older. Olive gives the impression that Tom swept her off her feet.

If one takes Olive's account of the events as fact, she may have, in her youth, lacked the critical judgment to make such inquiries about Tom's past.

Olive's version is incomplete. She described herself as "a country child" in her autobiography and gave the impression that she was a mere girl when she and Tom married.[24]

What Olive forgot to recount in her autobiography is that between her first encounter with Tom in St. Louis in 1904 and her reunion with him in 1909 that she had actually been married to another man. The marriage, to a man named Brown, was short-lived and occurred in 1905 and ended in 1906, when Olive was 18.[25]

What is also unknown are Tom's motivations for courting and marrying Olive. Did he pursue Olive because they had common interests—ranching and horses? Indeed, this is likely, as Tom gravitated toward women of the plains who could ride and rope and tomboy like a man. He had been strongly attracted to Lucille Mulhall when they met. He likely viewed Olive's ability to ride and rope and handle horses and cattle as an attribute. Clearly, Olive was far better suited to be Mrs. Tom Mix than either Grace Allen or Kitty Perrine. Both women were used to living in towns with the modern creature comforts, and both viewed Tom's footloose cowboy life with disdain.

What is interesting to contemplate is the fact that by the time Tom had married Olive he had been married twice and divorced twice, seemingly without missing either woman when they were gone. Tom apparently breezed through both relationships without missing a step, and it begs the question: Did Tom approach marriage as a commitment or as a venue for female companionship?

Indeed, women on the frontier in the first decade of the 20th Century fell into two categories—those that did and those that didn't have sex with men outside of marriage. While the popular conception of frontier women is that only prostitutes slept around in that time, there is much data to suggest that there was less virtue among proper women on the plains than was commonly believed. Indeed, "marriages" in the old west were often short term "shack ups" that ended quickly. In this case, Olive depicted herself in her autobiography as a virgin when she married Tom. If Tom did not know of Olive's prior nuptials, it is likely he believed that in order to woo her into his bed, he would have had to marry her.

A rare photo exists of Tom and Olive. It was taken in the summer of 1909 in Flemington, Missouri during production of *Ranch Life In the Great Southwest*, one of Tom's first movies. The young couple are still newlyweds, barely six full months into their marriage. They are standing in front of a split rail corral somewhere on a barren, windswept plain. Tom is lean, tanned and clean-shaven. He wears a tan hat with a high-peaked crown, much like the hats he would wear in most of his Selig movies. A large, brightly colored bandanna is tied around his neck and his shirt is a broad checked pattern shirt with large buttons. He is wearing a dark mackinaw, and dark pants which are tucked into finely tooled cowboy boots. He is wearing large spurs. Interestingly, around Tom's waist is a sash and a gun belt. In his right hand is a hand-braided lariat. Tom's left hand is in his pants pocket and he has propped his left foot onto the rail in a jaunty stance. Behind him, Olive is dressed in a dark dress with a coat over it. The dress and coat have matching buttons. She is wearing a tie which is fashioned into a loose bow. She is wearing a dark, broad-brimmed hat and her thick, dark hair is braided and pulled up behind her head.

What makes the photo intriguing is that neither Tom nor Olive is smiling. Tom is turned away from Olive. Olive is leaning against the corral while Tom is turned sideways. One wonders what the body language of this photo conveys. Clearly, in Tom's mind he is the subject of the photograph and he is posed for effect. Olive seems slightly uncomfortable, as if the photo was taken without much preparation. One wonders if they are posed in this serious manner because of the 19th century belief that photographs should be dignified, or because they were distant from each other.

Another photo taken that same day at that same corral is strikingly different. It is a photo of Tom, director Frank Boggs and several cowboys. All of the men are either sitting or squatting on the ground or propped against the corral fence. In this candid photo Tom, Boggs and a cowboy directly to Tom's right are intently looking at another cowboy to their right, whose face is obscured. Tom, Boggs and the second cowboy are smiling, as if sharing a joke or a funny story. In this photo we see Tom engaged in some male camaraderie, relating to the men around him.

The photo stands in stark contrast to the prior photo. In the photo of Tom and Olive he is not interacting with her. He stands at least a foot away from her with his back turned. He is not posing with Olive as if they were a couple interacting with each other. In the candid photo of Tom and the other men, the cowboys are so close together that their arms and legs are all touching. Boggs sits perhaps a foot away from Tom's left. What we are left with is the impression that Tom felt more comfortable among his cowboy friends than he did with women, even his own wife.

After their wedding, rather than return to the Stokes Ranch in Oklahoma, the couple decided to head west to honeymoon in Montana. They headed for Miles City and to spend several days enjoying the scenery.[26]

It is interesting that Tom chose Miles City for their honeymoon because he had cowboy friends there he wanted to see—and because he wanted to "show off" Olive to his friends.[27] In short, Tom sought male companionship even when he was on his honeymoon.

Olive recounted in her autobiography an incident on the train ride from Medora, North Dakota to Miles City. Tom and Olive were sitting together on the train when a big, drunken bully began to harass a young widow and her son. The man took offense when his advances were rebuffed and when her young son took up for his mother, the bully cuffed him. Olive said that Tom leapt to the women's defense, that the bully attempted to pull a gun on Tom, and that Tom disarmed the man and whipped him in a fist fight.[28]

Tom and the bully duked it out and the train screeched to a halt. The conductor ran down the aisle of the passenger car, arriving at the scene just as Tom knocked the bully senseless. Tom helped the conductor throw the man off the train and the train lurched forward to continue its journey, leaving the battered, drunken bully in the middle of the snow-swept prairie. The woman, a widow from Pennsylvania who was on her way to Helena, Montana to live with her brother, thanked Tom profusely. Tom reassured the woman that such incidents were uncommon in the west and that she would enjoy living in Montana, which

Tom called "the greatest part of the country." Tom allegedly spent the remainder of the train trip regaling the boy and his mother with windies of his daring exploits, much to Olive's chagrin.

"I smoldered a little, remembering that this was my wedding journey and that Tom should be talking to me." Olive recalled.[29]

The story is highly suspect, mostly because it contains all of the elements of a dime novel rescue, the kind of clichéd knight-of-the-plains-to-the-rescue tale that would become a staple of early silent movies. The most suspect part of the story is when the bully cuffs the boy. Such an element was a standard device in early silent movies to delineate a character as a villain. The story is also suspect because there is no other independent account of the event.

Olive related the tale as an illustration of Tom's character, noting that such elements would later appear in Tom's films. It is another chapter in the Tom Mix legend, likely a grain of fact embellished into a tale of derring do.

Olive said Sid Jordan told her that Tom was once the sheriff of Two Buttes, Colorado and that Tom was shot in the knee while arresting some rustlers. The scar on Tom's knee is, without question, the scar from his accidental shooting in Pennsylvania as a child.[30]

Tom and Olive arrived in Miles City in the dead of winter and Olive was shocked at what a "dreary" place Tom had picked for their honeymoon. The streets were calf-deep ruts of mud and the buildings were all unpainted and slapped together, much like most western boom towns.[31]

Tom shrugged off Olive's suggestion that they return to Oklahoma and took her to a ranch outside of Miles City owned by Bill Tambler. Tom had known Tambler since 1905, when the two men had ridden with Seth Bullock's Cowboy Brigade to Teddy Roosevelt's inauguration.[32]

Olive recalled that Tom told her that he had ridden with Roosevelt in Cuba during the Spanish American War, an obvious windy since Tom was stationed on the east coast of the United States with his artillery regiment during the war.[33]

The next day Tom and Olive went shopping. Tom bought himself and Olive matching saddles and bought Olive a matching skirt and jacket made out of buckskin. Tom then bought himself a fancy pair of batwing chaps which were festooned with silver conchas.[34]

It is interesting that Tom then led Olive to a pawn shop where he bought her a diamond wedding ring.[35]

That he bought his new wife—his third wife in less than seven years—a second hand ring begs the question. Did Tom simply want to spend his money wisely on his wife's wedding ring, or did he view such a thing as secondary in importance to a new saddle and chaps?

6

Tom likely found Olive to be a suitable female companion for his male-oriented lifestyle. She was very much like Lucille Mulhall, a rambunctious tomboy who was one of the guys. She was easy to be around. She admittedly was "never the overly romantic type," and never spent time in front of a mirror primping and preening.[1]

Olive allowed herself to be pulled into Tom's footloose and carefree world. She had initially tried to get Tom to settle down and live with her on the Stokes Ranch, but Tom liked the idea of living the wandering life of a wild west show cowboy, so she gave up "with misgivings."[2]

By 1909, Tom had gotten show business in his blood. He no longer wanted to be a cowboy working for $15 per month chasing cows along dusty trails. He no longer wanted to be an underpaid lawman, though he would continue working the off season as night marshal in Dewey, Oklahoma until 1912, when he became active in movie making. Tom realized, like many cowboys at the time, that more money could be made showing off his cowboying skills for an audience than could be earned actually cowboying on a ranch.

Tom wanted to strike out on his own and open his own wild west show but he and Olive didn't have enough money.[3]

Tom heard that a man named Widerman, whose first name is lost to history somehow, was hiring acts for his wild west show.[4]

Tom and Olive took the train to Amarillo, Texas to meet with Widerman about hiring on with the show.[5]

Olive remembered Amarillo as a "dry, dusty town swarming with cowboys, ranchers and gamblers." The town was still a collection of small adobe huts and wood-frame buildings. Tom led Olive to the hotel, where she cooled her heels in the lobby while Tom had a drink with Widerman in the bar and talked over the terms of Tom's employment.[6]

Olive's presence in the lobby caused quite a stir. Amarillo was, in her words, "short on women in those days."[7]

Tom hired on to do a rope act similar to Will Rogers' act and Olive came along as his assistant and even did some trick riding and shooting as a separate act. Tom's trick riding and roping act fit nicely into Widerman's menagerie and the show, while small, played to capacity crowds. Audiences applauded Tom heartily at each show and Olive saw Tom's popularity first hand.[8]

"Tom wasn't officially designated as the star of the show, but it was obvious from the very first that the entire exhibition revolved around him. The moment he came tearing into the arena on Old Blue [Tom's blue roan], his energy and fire seemed to reach out and seize the spectators," she recalled.[9]

Tom would trick ride, sliding down onto Blue's side, hiding from sight as Indians did on the attack. He would somersault off of Blue and land on his feet.[10]

After his trick riding, Tom would then put on a one-man roping act. Tom knew that Will Rogers used a 40-foot rope with a 25-foot reach. Always the competitive type, Tom had devised a routine using a 60-foot rope with a 40-foot reach.[11]

Tom's trick riding and roping acts are not lost to time and can be seen in *My Pal, the King* (1932). Even at 52, Tom is seen clearly doing all of his trick-riding and roping performances as part of his Tom Mix Circus.

Olive's recollection about Tom riding Ol' Blue in 1909 is significant because it dates Tom's ownership of the blue roan gelding as far back as that year.[12]

Ol' Blue was Tom's first movie horse, and it is widely known that Tom used the horse for years in his wild west performances and then in his movie career from 1910 until 1918. After the horse's death on January 29, 1919, Tom wrote an epitaph for Ol' Blue that dated its birth as July 1897.[13]

Tom never wrote down the date that he acquired the horse, but it is clear that he bought the horse sometime between his arrival in Oklahoma in 1903 and his wild west show performances in 1909. Tom rode Ol' Blue and a big black horse named Colt .45 in his early movies from 1910 until 1917.[14]

He then bought a sorrel gelding known as Tony Boy in 1917 from Pat Chrisman for $600.[15]

After Blue's death, Tom rode Tony (and Tony's stunt doubles) in all of his silent films. Tom later switched to another sorrel named Tony, Jr. for his sound films, and later a string of horses which he called Tony for his live performances.

Tom loved being back on tour, but Olive recalled that all touring meant to her was "spending half my time on trains and the other half in hotel rooms."[16]

During a stop in Kansas City, Kansas, Tom and Olive had a reunion with Will Rogers, who was also performing in the city. During dinner, Will told the couple he thought they'd end up together when the three of them were all at the exposition in St. Louis back in 1904.[17]

That night, Tom and Olive talked about Will's success in vaudeville and realized how little Tom was actually making, considering he was basically the star of the Widerman show. Olive encouraged Tom to ask Widerman for more money.

The next day the Widerman show left by train for Napa, Idaho. During a stopover in Denver, Tom asked Widerman's nephew, who was running the show, for a raise and was turned down flat. Olive recalled that Tom and the younger Widerman got into a heated exchange of words and that Widerman went for his gun. Olive said she pointed one of Tom's .45 pistols at Widerman and got the drop on him. Tom and Olive quit the show on the spot. Widerman changed tactics and begged them to stay with the show, but Tom refused.[18]

The couple decided to get a hotel room not far from the train depot. Tom wanted to form his own wild west show, but Olive was weary of the road and wanted to return to her ranch in Oklahoma. Before they left the train station, Tom ran into an old friend.

Charlie Tipton, a champion bronc rider who'd won the 1908 Cheyenne Frontier Days, was headed to Seattle, Washington, to see if he could find some work.[19]

Newspapers across the country were touting the opening of a gigantic world's fair-style exhibition in Seattle, Washington. It was called the Alaska-Yukon-Pacific Exposition and it was designed to lure trade and investment to the Alaskan territory.[20]

Tom thought that he and Olive might stage a successful wild west show if they could take advantage of the large crowds going to the exposition.[21]

The plan was simple: Open a wild west show just down the street from the exposition. Crowds that couldn't get into the exposition or had tired of it would come over and pay to see the show.

Tom gave Olive money to buy the train tickets to Seattle and then led Charlie down to the local saloon for a drink. Olive took a nap in the station. When the conductor called for passengers for the train, Olive—half-asleep—boarded the train. It wasn't until the train stopped at the next station that Olive realized Tom and Charlie weren't on the train. She had the telegrapher wire the Denver station. Tom and Charlie were still in Denver, having forgotten about the train as they drank beer and swapped stories.[22]

Tom wired back, telling Olive to go on to Seattle and that he and Charlie would come on the next train.[23]

Tom and Charlie caught up with Olive in Seattle. Olive described the weather as "terrible, full of torrential rains."[24]

Tom was enthusiastic about opening his own show and was seemingly oblivious to the bad weather, which could drive away any potential audience.

Tom was not dissuaded. Indeed, his luck held—as it always seemed to do—and he ran into Ezra Black, a former Montana rancher who was now getting rich in the timber business. Black invested money in Tom's show.[25]

Tom had only nine days to organize his wild west show in order to begin performances that would coincide with the opening of the Alaska—Yukon—Pacific Exposition. Tom began hiring performers. He hired cowboys and Indians, mostly Blackfoot, and began putting together a show. In the end, Tom had hired 65 people.[26]

A photograph of part of the troupe taken in 1909 shows Tom and Olive and 11 other cowboys standing side by side in a line. The men are all wearing chaps and wide-brimmed hats. They are a clean-shaven, well-groomed bunch of men. Tom is the tallest of the group, and is wearing a checkered shirt and fringed gloves and a bright bandanna. In his left hand he is holding an ornate bridle festooned with silver. Several other cowboys have brightly decorated bridles in their hands as well.

Tom rented a lot called the Western Washington Fairground and began advertising the show.[27]

To increase interest in the show, Tom put together a segment featuring knights in shining armor jousting and sword fighting on horseback.[28]

On opening day, The Tom Mix Wild West Show prepared for the crowds but was greeted with a torrential rain that turned the fairgrounds to a mud pit. Olive described the storm as a "heartless downpour."[29]

To their surprise, ticket sales were brisk and more than half the fairground stands were filled with enthusiastic, if slightly wet, people. The crowd loved the show and cheered wildly.

Tom did his trick riding, trick roping and trick shooting acts. Charlie Tipton rode some wild broncs. In an act reminiscent of Buffalo Bill Cody's show, Tom staged an Indian attack on settlers featuring his troupe of 40 Blackfoot Indians and 25 white performers. The Blackfoot attacked with such ferocity that the audience was spellbound.[30]

Tom also recreated another act similar to Cody's—the Indians attacking a stagecoach. Tom also put on an exhibition of bull-dogging.[31] Tom had learned bulldogging from Bill Pickett, the black cowboy who'd invented the sport and toured with the 101 Ranch.[32] He had a postcard created which featured him bulldogging a steer and proclaimed himself the champion of the event, a shrewd marketing trick that drew audiences to the fairgrounds.

The rain continued to vex the show but Tom remained optimistic. Olive wasn't so sure the show would survive. She could see that Tom was popular with the audiences—sometimes too popular.

It was in Seattle that Olive first realized that Tom was magnetic to women. It happened when she caught Tom in the arms of a love-stuck teenaged girl. The girl—whom Olive guessed was either 16 or 17 years old—had snuck into a rehearsal and was flirting openly with Tom, who didn't seem to mind. Olive saw what was going on and stormed up to Tom and the girl. When Tom cooly introduced Olive to the amorous girl as his wife, she was dumbstruck. Before she could recover her composure, Olive physically ejected the girl from the fairgrounds. It would not be the last time that Olive got violent over Tom's roving eye or the attentions of amorous female fans.[33]

The show was initially a success, but with each passing day the weather grew unpredictable and rain chased away the crowds.[34]

One dark, rainy night the show was particularly successful and, as Tom and Olive counted the receipts for the day by lamplight, three men rushed into their tent brandishing guns and tried to rob them.[35]

Tom fought back as Olive doused the light. Shots rang out in the darkness as Tom struggled with the robbers. Olive managed to knock one out with a metal chair. Tom knocked out the lead thug and the third man took off running. Tom grabbed one of the robber's pistol and shot the fleeing man in the leg.[36]

When Olive relit the lamp, she saw Tom dragging the wounded robber back to the tent. Tom's face was bloodied and his right hand had been creased by a bullet. The money was scattered all over the tent as if strewn by a tornado.[37]

When the Alaska-Yukon-Pacific Exposition closed, so closed Tom and Olive's wild west show. To Tom's surprise, he and Olive broke even on the venture and paid off the performers and their investor, Esra Black.[38]

Tom learned two things as a result of the effort—that he was grossly underpaid as a wild west show performer and that owning your own wild west show was a costly enterprise. Not only did he have to feed, clothe and house the performers, he also had to feed and house the animals used in the show, pay for costumes and props, and more.

Still Tom had learned a valuable business lesson that it was better to work for himself than to work for others. He was determined to have his own successful wild west show.

Tom and Olive left Seattle and headed east to Wyoming for the Cheyenne Frontier Days, a large-scale celebration of western culture, culminating with an enormous rodeo.[39]

Upon arrival, Tom and Olive got a room at the Plains Hotel and Tom went down to the fairgrounds and entered the bronc riding and calf roping events.[40]

Not much is known about the results of the calf roping, but Tom's bronc riding made history.

Tom drew a wild bucking horse named Sabile. The bronc was owned by Cheyenne promoter Charlie Burton Irwin, as big a legend in Wyoming as the Miller Brothers were in Oklahoma.[41]

Irwin was the owner of the Y6 Ranch, had his own wild west show, and was instrumental in the promotion of the sport of rodeo. He helped create the Cheyenne Frontier Days and later was a founder of the Professional Rodeo Cowboys Association before his untimely death in 1934 in an auto accident similar to the car crash that would kill George Miller and the accident which killed Tom six years after Irwin's death.[42]

Irwin billed his bucking horse as "the horse that cannot be rode." Tom predicted to Olive that he would ride Sabile. Before the event, Olive asked Clayton Banks, the cowboy who'd won the bronc riding in Cheyenne the year before, about the horse. Banks told Olive the horse was "the crookedest horse in the world."[43]

Worried that Tom would be seriously hurt riding the famous bronc, Olive went to the grandstand to watch the bronc riding. As she took her seat, she saw promoter Irwin's massive, 300-pound frame seated not far from her. As Tom climbed over the bucking chute to prepare for his ride, Irwin bellowed loudly that he'd bet anyone $500 that Tom wouldn't last three jumps on the horse.[44]

Sabile was a crazy horse, known to twisting and sunfishing his belly and throwing a cowboy within one of two seconds. Olive remembered Clayton Banks' words, then made a decision. She reached into the bosom of her dress and pulled out five $100 bills.

"I'll take that bet, Mr. Irwin!"[45]

Irwin gave Olive a suspicious look and took her bet, asking the owner of the Plains Hotel to hold the stakes.[46]

Tom leapt aboard Sabile and rode the bronc like he was tied to the saddle. Sabile leapt and turned and bucked and twisted, but Tom kept his seat. The crowd went wild and Tom finished the ride just as Sabile gave up.[47]

When Tom went to the pay window to collect his day money, he got $100. Olive made ten times that amount off of her bet with Irwin.[48]

She had the money to bet because during the time that she and Tom were in Seattle oil had been discovered on the Stokes Ranch in Oklahoma. Olive bet part of the money she'd just received by wire that had been sent to her as part of her share of the oil proceeds.⁴⁹

While in Cheyenne, Tom received a letter from Will A. Dickey, a wild west show promoter, whom Tom had known since early in his 101 Ranch days. Dickey was now involved in making motion pictures with William Selig, the owner of a film company called Selig Polyscope Company.⁵⁰

The Selig company was owned by William N. Selig, who added the sobriquet "Col." to his name. A former vaudeville magician, Selig had gotten in on the ground floor of the newfangled movie business by signing a compact with Thomas A. Edison, who was one of the inventors of the motion picture technology. Edison had joined with Biograph Company, Vitagraph Company of America and several other companies and formed a monopoly called the Motion Pictures Patents Company.⁵¹

"The trust," as it was often called, sought to prevent other independent producers from making movies. It resorted to all sorts of tactics to keep its stranglehold on the movie business, including the use of violence. The viciousness of "the trust" drove independent producers westward across the expanse of the United States. Back in the early 1900s, it was difficult to travel cross-country, and producers used that 2,000 mile separation to operate outside of the influence of the east-coast bound monopoly.

Dickey wanted Tom to work for the Selig company.⁵² Dickey told Tom to meet him in Flemington, Missouri.⁵³

When Tom arrived in Missouri, there was some friction at first because the Circle D cowboys—most of whom were from the wilds of Montana—couldn't tell if Tom was a real cowboy or pretending to be one. Tom quickly earned their respect with his ability with a lasso and with livestock, and with his friendly nature.⁵⁴

In the early years of his life Tom was not known for telling windies. His penchant for spinning tall tales, for which he would become infamous, surfaced during his rise to stardom. This was, no doubt, part of his self-driven public relations, but it was likely more. Tom's natural gregariousness, coupled with his desire to avoid public knowledge of his status as an Army deserter, caused Tom to adopt the exploits of others and graft them onto his legend. Indeed, stuntman Yakima Canutt called Tom, "the goddamndest liar I ever saw."⁵⁵

"Tom used to chum around with some of our bunch," Circle D cowboy Harry Hazelleaf would remember years later, "but you could never say that he believed in tooting his own horn. Ask him a question and he'd answer it honestly, but he wasn't much on volunteering information about his past."⁵⁶

Western artist Joe De Yong, who worked on the film, recalled that some of the scenes were shot at Sherman Moore's Horshoe L Ranch near Dewey, Oklahoma, where Tom was still working as night marshal. Cowboy Johnny Mullins, who appeared in the film, remembered the movie being shot in tiny Flemington, Missouri as did Olive Mix in her autobiography.[57]

The roster of cowboys who appeared with Tom in the earliest Selig films is a who's who list of Oklahoma cowboy notables. Pat Long, the champion bull-dogger appears along with champion ropers Johnny Mullins and Charles Fuqua. Champion steer roper Harry Grammar ropes and ties a steer in 14.5 seconds in the film *Ranch Life in the Great Southwest*, and Tom bucks out a bronc and bull-dogs a steer in the same movie.[58]

It is interesting to note that Olive recalled Tom's first film was *The Range Rider*.[59]

Other historians insist that Tom's first film was *Ranch Life In the Great Southwest*.[60]

It appears that *The Range Rider* is the first movie Tom actually appeared in, but the first movie to be released to the public which featured Tom was *The Trimming of Paradise Gulch* (1910).[61]

In *Ranch Life in the Great Southwest*, Tom was billed as a former United States marshal. The film is basically a series of shots of the cowboys going about their tasks. It is visually akin to watching a rodeo.

The film would be a hit for Selig, who was taking risks by traveling far and wide to find subjects that would interest movie audiences. Even in a time when movie tickets only cost a nickel, the film made a good profit for the studio.

Motion picture production was in its infancy, but already enterprising producers were looking for new topics at which they could point their cameras. The films they produced were short subjects, often without plots. The hand-cranked cameras produced jumpy images that, when under cranked by the projectionists would flicker wildly, thus the films were nicknamed "flickers." The term was not one of endearment. Much of established, civilized society viewed these new motion pictures as cheap, tawdry entertainment, partly because the poorer immigrant classes who could not afford tickets to symphonies, ballets and legitimate theater gravitated toward the cheap nickelodeons, so named because a ticket cost a nickel.

Most of the Selig films were flickers, short one-reel films lasting about five minutes.

Tom and Olive talked it over and decided that the motion picture industry might be a way to make money to buy and build Tom's dream ranch.[62]

In 1910, Tom went back to his old stomping grounds and signed on with Zack Mulhall and his wild west show.[63]

Tom had considered going back to work for the 101 Ranch but thought he'd have a better time with Zack and Lucille, now that he was married to Olive. Zack Mulhall could tolerate Tom's presence now that he knew the roustabout cowboy was married and not trying to court his daughter.

The show went on the road and Tom did his usual roping and riding tricks much to the delight of audiences. The Mulhall show hit Knoxville, Tennessee on September 12, 1910 for a thirty-day stand at the Appalachian Exposition.[64]

The highlight of the month-long event was the appearance by former President Theodore Roosevelt. Tom rode up to the grandstand and chatted with Roosevelt, no doubt recalling his ride with Seth Bullock's Cowboy Brigade to celebrate Roosevelt's inaugural.[65]

Roosevelt insisted that Tom and Olive join him for dinner after the show. During dinner Roosevelt presented them with an autographed set of his multi-volume *The Winning of the West.*[66]

During the show's run, Tom did double duty. He performed with the show and also filmed a movie for Selig called *Two Boys In Blue*. While in Knoxville, Tom received a check for $250 from William Selig, who wanted Tom to use the money to hire a contingent of cowboys and Indians for upcoming movie productions.[67]

Mulhall caught wind of Tom's deal with Selig and tried to get Tom to hire his show for the movie. Mulhall's show was on the verge of bankruptcy and he wanted in on the deal. Tom didn't think the Mulhall show Indians would be right for the movie.[68]

"The Indians employed with the Mulhall show would not do for picture purposes as they are mostly short haired and young and do not look the part," Tom wrote to Selig on September 26. He added that Selig should "send a man to the reservation to secure good picture workers or get them from some show that is just closing, the latter would be rather hard as the Indians all like to go home after closing season." Tom recommended using a man who called himself "California Frank" to secure a contingent of Cherokee Indians from North Carolina for the movies.[69]

Tom told Selig it would be no problem hiring as many cowboys as needed. "I can gather at any time all the typical real cowboys at a remarkably low salary—they to furnish their own horses if necessary…"[70]

Tom told Selig he could leave the Mulhall show and come work for the studio. Mulhall was furious at the idea of Tom leaving and even more furious that Tom wasn't steering Selig's money his way.[71]

While the show was in Knoxville, Tom was arrested for horse-stealing on a warrant from Oklahoma. The incident caused Tom great alarm as horse thieves were still being hung in 1910. Tom was extradited back to Kay County, Oklahoma. To his dismay, the man accusing him of horse theft was none other than Zack Miller. Tom was stunned. He had thought his relationship with the Millers was a cordial one, but he soon learned the Miller brothers could be crafty and downright dangerous when they wanted to be.

The allegation was that, in 1905, Tom had borrowed a 101 Ranch horse to ride from the ranch to a rodeo. During the rodeo Tom was riding a bronc, which stumbled and fell and Tom went down with it, breaking his leg. While Tom was convalescing, the 101 ranch horse that Tom had borrowed was taken to Zack Mulhall's ranch and then suspiciously disappeared.[72]

The complexity of the story worsens at this point. Some accounts make is clear that Zack Miller used the horse-stealing charge as a vehicle to get Tom to return to the 101 Ranch. Other versions contend that Zack Mulhall conspired with Zack Miller to dredge up the disappearance of the horse and slap Tom with a criminal charge to tie up Tom in Oklahoma, thus ensuring that Selig would use Mulhall's show in his movies.[73]

What is not clear is why Miller would accuse Tom of horse-stealing to help out Mulhall, or why Mulhall would assist Miller in trapping Tom into working for a rival show. Mulhall was competing directly with the Miller Brothers 101 Ranch and Wild West Show. Most likely the two ranchers came up with the plan to further their mutual interests. Tom would not interfere with Mulhall's efforts to get Selig's money and Miller would have Tom back in the fold for a second winter tour in Mexico. It would be the second time in two years that the 101 show, rather than shutting down for the winter, would head south of the border for a series of shows.

Tom's bond was set at $1,000. On October 31, 1910, Tom appeared before Judge Claude Duvall. County Attorney J.E. Burns prosecuted. Tom waived his preliminary hearing. Tom and Olive scraped up his bail money and hired attorney Sam K. Sullivan to represent him. The case was docketed with District Judge William Boles, who set the trial for January 16, 1911. Tom skipped bail and the case disappeared off the docket.[74] Only the powerful Miller brothers could have engineered Tom skating on a felony horse-theft charge.

Tom got his neck out of the hangman's noose by quitting the Mulhall show and rejoining the 101. Selig opted not to use Tom for the films because Tom was too busy clearing his name. Tom wrote to Selig, trying to explain his predicament, on November 1.

"[Mulhall] wanted me to recommend that you advance $1,000 [to Mulhall] to spring his outfit…Certainly I would not enter into any such deal, and they attempted to crowd me out and brought this Oklahoma charge against me…"[75]

Tom boarded the train and again headed south of the Rio Grande with the 101 show.[76]

The show traveled in a special train that was brightly painted in the circus style. Per order, the troupe was always dressed in its finest wardrobe to entice the audiences to come to the show. As the garishly painted train passed one impoverished village after another, the villagers would come out of their homes and businesses to watch it pass by.[77]

When the show reached Mexico City there was great interest in Bill Pickett, the famous black cowboy who invented the sport of bulldogging, also known as steer wrestling. Bulldogging is when a cowboy rides up alongside a running steer and then leaps onto the steer's back, grabs its horns and then throws the steer onto its side. Pickett invented the sport and, in addition to throwing the steer, would often immobilize it by biting the steer's lip with his teeth.

Tom had known Pickett since his early days at the 101. There is no information as to whether Tom and Bill were friends, but all indications were that they got along well. Indeed, the cowboy culture was far more integrated as a culture than the rest of American culture at the time. Modern films and books fail to accurately portray the climate of the day. Black, Mexican, Indian and mixed breed cowboys were commonplace and they worked together without rancor.

It is amazing that Pickett, billed as the "Dusky Demon," agreed to return to Mexico. He was at the center of a violent and almost fatal performance during the 1908 tour. That year, Pickett had stayed at the 101 Ranch when the show left for Mexico but Joe Miller sent for him when Mexican officials began fining the show for falsely advertising that Pickett was to perform.[78]

When Pickett arrived in Mexico, Joe Miller had goaded Mexican bullfighting promoters at the El Toreo bullring, betting them large sums of money that Pickett could bulldog a Mexican fighting bull and keep it immobilized for five minutes. The wagering was fierce.[79]

During the December 23, 1908 performance in Mexico City, Pickett rode his beloved bay horse, Spradley, into the arena. Joe, Zack, and cowboy Vester Pegg were all mounted on horses to act as Pickett's hazers. Their job was to steer the bull into position so that Pickett could leap off his horse and throw the bull.[80]

As bulls are considerably more aggressive than castrated steers, things went horribly wrong. Instead of being hazed, the bull turned sharply and hooked a horn deep into Spradley's rump. The pony screamed and stumbled, sitting down on its rump in shock. Pickett leapt from the horse onto the bull's horns, more to save his horse than to bulldog the bull for the audience. The bull, unaccustomed to such a tactic, went berserk, but no matter what it did, Pickett never lost his grip. For an agonizing seven and a half minutes, Pickett hung onto the bull's horns, bulldogging the bull. Rather than cheering Pickett's feat, the audience reacted with fury. Filled with anti-American nationalism, the Mexican crowd began pelting Pickett with debris, including rocks and bottles. Pickett's face was badly cut twice by sharp rocks thrown by strong spectators and another beer bottle hit him so solidly in the side that two ribs were broken.[81]

Picket finally fell to the ground in agony and Vester Pegg leapt in front of the bull waving his red shirt to distract the deadly animal while Pickett was helped from the ring. Badly wounded, Pickett refused treatment and went immediately to his beloved horse. Spradley was so weak from loss of blood and shock that the horse could not stand. Pickett was inconsolable. An old Mexican approached hesitantly and offered to help. Pickett nodded, a look of desperation on his dusty, brown face. The old man sent a boy down the street to obtain two red bananas. The boy returned and the old man peeled the bananas and pushed them into the deep wound. Surprisingly, Spradley stopped shaking from shock and was soon able to stand. The horse soon healed and was left with no aftereffects of the injury, except a scar.[82]

In the end, Pickett had kept the bull immobile for seven and a half minutes. When the promoters paid off the bet, the Miller brothers netted $53,000.[83]

It is not known if Bill Pickett shared in the winnings. As tight with a buck as the Millers were, it is unlikely.

During the 1910 tour of Mexico, Tom once again recreated the incident that had made Will Rogers famous. Stack Lee, the show's marksman, turned a steer loose in the stands with Tom's help and Bill Pickett rode out, roped the steer and pulled it back into the arena to great applause.[84]

During the Mexico tour Zack Miller got wind of a tragic incident at a Mexican circus where husband and wife lion tamers were killed by lions. Their son, called Machacha in some accounts and Muchacho in others, was ten years old at the time. (It is likely that the boy's name was Muchacho because it means "boy" in Spanish.) Muchacho had also been attacked and one of his arms was mangled.

Zack and his wife, Mabel, adopted the crippled boy and took him on tour with the 101 as a mascot.[85]

When the Mexican tour ended, Tom worked the balance of the off-season on several Selig films.[86]

Selig saw early on that Tom had a charisma on film. Selig's first stars, Gilbert M. "Bronco Billy" Anderson and Hobart Bosworth were portly, un-athletic men who could hardly ride a horse and had no cowboy skills. They barely fit the bill as cowboy heroes. This was not so with Tom. Tom had an athletic grace.

Even with the primitive flicker images, Tom's personality seemed to transcend the medium. Additionally, Tom was able to do all of the things a cowboy hero was supposed to do. Tom Mix didn't need a stand-in to do his riding, roping, fighting or shooting. Tom was the real deal.[87]

Selig cast Tom in nine one-reel films which were made in a flurry of activity in the winter of 1909-1910. Some were straight adventure stories, while others were westerns. *Briton and Boer, Taming Wild Animals* and *Up San Juan Hill* were adventure films and *Pride of the Range, The Pony Express, The Millionaire Cowboy, Briton and Boer, An Indian Wife's Devotion* and *The Range Riders* were westerns.[88]

Olive played a featured role in *The Range Riders*. Tom's pal, Hoot Gibson, who would later become a big cowboy movie star and Tom's main competitor in Hollywood westerns, made his first appearance on film in *Pride of the Range*. *Briton and Boer* and *Up San Juan Hill* were filmed along the Des Plaines River near Chicago, Illinois.[89]

Many of the cowboys who appeared in the Selig movies were from Will A. Dickey's Circle D Wild West Show and Indian Congress. This wild bunch of Montana cowboys liked to hurrah around and raise the roof whenever there was a dull moment. Tom got along well with the cowboys but kept a low profile and was not remembered as a particularly loquacious person.

Tom's star began to rise at Selig as the company began to realize how well Tom's looks and manner translated into charisma on screen. He was dark and handsome and athletic and seemed to have a sharp wit. When it came time for comedic scenes, Tom was funny. When it came time for no-holds-barred action, Tom was thrilling.

Not content to make Tom just a cowboy hero, Selig was determined to make him an all-around adventure hero. The studio decided to make some films with Tom in colorful locales, such as the mountains of Tennessee and the bayous of Florida, where Selig had a studio. The westerns would be shot in Prescott, Arizona.[90]

Tom was already showing his daring on film as early as 1910. In one film he jumped a horse off of a 30-foot cliff into a lake. He is reported to have broken two ribs and knocked out several teeth.[91]

There are varying stories about Tom's teeth—or lack of them. By 1910, some of Tom's teeth were already knocked out and others were covered with gold. By the time Tom signed with Fox Studios in 1917, he was wearing a full set of dentures.

Tom and Olive went on to Florida to film *Taming Wild Animals*.

Taming Wild Animals was a jungle adventure film. Tom played the hero and silent movie serial queen Kathlyn Williams played the heroine. The film was shot at Selig's Florida studio and featured several leopards, a lion, a camel and an elephant, all of whom were owned by animal trainer Tom Persons.[92]

Filming with wild animals, even ones handled by trainers, is extremely hazardous, as Kathlyn Williams found out one afternoon when one of Person's leopards attacked her. The trainer later speculated that the leopard was reacting to Williams' long blonde hair. The leopard turned on Williams and knocked her to the ground. It straddled her and was about to maul her when Tom pulled his pistol and shot the leopard dead.[93]

"The hungry leopard sprung for Miss Williams an' drove the claws of his forepaws into her scalp," Tom recalled years later. "I saw but one thing to do, an' I grabs Mr. Leopard by the tail, gives him a yank, and swings him clear…Finally I saw what I thought was a clear chance an' turned Mr. Leopard loose. He…started back at me…I got my old six shooter loose an' sent two shots in the direction of the leopard."[94]

Luckily for Selig, the cameraman caught the entire event on camera and the scene was included in the final film, much to the delight of film audiences.[95]

When Tom finished the series of films for Selig he had fulfilled his contract and was suddenly unemployed.

He reportedly worked a short time in 1910 for the Crescent Cattle Company at Four Mile Ranch in the Pike National Forest.[96]

In 1911 Selig realized he had a gold mine in Tom Mix. The versatile performer could carry action scenes as well as "dialog" scenes with ease. Selig saw that Tom could devise outlandish action sequences that left audiences breathless. One such stunt was recounted in the November 16, 1911 Canon City Record. "Another 'stunt' done by Mr. Mix at the show grounds on Friday was the 'bulldogging' of a large steer in something like twelve seconds, which, perhaps, in celerity has never been equaled in Colorado…In the instance alluded to, Mr. Mix was driven in an automobile at a high rate of speed to within a few feet of the steer selected for the experiment when he leaped from the machine to the back of the animal and threw it to the ground in the manner described. The whole thing was done so quickly as to astonish spectators...Many of the sports 'pulled off' by Mr. Mix and his associates here for photographic reproduction are hazardous in the extreme and require a degree of skill that is truly marvelous."[97]

The footage of this stunt, or a re-enactment of it, was included in the 1912 Selig film entitled *The Diamond S Ranch*.

The company wired Tom and asked him to come to Chicago to sign a new contract and join the company's production unit which was heading to Canon City, Colorado to film several outdoor films.[98]

They reportedly offered Tom the princely sum of $100 per week. In 1911 terms, that was big money for playing cowboy for the movies.[99]

Little did Tom know that in ten years he'd be making a reported $17,500 per week at the height of his film career.

Hollywood had still not been established as the movie capital of the United States, and many studios were trying out different locales. Canon City made sense because it had a railroad terminus and breathtaking scenery. Other studios were using Las Vegas, New Mexico. Tom eventually worked in both locales before moving on to Hollywood.

Movie studios have, throughout the history of filmmaking, had an edge when it comes to dealing with communities. Every town wants a movie company to locate within their confines. It is both glamorous and also profitable to have movies filmed in your town. It is also disruptive, but few complain when movie stars are in their midst. Such was the case with Canon City, Colorado. The town's fathers welcomed the Selig production unit with open arms. Selig rented most of the available houses in town. The company hired the entire contents of the livery stables, including the horses, saddles, wagons and teams. Townspeople were hired as extras at a whopping $5 per day, better than any job available in town. Children were often hired as errand boys for $1 a day. Entire cattle herds and the cowboys who herded them were hired for certain scenes.[100]

Tom arrived in Canon City in 1911 along with the studio's big name stars, William Duncan and Myrtle Steadman, who were enjoying their brief moments of fame and fortune.[101]

The actors were encouraged to integrate into the local community, to attend church and other social club functions.

Olive recalled in her memoir that Tom was popular with the cast, production crew and the residents of Canon City while filming in Colorado.

"He would treat a prop boy as though he were his closest friend. His warm regard for people reached out and permeated everyone he came in contact with," Olive said. "He was always thinking of what he could do for others. Even when we were isolated in the mountains of Colorado, he thought of a plan to bring some cheer into some very gray lives."[102]

Olive recalled that Tom staged a wild west show for a penitentiary while in Colorado, including his roping act. Actress Myrtle Steadman sang for the prisoners. Olive said the prisoners were "rapturous" with appreciation.[103]

Tom was often asked to give speeches. One thing Tom hated throughout his entire career was speaking before live audiences.[104]

He simply hated it, loathed it, feared it and would flatly refuse to give a speech. Tom would spend considerable time performing for an audience with rope and gun tricks, horse stunts and other wild west show feats, but he would not talk unless he had to. Many who knew him believed it was because Tom wore dentures. Indeed, Tom had knocked most of his teeth out during his wild west show, rodeo and early film days. There is a photo of Tom taken around 1911 that shows Tom smiling at Myrtle Steadman and he is clearly missing some of his upper left incisors.[105]

Each major stunt in a Tom Mix movie took a physical toll on Tom, and often that toll was taken on his teeth. When Tom finally got dentures, they slipped often and did so with such a loud click that he was often taciturn simply to avoid the embarrassment of his audience learning of his false teeth. Tom would later continue to make silent movies after the advent of sound in motion pictures simply because he dreaded speaking on camera.

Selig rented a two-story building in Canon City, located at the intersection of Third and Main Streets.[106]

Residents of the town often saw the movie company about town filming scenes, often racing horses back and forth in front of the cameras. Steadman, a petite and innocent-looking woman, received considerable attention from both men and women who lived in Canon City. She was the darling of the town.

Tom, on the other hand, had gotten a reputation as a rowdy. He was always restless, relieving his boredom in Canon City by getting into trouble with women and whisky. Reports of Tom's drinking at Hell's Half Acre Saloon began to circulate. Tom often ended his work day in the saloon drinking its nickel beer and playing pool. Woody Higgins, a resident of Canon City at the time, remembered the high jinx at the Hell's Half Acre Saloon. Tom and the movie cowboys would put lemons on top of upended shot glasses at one end of the bar and then take turns standing at the other end of the bar shooting the lemons off of the shot glasses. Whoever missed had to buy the next round of drinks.[107]

One night Tom riled a local cowboy during an argument by pulling his gun. The cowboy pulled his gun and told Tom he was going to shoot the buttons off of Tom's shirt. Tom holstered his gun. By the end of the evening the two were fast friends, Higgins said.[108]

F.L. "Peanut" Bunten was Canon City's first car dealer. He used to hang out in the saloons when Tom and the Selig company were in town. He recalled an incident when Tom began boasting about his cowboy skills. "Often on a Saturday night, Tom and three or four of the boys would hire a car for a trip to the surrounding towns. When he got a few drinks, he was inclined to become boastful. I remember one time when he was boasting about his ability as a rider and bulldogger and Abe Humphries stopped him cold. He said, 'Tom, I believe you have things reversed. You know down in Old Mexico the bulls throw the people.'"[109]

Tom also began carousing with women, who found him irresistible.[110]

He alternated between playing heroes and villains in on film, but Tom was different from the other movie actors with the company. The other men were largely soft-bellied Easterners with cultured manners and a diffident air. Tom was dark-eyed and masculine, with the lean, sinewy grace of a cowman of the plains. He was tanned and rugged and exuded a solid manliness. By the time Tom reached Canon City in 1911 he had also learned the value of self-promotion and had begun telling windies about his days as a soldier of fortune, an Oklahoma sheriff and U.S. marshal and a member of Teddy Roosevelt's Rough Riders.[111]

These tall tales endeared him to the people of Canon City, especially the women, who began to flirt openly with him.

Suddenly Tom was a ladies' man and Olive was not a bit happy about it. She began to quarrel with Tom about his roving eye and wandering hands.[112]

One night Tom and Olive had a nasty argument which resulted in Tom fleeing for his life. Olive, who was part Indian and had a short fuse, pulled a gun on Tom. Tom took off on foot with Olive in hot pursuit. Tom ducked into the Smith Hall Elks Club and enlisted the doorman's help. As the doorman barred Olive's way, Tom bolted upstairs and climbed out a window, hiding in the rolled-up awning. Pistol in hand, Olive conducted a room-to-room search for Tom. Unable to find him, Olive camped out on the steps in front of the Elks Club and waited. The next morning the daytime doorman came on duty and, as was his custom, he unrolled the awning. Tom rolled out with it and fell like a sack of potatoes onto the sidewalk where Olive was still waiting.[113]

Another time Olive was so sick of Tom's womanizing that she lost her temper while Tom was filming a kissing scene and, pulling her pistol, sent Tom's lovely co-star scurrying in terror for her dressing room.[114]

On another occasion, Tom and Olive were at the Stokes Ranch and Tom took Olive's fancy horse and buggy to Bartlesville to visit some friends, promising to return by dinner. Instead, he didn't come back home until nearly dawn the next day. Olive met Tom at the front door, pointing a Winchester rifle at him. Olive told Tom to hide behind a tree in the front yard. When he demurred, Olive fired off a round at Tom that was too close for comfort. Tom took refuge behind the tree and stayed there until Olive told him to come out.[115]

Olive's distress at Tom's womanizing was understandable. She was barely 24 and Tom was 31. She was a rancher's daughter, a tomboy and rough around the edges, with a straightforward earthiness and Victorian faithfulness. Suddenly Tom was thrown into the company of gentile women possessed with womanly wiles who sought a husband and, even worse, actresses with an easy sexuality who were attracted to Tom's celebrity.

The Selig days at Canon City were some of the earliest forays into location filming. Actors did their own stunts, especially Tom, who was called upon to do some harrowing stunts for the films. Filming was often fraught with risk. Contemporary accounts of that time give testimony to the dangers.[116]

The October 11 and 12, 1911 issues of the *Canon City Record* recounted a stunt gone awry during the making of *The Telltale Knife* in which Tom and another actor nearly drowned. The two accounts are combined here for clarity.

"The two outlaws, who were represented by Tom Mix and Charlie Farrar, rode their horses at breakneck speed down the side of the mountains on the south side of the [Arkansas] River, some four or five hundred yards across the mouth of Grape Creek and plunged into its current from a rock fully ten feet above the bank; creating a mighty splash in water as they did so. A few minutes later the sheriff and a posse followed and repeated the same performance; a regular fusillade of shots being fired by the pursued and the pursuers…The great volume of water pouring out of Grape Creek forces its way at right angles almost across the river and imperils the life of any living thing that gets into it except waterfowl. A sandbar has been created by its current for, perhaps, a quarter of the distance across the river on its eastern border and it was to that haven of refuge that Mix and Farrar were swimming their horses when the latter nearly lost his life. Farrer in some manner got too far out from the bank and was swept around the end of the bar by the rushing waters and horse and rider were repeatedly submerged in a swirling current that nothing could withstand.

"Frank Carroll, who was one of the sheriff's posse, was nearly drowned in the same place and in almost precisely the same manner a few minutes later. Leon Watson was also in great peril for a short time from a similar cause…Eddie Cull [sic], the photographer of the company, while wading out in the river to avail himself of the most advantageous point in which to take the pictures, was swept from his footing by the water and in his struggles to reach a place of safety got into some quicksand from which he was extricated with considerable difficulty by his friends. 'It looked for a few minutes,' said Mr. Thayer, 'that the undertaker was about to have the biggest job of his life. Happily all's well that ends well and his services were not needed.'"[117]

Another account of the incident, reported in the October 11, 1911 *Florence Daily Citizen*, finishes the tale: "Both horse and rider (Farrar) were drowning. Occasionally the rider's head appeared above the water for a moment and it was during one of these moments that [a] big Mexican who is one of aggregation threw a lariat about 100 feet and made one of the neatest ties on record, then he landed the desperado while the crowd cheered."[118]

Throughout 1911 Tom was a featured player or the star in a flurry of Selig films, including *In Old California, When Gringos Came, In the Days of Gold, The Schoolmaster of Mariposa, Rescued by Her Lions* (possibly a reissue of *Taming Wild Animals*), *Kit Carson's Wooing, Lost in the Arctic, Lost in the Jungle* (possibly a reissue of *Taming Wild Animals*), *The Cowboy and the Shrew, Back to the Primitive, The Rose of Old St. Augustine, Captain Kate, Saved by the Pony Express, Dad's Girls, Told in Colorado, Why the Sheriff Is a Bachelor, Western Hearts, The Tell-Tale Knife, A Romance of the Rio Grande,* and *The Bully of Bingo Gulch*. All of these films were short one-reelers, but each contained short, often inventive stories which showcased Tom's charisma. Even when Tom played the villain or a secondary character, his magnetism was apparent. It was evident that Tom Mix was a real cowboy, and this added to the credibility of his onscreen portrayals. The Selig company began to see that Tom Mix might very well be the next big western star.

7

In 1912, The Miller Brothers 101 Ranch and Wild West Show was in its heyday. Thousands of tourists visited the ranch each year and tens of thousands came to see their traveling wild west show. Tom Mix's stature as a performer grew as well, thanks in part to his Selig movie work. Additionally, many other cowboys joined the show and stayed for years—and many went on to Hollywood to become popular cowboy stars, often in direct competition with Tom. The most notable of these were Hoot Gibson, Ken Maynard and Buck Jones. Gibson was a close friend of Tom's and can be seen in bit parts in some of Tom's earliest Selig films, including *Pride of the Range* (1910). In *The Man From Texas* (1915), Hoot is clearly seen as a member of the posse.

Hoot came to fame when he won the All-Around Cowboy championship at the Pendleton Roundup in 1912.[1] He would go on to enormous success as a cowboy star, using his quick wit and charming personality rather than just his fists and guns. Hoot was popular in Hollywood and worked steadily into the 1940s in low-budget matinee westerns called "B westerns." When age overtook him, he continued acting in small character parts, including working with John Wayne on the big-budget cavalry epic, *The Horse Soldiers* in 1959.[2] The film was directed by John Ford, the rapscallion film director who began his career in silent films under the name Sean O'Fearna. Ford's first successful silent film was *Straight Shooting*, starring Hoot and silent movie icon Harry Carey.

Ken Maynard was a brilliant rider, capable of some of the most daring riding stunts ever seen by wild west show and movie audiences. He was born on July 21, 1895 in Indiana, but claimed he was from Mission, Texas.[3] He went on to tour with popular circuses and then jumped to movies. A big, broad-shouldered man, Ken had enormous appetites. He loved to eat and drink and, unfortunately, when he drank he became a violently depressed demon.[4]

His deeply rooted emotional problems would come to the surface without warning and in less than 20 years he had worn out his welcome in Hollywood. He would die a bitter man, broke and forced to live in a mobile home with his daughter.[5]

Buck Jones was born Charles Gephardt and lived the adventurous life that many cowboy stars—especially Tom—would have their publicists invent. He was a soldier in Mexico and in the Philippines. He joined the 101 Ranch around 1911. Chuck Gephardt became Buck Jones when he went to Hollywood and signed with Fox Studios. His career took off at Fox, the studio at which Tom had his greatest success.[6]

Fox executives had decided in the early 1920s that Tom was being overpaid, even though Tom's films brought in such profits that the entire studio operated off of the revenues from Tom's movies. Fox brought in Buck Jones to try to build him up into a younger version of Tom Mix—at a much lower salary. Indeed, the entire budget of a Buck Jones western was equal to Tom's salary. Tom and Buck remained friends for many years, even after Buck's star eclipsed Tom's at Fox Studios. They kept in touch right up until Tom's death in 1940. Just months before Tom died, they staged a chariot race in Hollywood in 1940 to benefit charities.[7]

Of them all, Hoot Gibson was Tom biggest competitor. He was born Edmund Richard Gibson in Tekamah, Nebraska on August 6, 1892.[8] Ed was given the nickname "Hooter" as a teenager when he delivered drugs for the Owl Pharmacy. As he grew to manhood, the nickname was shortened to "Hoot." A somewhat homely man with a sad, puppy dog face, Hoot went on to become one of Tom's best friends and chief rival during Tom's heyday in Hollywood. Hoot was famous for his devil may care attitude. He was by far the best horseman in the movies, better even than Tom, and he was fearless. When a producer asked Hoot if the studio could pay him money to let a horse drag him for a scene, Hoot replied that for the right price he'd let the horse kick him to death.[9]

Hoot appeared in some of Tom's earliest films when he was still an unknown. He became famous in 1912 when he won the All-Around Championship at the Pendleton, Oregon Roundup and the roping championship at the Calgary Stampede.[10] He returned to Hollywood in 1913 and wrangled a job as a stuntman for various other cowboy stars before working as an actor and becoming a star.

As far back as 1908, the Miller brothers, ever mindful of keeping abreast of the newest ways to market and promote their enterprise, discovered to their delight that movie-making served a dual purpose. Not only would the films promote the ranch and wild west show to new audiences, the 101 could make money by hiring out its performers to film studios and also take a share of the profits. They began associating with Selig Polyscope and the studio sent a production unit to the 101 in 1909. While filming at the 101 Ranch, producers filmed Tom riding a blindfolded horse off of a 30-foot high bluff into the Salt Fork River. It was likely Tom's first appearance in front of a movie camera.[11] William Selig would remember the cowboy who made the insane jump, knocking out his teeth in the process. Two years later he would tell Will Dickey to use that daredevil cowboy in some western movies being shot in Missouri and Tom's movie career began.

Little did the Miller brothers know that Tom Mix, their $35 a month cowboy, would turn that insane jump into a movie career that would make him richer than their wildest dreams—and even more famous than they were.

Western movies were fast becoming a staple of the new cinema. Audiences related to the iconography of the American cowboy, and they wanted more authentic cowboy heroes. Westerns had come along way since Edwin C. Porter had scored a ground-breaking hit with *The Great Train Robbery*, which was shot in New Jersey and released in 1903.[12]

8

The world around Tom was changing as the year 1912 began. Modern mechanized society was advancing westward with blinding speed. The old west was long dead and it was obvious that making a living as a cowboy was far less lucrative than working as a performing cowboy.

Tom was intrigued by the movie business. The idea that he could get paid for clowning around on camera, tossing a rope or riding a horse appealed to him. It seemed like a way to make a quick buck. The $100 per week he had been paid by Selig in 1911 was big money.

Tom realized that he loved the sawdust trail of the wild west shows as much for the footloose nature of the lifestyle as for the performing in front of audiences.[1]

He loved the freewheeling life of the tour. He loved rodeos and he loved county fairs. He loved drifting around the country playing cowboy for audiences. It simply wasn't work. It was just fun.

But Tom wanted to make big bucks playing cowboy—and in the process made history.

A little-known fact is Tom's involvement in the creation of the Calgary Stampede, an annual rodeo of enormous proportions that began in 1912 and has continued annually for nearly a century.

In the winter of 1912 Tom received a letter from Guy Weadick. Weadick was in New York City trying to put together a rodeo and wild west show combination that would be staged in Calgary, Alberta, Canada.[2]

Tom wired Weadick and agreed to help him put on the event. Tom had agreed to appear in a wild west show owned by Fred T. Cummins but the tour wasn't scheduled to begin until April.

Tom, Olive and Weadick arrived in Calgary in March of 1912 and their proposal to create a week-long celebration of the frontier was widely covered in the press.[3]

The *Alberton* newspaper carried an article about the two men in its March 25 issue. The newspaper noted Tom Micks (sic) "of Bliss, Oklahoma" was heading the effort to create "an annual national event that will mark the last stand of the picturesque western cowboy on the outer edge of civilization...who are now rarely seen or heard of, except in Russell pictures or western novels." Two days later the *Calgary News Telegram* carried a story that made it plain that the effort to establish the Calgary Stampede was "headed by Tom Mix, Champion Roper of the World..." and posited that Tom planned "to bring to Calgary the best aggregation of ropers, riders and general all-around cowpunchers that has ever been gathered together on the American continent." Tom and Weadick began working with a local livestock contractor named A.P. Day, who planned to supply the stock for the event.[4]

Not four days later a rift developed between Weadick and Tom. Tom got cross ways with Weadick over Weadick's comments about Joe Miller of the 101 Ranch. Weadick apparently had an axe to grind with Miller and made his feelings known to Tom. Tom wanted to involve the 101 Ranch in the Calgary event and Weadick apparently did not.[5]

Tom felt that Weadick had insulted Miller. Tom was so upset with Weadick that he wrote to Joe Miller to advise him of the situation. Tom told Joe Miller in a letter that Weadick was "sure sore on you and is knocking the show right and left." Tom wrote that Weadick and others thought that the 101 Ranch show had declined in quality and that there appeared to be a scheme to cheat the 101 Ranch out of $1,000 by charging a "license" for the show to appear.[6]

Tom closed his letter by reiterating that he thought Weadick was being unfair. "Now, I don't know what you and Guy's troubles are, but I know this much, that you gave him work when no one else would have him and as far as I know, treated him with more consideration he retaliated with."[7]

Tom asked Joe Miller to keep the letter confidential.

Joe Miller's response was not what Tom expected. Miller defended Weadick and left Tom in the cold, creating a rift between the two men that would widen over the years into an all-out hatred.[8]

Miller sent Tom a letter on April 10 that expressed anger and dismay over Tom's allegations about Weadick. He told Tom that he was going to write Weadick and send Tom's letter to find out what was going on. Miller wrote Weadick that same day and included Tom's letter. Joe demanded to know what was going on and asserted that "somebody is either a damned fool or crazy."[9]

The result of this exchange was Tom was summarily booted from the Calgary group. Most likely Weadick felt that Tom was a spy in his midst. There is no record of what occurred between the men, but Tom did not take any further part in the creation of the Calgary Stampede, nor did he appear at the inaugural event during the week of September 2, 1912.[10]

Tom and Weadick did not like each other thereafter. Years later, when Zack Miller sued Tom for breach of contract, Weadick sent a barrage of letters to Zack urging him on, making derogatory comments about Tom.[11]

In 1912 Olive grew weary of Tom's roving eye, bent elbow and rootless life. She encouraged him to leave the movies and the sawdust trail and take up ranching, where they could spend more time in each other's company.

There is some dispute as to what Tom did next. Some historians contend that Tom returned to the 101 Ranch, while others insist Tom toured with Guy Weadick's show. Olive remembered that Tom joined Vernon Seiver's Young Buffalo Show in Peoria, Illinois.[12]

Olive asserts that she and Tom traveled to shows at Dominion Park and in Montreal.

Tom went on to compete in a rodeo and wild west show organized by Weadick in Dominion Park, Montreal. During the show's Sunday night performance Tom was bulldogging a steer when disaster struck. The steer was savvy and didn't care to be bulldogged. As Tom leaned off of his horse and wrapped his arms around the steer's horns the steer stopped short and twisted its head, hooking Tom in the jaw. Tom was knocked unconscious. He was carried out of the arena and taken to the dressing rooms. A doctor was summoned but Tom refused to be treated. Tom shook off the cobwebs because he wanted to compete in the bronc riding contest. Later that evening Tom headed to the bucking chutes, his jaunty smile intact, assuring his fellow cowboys that he was all right.[13]

Tom's bronc was particularly wild that night, bucking and kicking and rearing with great force, twisting and sunfishing as it bucked. Tom had a good seat for the first part of the ride but lost his seat and pitched forward, landing on the back of his head and shoulders. The impact knocked Tom out for the second time that evening.

Johnny Mullins, the champion roper who appeared with Tom in Tom's first movie, insisted that Tom accompany him to a local hospital.[14] Thankfully, Tom recovered quickly.

Prior to their arrival in Montreal, Olive told Tom that she was pregnant. She recalled that Tom reacted to her pregnancy by becoming overprotective, which got on her nerves. She said Tom began to handle her like fragile china.[15]

Olive said she was with Tom in Montreal during the final weeks of her pregnancy and she was growing apprehensive about having the baby in Canada. She insisted that she return home to Oklahoma to give birth. Tom sent Olive home by train and said he'd be along as soon as he finished the show.[16]

Olive gave birth to their daughter, named Nadine Ruth Jane Mix, on July 11, 1912 at the Stokes Ranch near Dewey, Oklahoma. Other accounts list her birthday as July 13. Tom arrived three days later on the train from Montreal.[17]

He was struck by the awesome responsibility of parenting little Ruth and he told Olive that he thought that he should give up the wild west shows and movies and settle down to a life of ranching or law enforcement. Olive didn't think Tom could do it. She realized, sadly, that "there was never going to be a real 'settling down' in our lives."[18]

Tom got his job as part-time night marshal back. The oil boom was in full swing and vice was running rampant throughout Dewey. Tom had his hands full keeping the lid on the rowdies who were drunk on cheap moonshine.[19]

"It was a hard job! It was a great job too," Tom wrote years later. "I tell you the bootleggers led me on a fine chase in those early days in Dewey, Oklahoma."[20]

After finishing his term as night marshal in Dewey, Tom returned to the 101 Ranch for the 1912 season. An incident recorded from that season was when Tom roped a buffalo cow that went berserk when the orphan, Muchacho, and Mabel Miller's ten-year-old cousin, Jack Cleo Baskin, were teasing the cow's young buffalo calf. The mama buffalo, all one and a half tons of her, charged the boys. The buffalo made a ruckus as she charged and Tom, who was wrangling some dudes with Stack Lee and Bill Pickett, came to the rescue. Stack, ever the marksman, went for his rifle, but Tom and Bill leapt aboard their horses and chased after the mad buffalo cow. Stack, rifle in hand, got in front of the boys so that, if Tom and Bill failed to stop the buffalo, he could shoot it without the boys getting hurt. Tom and Bill dropped their loops on the mama buffalo and, dallying their stout ropes on their saddle horns, dragged the buffalo back to an empty corral.[21]

In the fall of 1912 Tom received an offer from Selig to return to the studio and make additional movies.[22]

Tom took the train to Chicago, signed the contract, and then headed to Prescott, Arizona, where the Selig company was using William Selig's Diamond S Ranch for a western location. Tom stopped in Oklahoma long enough to pick up Olive and Ruth and the family headed west to the scorching Arizona desert.[23]

William Selig's Diamond S Ranch was actually the Bar Circle A Ranch owned by Ed and Elizabeth Albertson and located in a region called Slaughterhouse Gulch. The Albertsons settled on the land in 1883 and leased the property to Selig in 1913.

Tom liked Prescott a great deal. Arizona was just achieving statehood but there was a wild and open feel to the high desert. The town was small but friendly, and there were plenty of opportunities to have a good time when the cameras stopped rolling. Tom even competed in the local Prescott Frontier Days Rodeo, where he won first place in the bulldogging contest.[24]

Prescott writer Budge Ruffner was a boy when Tom lived in Prescott, and he remembered years later when Tom visited Prescott one time and was having fun doing roping tricks with other cowboys at the American Ranch in Williamson Valley. Ruffner said his father was good friend of Tom's so they were invited to come along.

Ruffner remembered that Tom was galloping Tony, his movie horse, when suddenly Tom's hat blew off. Ruffner recalled that Tom turned Tony and galloped back, bending low off the galloping horse and picking up the hat without slowing down. Ruffner said that every child who was there that day tried to learn the trick and managed to break some bones in the process.[25]

What is interesting about this reflection is that Ruffner recalled that Tom was aboard Tony. This is important because it helps to date the incident. Tom did not take Tony with him wherever he went. Tony only went where Tom was performing. Tom often rode other horses when he was off camera to give Tony a break. Ruffner recalled that this memory comes from a time when Tom was only visiting Prescott, but it is likely that Tom was in Prescott making a movie. It also dates the event to after 1915 as Tom did not begin riding Tony until that time. He did not begin riding Tony exclusively on film until he retired Blue. The event Ruffner recalled most probably took place in late 1919 or early 1920 when Tom was in Prescott to film *Three Gold Coins* and *Sky High*, both films in which Tom rode Tony.

Tom would return to Prescott often throughout his life. He conveyed his feelings for Prescott in a July 26, 1939 letter to Lester and Grace Ruffner, writing, "when I come home, I will come by way of Prescott and see you all, as you know my heart always leans toward old Yavapai."[26]

Years later, the town named several streets after the titles of Tom's movies.

Selig realized by late 1912 that Tom Mix was a bankable movie star. The company wanted to keep Tom happy so, when he and Olive arrived in Prescott, the company gave the new parents their first home. The house still exists. It is now the clubhouse for residents at the Yavapai Hills Housing Development on the outskirts of town.[27]

In short order Tom completed *Outlaw Reward*, *The Cowboy's Best Girl*, *The Diamond S Ranch* and *A Reconstructed Rebel* for the studio.

Tom was, by now, eating, sleeping and breathing the movie business. He had story ideas which he shared with the studio and many of them were incorporated into scripts. Shortly thereafter, Tom began to write and direct his films. In late 1912 Tom filmed *How It Happened* and then directed his first film, *Cowboy Millionaire*. The most memorable of the 1912 films is *The Diamond S Ranch*, which featured the type of stunt that Tom would become famous for. In the film, Tom bulldogs a steer by tackling it from a speeding car.

In these and the majority of the Selig films Tom is dressed in a manner which is more subdued that his attire in his Fox films. Tom wears a big black hat with a peaked crown and wide brim. He wears a simple, light-colored shirt and chaps. His gun belt is simple and he looks more like a traditional cowboy. In short, he had not developed the circus-style wardrobe which would become his trademark.

Selig Polyscope was typical of most studios of the silent era, turning out product at a dizzying rate. Most one-reelers were completed at a rate of one film per week.

In 1913 Tom appeared in 44 one-reelers for Selig. They were *How It Happened, Cowboy Millionaire, The Range Law, Juggling with Fate, The Sheriff of Yavapai County, Pauline Cushman—the Federal Spy, The Life-Timer, The Shotgun Man and the Stage Driver, A Prisoner of Cabansas, That Mail Order Suit, His Father's Deputy, The Noisy Six, Religion and Gun Practice, The Wordless Message, Taming of a Tenderfoot, The Law and the Outlaw, Made A Coward, Songs of Truce, The Marshal's Capture, Sallie's Sure Shot, Bud Dobie Comes Back, The Only Chance, The Taming of Texas Pete, The Stolen Moccasins, A Apache's Gratitude, The Good Indian: A Saving Service Rewarded, How Betty Made Good, Howlin' Jones, Tobias Wants Out, The Rejected Lover's Luck, The Cattle Thief's Escape, Saved from the Vigilantes, The Silver Grindstone, Dishwash Dick's Counterfeit, A Muddle in Horse Thieves, The Sheriff and the Rustler, The Schoolmarm's Shooting Match, The Child of the Prairies, The Escape of Jim Dolan, Local Color, Cupid in the Cow Camp, Physical Culture on the Quarter Circle V Bar, Buster's Little Game,* and *Mother Love vs. Gold.*

By summer of 1913 Tom's old pal, Sid Jordan, had come to Prescott to see what making movies was all about. He'd spent his life in Oklahoma and after growing up had worked with his father, who was a county sheriff in Oklahoma. Sick of the newer, more civilized Oklahoma, Sid had gotten the notion to travel to the wilds of South America. While on the train somewhere in Colorado, Sid saw a newspaper article about Tom's success in the movies and decided to go have a look at his friend, the movie star, in action.[28]

Tom was delighted to see Sid and hired him on the spot. Jordan would work for Tom for the next 15 years both at Selig and until the end of Tom's Fox Studios contract. Sid's first appearance on film appears to be in *How Betty Made Good*. Sid was Tom's kindred spirit. Both men were wild, leather tough, strong and capable cowmen and excellent riders, ropers and marksmen.

Many of Tom's ingenious stunts were devised by Tom and Sid during the rough play the two men engaged in. Olive recalled that Tom and Sid were always doing dangerous stunts, even at home. Tom and Sid once packed themselves into a wooden barrel and rolled down a steep hill until the barrel crashed and splintered. Tom and Sid emerged, bruised and cut and laughing like lunatics. They would recreate the barrel roll stunt in a film later that summer.[29]

Tom made 54 films in 1914. They were *The Sheriff's Girl, Buffalo Hunting, By Unseen Hand, A Friend in Need, The Little Sister, Shotgun Jones, Me an' Bill, When the Cook Fell Ill, The Leopard's Foundling, In Defiance of the Law, The Wilderness Trail, Wiggs Takes the Rest Cure, Law of the Ladies, Etienne of th Glad Heart, His Fight, The Reveler, When the West was Young, The White Mouse, Chip of the Flying U, To Be Called For, The Fifth Man, Jim, The Lonesome Trail, The Livid Flame, Four Minutes Late, The Real Thing In Cowboys, Hearts and Masks, The Way of the Bad Man, The Moving Picture Cowboy, The Mexican, The Going of the White Swan, Jimmy Hayes and Muriel, Why the Sheriff Is a Bachelor, Garrison's Finish, The Losing Fight, The Ranger's Romance, The Tell-Tale Knife, Out of Petticoat Lane, The Sheriff's Reward, The Scapegoat, If I Were Young Again, Young Girl and Mine, The Tell-Tale Knife, Save by a Watch, The Rival Stage Lines, In the Days of the Thundering Herd, The Soul Mate, Lure of the Windigo, The Man from the East, Wade Brent Pays, Cactus Jack-Heart Breaker, Flower of Faith,* and *A Militant School Ma'am.*

The year would be a banner one for Tom as he began to take the reins of his film career, insisting on writing and directing many of his own films. He had gone from journeyman cowboy and dude wrangler to wild west show star to novice film actor to now experienced film maker in just a few short years. Tom began to turn story ideas into usable scenarios, which he would film using actors he enjoyed working with, many of them cowboys from the 101 Ranch such as Hoot Gibson and Leo Maloney. Some stories were reused and recycled.

Tom used the title *The Tell-Tale Knife* for three separate movies.

In the Days of the Thundering Herd was Tom's most important five-reeler to date. Filmed on the Oklahoma ranch owned by wild west show impresario Gordon "Pawnee Bill" Lillie, it was the first feature-length film in which Tom played a starring role. The film showed Selig that Tom could carry a full-length film and it was popular with audiences when it was released in November 1914.

The film survives today and is a remarkably big production for its time. It opens with Tom—a Pony Express rider—riding hell for leather, leaping off a running horse and landing on his feet at a dead run, leaping aboard another horse and riding away at a full gallop. Shortly after that Tom rescues Bessie Eyton from a thundering herd of buffalo by pulling her aboard his galloping horse and riding up a steep draw. In the early sequence Tom rides a fine chestnut horse, not Tony, but later on he rides Blue. The film contains some exciting Indian attacks and buffalo hunts and is head and shoulders above the one-reelers Tom made with Selig.

Tom is dressed much like William F. "Buffalo Bill" Cody, in a mid-peaked white hat and a fringed buckskin jacket festooned with Indian beads. He wears a wide, square belt buckle similar to the one made famous by Cody, and boots similar to the knee-high boots the frontiersman also wore.

With the success of *In The Days of the Thundering Herd*, Tom was given permission to make more serious Westerns. In late 1914, Tom wrote, produced, directed and starred in two westerns which served to cement his reputation as a bankable western star.

The first was *The Man from Texas*, which was released in early 1915. A well-crafted adventure, this film features Tom as a man tracking down a lowlife scoundrel who took his sister's virtue and then left her to die of shame. Tom is first seen dressed in an uncharacteristically low-brimmed hat and traditional cowboy garb. He receives a letter about the tragedy that has befallen his sister and goes on an odyssey of revenge. The film is packed with action, including a scene where Tom is ambushed while breaking camp. We see Tom's hat shot off of his head and he picks it up to reveal a bullet hole. Tom's hat was actually shot by Sid Jordan, whom Tom trusted to make the shot without hurting him. Later in the film, Tom is pinned down by the wall of a house and a bullet, again fired by Sid, creases the wood right above Tom's head, coming within inches of Tom's skull. Tom often referred to Sid as "Big Chief Rifle Shot," a testament to how much Tom trusted Sid's skill as a marksman.

In one scene, Tom rescues the virtuous heroine from the clutches of the licentious womanizer. In the scene Louella Maxam, the actress portraying the heroine, rides Tony. By this time Tom had acquired Tony but wasn't calling him a "wonder horse" or riding him as his mount on film. Indeed, Tony is relegated to the status of an extra horse in the production. Fox Studios public relations would later claim that Tom was the only person who had ever ridden Tony, which was not true.

The Man from Texas was a big production of comparable quality to the best films of William S. Hart, the top movie cowboy at the time. The film showcased Tom's ability to be a serious action hero in a well-crafted western and it is certain that Hart saw that Tom was a challenger on the horizon.

The second major film of 1915 was *The Stagecoach Driver and the Girl*. The film, like *In The Days of the Thundering Herd* and *The Man from Texas*, hints at the greatness to come. In the film, Tom plays a stagecoach driver bringing a shipment of money to a town and he is beset by bandits.

During the stagecoach robbery scene Tom whips the team of four into a run and a horrible accident is captured on film and left in the final cut with great dramatic impact. Suddenly the left rear horse collapses and is dragged by the rest of the team as Tom hauls back frantically on the reins trying to keep the coach from running over the fallen horse. Several cowboys rush over to unhitch the downed horse and Tom takes off with three horses. The fallen horse is seen lying on the ground, occasionally flailing. There is no record if the horse was injured or killed during the scene, but the blur of reality and fantasy is compelling. No modern actor could have driven the coach as expertly and Tom's credibility as a real westerner is enhanced by this chance episode.

Later in the film, Tom again does his own stunt and turns the racing stagecoach sharply, flipping it onto its right side. Tom can be plainly seen leaping from the seat and landing on his feet, hauling on the reins to stop the three-up. It is an action-packed one-reeler that shows just how much real excitement could be packed into a short film by daring cowboy actors who did their own riding, roping, shooting and other stunts. Released in February 1915, *The Stagecoach Driver and the Girl* was a hit for Tom and made Selig a hefty profit.

Most of Tom's Selig films were short comedies, thus these three films stand out for their length and emphasis on action. Despite their success, Selig again relegated Tom back to comedy westerns. Indeed, the bulk of Tom's films continued to be comedies and short one-reelers because the films could be shot cheaply and reap big profits.

9

Western were extremely popular with silent movie audiences. As a result the studios all sought capitalize on their popularity by churning out westerns at a dizzying rate.

Selig Polyscope was the first studio to create a bankable western star when it featured Gilbert M. "Bronco Billy" Anderson in a series of films. Anderson went on to form his own studio, Essanay, and star in more than 500 western shorts.

William Surrey Hart, a stage actor who had spent his youth wandering the Midwest with his millwright father, was building a loyal following portraying stern badmen who redeem themselves by the fadeout of each film.

Tom's movies were popular with audiences as well. Suddenly, he was becoming a movie star.

Tom and his Selig production unit arrived in Las Vegas, New Mexico in early July 1915 and produced a considerable number of one-reelers in the town within the next six months. The citizenry welcomed their new celebrity resident and Tom's exploits were often covered in the local newspaper.[1]

Tom rented a brick block house at the corner of Ninth and Galinas Streets, within walking distance to the local saloon and the park. Around August of 1915, Victoria Forde joined Tom's unit as a leading lady. Tom took an instant liking to Victoria, who was vivacious and was rapidly becoming a movie star in her own right. She was as enthusiastic about movie-making as Tom was, and they spent considerable time together working on the Selig films. Indeed, much of the 1915 output by Tom's unit survives today. Victoria Forde was a better leading lady for Tom than Myrtle Steadman and some of the other heroines. She was more energetic, more interesting to watch. There was a chemistry between her and Tom that was obvious.

By the time Tom and Victoria began working together, Tom's marriage to Olive had begun to unravel. He was no longer just a man of the plains. He was now a movie star. Conversation around the dinner table or the chuck wagon during shooting was not about horses and herds of cattle, but camera angles and box office grosses and marketing of movies and distribution efforts. These topics were foreign to Olive, but not to Victoria. She had grown up in show business and Tom learned a great deal about the movie business from her.

Tom's time in New Mexico was spent working, partying with his fellow actors and crew, and socializing with Las Vegas residents at a variety of public events, such as basket socials, receptions at the Commercial Club, horse races at Galinas Park, and other picnics and town fairs.[2]

Tom was always present at these family-oriented events, but his wild streak sometimes got the better of him. In mid-October he took a car ride down to Albuquerque to "paint the town." After having a bit of fun, Tom fired up his car and began to drive around town in the wee hours of the morning while the residents were trying to sleep.[3]

From the earliest days of automobile and motorcycle development, Tom was a speed freak. He liked to drive at breakneck speeds, so fast that most of his friends refused to ride with him. If Tom's car had a top speed of 100, Tom drove it 110. He was an adrenaline junkie. His antics on screen such as jumping horses off of moving trains, off of collapsing bridges, off of balconies, all paled in comparison to his near-suicidal antics behind the wheel. Indeed, it was Tom's driving that killed him in 1940.

That brisk October night, Tom was driving a car that had no mufflers. Tom liked the noise of a car engine and this car was so loud that is sounded to bystanders like "a machine gun platoon in action." An Albuquerque policeman named Schuff arrested Tom for having an open muffler in violation of the town's noise ordinance. Tom was fined $10.[4]

In late 1914 and throughout 1915, Tom made 56 films. They were *Weary Goes A Wooing, Western Justice, Harold's Bad Man—A Story of Luck and Love, Cactus Jim's Shop Girl, Heart's Desire, The Grizzly Gulch Chariot Race, Forked Trails, Roping A Bride, Bill Haywood—Producer, Hearts of the Jungle, Slim Higgins, A Child of the Prairie, The Man from Texas, The Stagecoach Driver and the Girl, Jack's Pals, The Puny Soul of Peter Rand, Sagebrush Tom, The Outlaw's Bride, Ma's Girls, The Legal Light, Getting a Start in Life, Mrs. Murphy's Cooks, The Face at the Window, The Conversion of Smiling Tom, An Arizona Wooing, A Matrimonial Boomerang, Saved by Her Horse, Pals in Blue, The Heart of the Sheriff, The Girl of Gold Gulch, The Parson Who Fled West, The Foreman of the Bar Z Ranch, The Child, the Dog and the Villain, The Taking of Mustang Pete, The Gold Dust and the Squaw, The Lucky Deal, Never Again, Rancher's Daughter, Country Drugstore, The Range Girl and the Cowboy, The Auction Sale of Run Down Ranch, Her Slight Mistake, The Girl and the Mail Bag, The Stagecoach Guard, The Brave Deserve the Fair, The Race for a Gold Mine, The Foreman's Choice, Athletic Ambitions, The Tenderfoot's Triumph, The Chef at Circle G, The Impersonation of Tom, With the Aid of the Law, Bad Man Bobbs* and *On the Eagle's Trail.*

Some of these films survive today.

In *Weary Goes A Wooing* (1915), Tom is a cowboy out to woo a lovely schoolmarm. He takes part in a horse race in which the cowboys set it up for his horse to run away with him. Tom gains control of the horse, played by his trusty roan, Blue, and ends up at the schoolmarm's house. He invites her to go to a dance. In the film Tom wears traditional cowboy garb but it hatless until the final scenes where he dons a white, high-crowned hat that would become his trademark. Tom produced, wrote and directed the film.

In *Never Again* (1915), Tom plays a cowboy who goes on a drunken shooting spree, shooting another cowboy named Ned. Believing his has killed his pal, Tom flees town. Tom rides hell for leather throughout much of Las Vegas, New Mexico before jumping a train. We next see Tom at a rodeo in Los Angeles riding bucking broncos. The sheriff, played by Sid Jordan, discovers who Tom is and decides to take him back. He arrests Tom at the rodeo and brings him back to Las Vegas where Ned drops the charges and Tom is let go. Ned is played by Leo Maloney, who would go on to fame as a silent movie cowboy star in his own right in the mid 1920s.

In *Using His Brain* (1915) (most likely a reissue title), Tom rescues a woman from Mexican bandits. By this time, Tom began experimenting with his wardrobe. He preferred black hats to white on film, but the primitive film of the day often failed to capture the detail of the hats and the people wearing them. Tom had a light grey hat band and brim band sewed onto his hat, making the hat's shape more visible on the primitive film.

Sagebrush Tom (1915) is a comedy. It begins with a scene in which Tom, wearing all black, except for a white bandanna, picks his favorite movie star on a postcard. He rides back to the ranch and writes a fan letter. Tom's return address on the letter is "Diamond S Ranch, Prescott, Arizona." The movie company—Selig Polyscope—decides to send the actress west to make a movie at the Diamond S. In a funny scene, Tom brushes the alkali from his black clothes using a broom, raising a cloud of dust. The movie company arrives by stagecoach and the actors cavort in the open space, even having a foot race. The leading lady, played by Myrtle Steadman, runs right into Tom, knocking him down. Tom can't believe his eyes. He tells the actress that he is the cowboy who wrote to her. They sit on a wooden bench and flirt while the leading man from the movie company fumes. The actor pushes Tom and Tom punches him, knocking him cold. The actress scolds Tom and sends him packing. The next day the leading man can't work because his jaw was broken by Tom's punch. The director decides to use Tom for his leading man. The actor gets jealous and decides to get even. The leading man convinces Tom that to be an actor he needs to be strong, showing a photo of a nude gladiator wrestling a bull from Quo Vadis. The actor tells Tom that to be the hero he must throw a bull to the ground much like the actor in Quo Vadis. Tom resolves to throw a steer. He rides out into a pasture and ropes a steer which he herds into a corral. Dressed in his longjohns and boots, Tom tries to tame the large steer. He realizes that his efforts to impress the actress are for naught when the leading man tells him that she has gone back east to her husband. It is a funny vignette, written, produced and directed by Tom in spring 1915.

By *Sagebrush Tom*, Tom had begun to make his wardrobe a little flashier. There are silver conchas on the outseam of his chaps and he is using a silver laden bridle and his championship saddle in his films.

Some biographers assert that Tom moved his production unit to Los Angeles in the summer of 1915, but contemporary newspaper accounts of Tom's exploits in Las Vegas clearly show that he left town on December 27, 1915.[5]

Tom's burgeoning movie career was going well, so much so that when the company moved production to Hollywood, he felt secure enough with his employment at Selig that he built a large 18-room log cabin in Laurel Canyon, north of Hollywood. Little did Tom know that dark clouds were looming.

In 1916, Selig began cutting back Tom's output of movies. Instead of turning out a film a week that year, Tom rode across the screen in 40 movies in 1916. Tom starred in *The Wagon Trail, The Long Trail, The Desert Calls Its Own, A Mix-up in the Movies, Making Good, The Passing of Pete, A $5,000 Elopement, Trilby's Love Disaster, Along the Border, Too Many Chefs, The Man Within, The Sheriff's Duty, Crooked Trails, Going West to Make Good, The Cowpuncher's Peril, Taking a Chance, Some Duel, Legal Advice, Shooting Up the Movies, Local Color, An Angelic Attitude, A Western Masquerade, A Bear of a Story, Roping A Sweetheart, Tom's Strategy, The Taming of Grouchy Bill, The Pony-Express Rider, A Corner in Water, The Raiders, The Canby-Hill Outlaws, A Mistake in Rustlers, An Eventful Evening, The Way of the Red Man, A Close Call, Tom's Sacrifice, When Cupid Slipped, The Sheriff's Blunder, Mistakes Will Happen, The Golden Thought, Twisted Trails* and *Starring in Western Stuff.*

The films that Tom made in 1916 were mostly short comedies, which turned a quick profit for Selig. Tom made only one major feature that year when he starred in *Twisted Trails*, but Selig held it to only three reels instead of five. The film once again gave audiences a glimpse of what was to come when Tom raced his horse along a narrow log bridge across a deep, yawning chasm.

In *Local Color* (1916), Tom portrays a cowboy who schemes to give an Eastern writer some of the wild and wooly local color of the lawless west. Tom dons a buffalo bill mustache and goatee and tells her that he came to Texas after he shot his grandma. He jumps aboard Colt 45, his big black horse, and rides down a bandido and shoots him full of holes. The men then rope the bandit's body and drag him across the desert. The writer doesn't realize the body is just a dummy. She and Tom begin flirting. She is interested in him but he has convinced her that he shot his last two wives, which shocks her. The cowboys tell her that flirting requires marriage and a parson appears to marry them. Tom thinks it's part of the joke, but the joke is on him. In a plot device that mirrors Tom's charade that resulted in his marriage to Olive, the parson who marries them has actually joined Tom and the writer in matrimony.

In *An Angelic Attitude*, (1916) the story of *Local Color* is recycled and this time the heroine is an artist instead of a writer. Tom is again riding Blue and dressed down, except he has a large eagle feather in his hatband. Tom used feathers in his hatband early on with Selig but dropped the habit as his film career progressed. Feathers in hats often denoted that the character was an Indian. In one scene, Tom is spying on the lovely artist. He slips and slides down a 50-foot embankment. In a particularly funny scene, Tom and his father compete for the artist's affections. Tom hatches a plan to get his father to dress up like an angel to have his portrait painted. Tom then suspends him from a rope so he can "fly" like an angel. In the meantime Tom makes his getaway with the girl of his dreams.

In *Roping A Bride* (1916), Tom and Sid Jordan compete for the affections of Vera (Goldie Colwell). The two men are friends and come a'courtin' on the same day. Vera sits between them as they drink lemonade and eat cookies. Tom drops much of his cookie on the ground and picks it up to eat it, saving the camera take and Selig's money by not wasting film. In the film Tom is again dressed all in black, except for a pale bandanna. The two men engage in a friendly roping contest by roping a pole next to the barn. Tom and Sid learn that Vera's father has devised a contest in which the two men will race and the first to cast his loop over Vera's head will win her hand in marriage. Tom practices his roping on a donkey while Sid practices on a calf. Both men are seen on their knees proposing to their respective catches. Tom even kisses the donkey on the nose. Vera spies the silliness and laughs at the two men. A funny title card in the film says: "The day of the match the whole town turned out and all twelve of them were rewarded for their trouble." Tom and Sid race for Vera and Tom catches her, only to discover that she is hot-tempered. The film ends with Tom and Sid, the "two lucky losers" sitting by the barn smoking and congratulating each other on not marrying Vera.

This is one of the rare times when Tom, who smoked his entire adult life, smoked on camera. The film was shot in late 1914 and produced and directed by Tom.

In *A Bear of A Story* (1916), Tom and Sid decide to bring a bear back from the wild for Vickie (Victoria Forde), who has taken a liking to bears. In an amazing stunt, Tom and Sid actually chase down and rope a wild bear, which fights like crazy to get away, often lunging straight at Tom or Sid when they get too close. By the time they manage to get the bear home, they are torn to pieces and disheveled. They bring the bear back to Vickie who decides she doesn't like bears after all.

One notices several mannerisms of Tom's in these early films. He is lanky and muscular, and often stands with his hands resting on his lower back, palms in and thumbs down, in a kind of sway-backed stance. It is comical to look at but seems natural and not designed to be funny. In modern film only comedians such as Benny Hill stand in this manner to be funny, but it appears to have been a common practice back during Tom's Selig days. Several other cowboys stand that way at various times, suggesting it was a stance favored by Plains cowboys.

Silent movie acting required the ability to convey thought without the spoken word. Many actors adopted set mannerisms to convey certain emotions, while others worked to find other ways to transmit their feelings to their audiences. By mid 1915, Tom had learned a lot about body language and how it conveyed attitude on screen. He would show his easy-going attitude by tipping his hat back on his head and allowing a thick shock of black hair to fall across his right eye. He would raise the brim of his hat and scratch his head all with the same hand to convey confusion or dismay. He would swing his arms comically to convey enthusiasm. While these efforts seem dated when Tom's films are watched today, they nonetheless still convey the emotion or attitude that Tom intended, thus they stand the test of time.

For example, in *A Bear of a Story*, Tom and Sid Jordan have caught the brown bear to impress the beautiful girl. When the bear is finally tethered, Tom and Sid are dismayed to find out that she is not impressed and they slump to the ground, back to back in exhaustion. The scene is played broadly and for comedic effect, but it conveys the emotions of both men.

Another interesting mannerism is Tom's wave. In dozens of movies, when Tom is supposed to wave to someone, he extends his arm straight up at the shoulder and holds it there. This type of wave was common on the Great Plains because it could be seen by cowboys on the flat prairies from great distances.

10

One of the greatest mysteries surrounding Tom Mix's life is whether or not he actually traveled to Mexico and met with Pancho Villa.

The alleged trip has been the subject of tremendous mythology, including a wonderful novel by Clifford Irving, entitled *Tom Mix and Pancho Villa,* that is pure fiction.

There are many questions surrounding the escapade. Tom is said to have gone to Mexico and attempted to join up with Pancho Villa's Norteño army in hope of seeing action in the Mexican Revolution.

This is a far-fetched story. From 1910 to 1915, the Mexican Revolution raged throughout that country, resulting in the deaths of tens of thousands and the destruction of much of Mexico's economy. It was a brutal time, with wholesale killing and treachery and brutality on all sides. To believe that Tom would shelve a budding movie career and its carefree moneymaking to head south of the border and risk death is simply incredible. Also, Tom's whereabouts from 1910 to 1915 can be tracked with considerable certainty. Given Tom's penchant for exaggerating his exploits, it is more likely that Tom met Villa after the struggle ended and prior to Villa's assassination on July 20, 1923.

Did Mix actually meet Villa? It appears so. Ironically enough, the proof comes from fellow 101 Ranch alumnus Jack Hoxie, the Oklahoma cowboy who went on to stardom in silent and early sound westerns. Tom and Hoxie knew each other from back in the 101 Ranch Days and from various movie and rodeo events. Both men were Oklahoma cowboys, and had a kinship from their common background.

Hoxie insisted for years that he and Mix had gone to Mexico together—and he had proof.

"Tom Mix and I went down to Naco in Old Mexico to see Pancho Villa," Hoxie recalled. "Tom wanted to get some pictures of him so we could use them in our pictures. He [Villa] was camped on Mount Pedro, out of Naco. We went up there to see him. Boy, he was sure nice. He gave Tom Mix his bridle and spurs and a gun. And he gave me one of his saddles. He had a dozen or so. I still have that Mexican saddle."[1]

It is possible to date the encounter thusly: Jack Hoxie noted in his recollection that he and Mix went to Mexico to photograph Villa for use "in our pictures." Hoxie did not become a star until 1919. While he dabbled in movies from 1910 to 1918, he did not have any major parts and spent as much of his time on the wild west show and rodeo circuit as he did making movies. After 1919, Hoxie was a bonafide movie star, earning as much as $1,000 per week at Universal. While Tom was making much more at the time, both men were considered big stars by their studios.

Naco is in Sonora, Mexico, just across the U.S./Mexico border from Bisbee, Arizona, and fifteen minutes south of Tombstone.

If indeed Tom and Jack Hoxie crossed the border and met with the retired bandido, it is likely that they did so between 1919 and 1923, when both men were big cowboy stars. Villa was, by this time, living as a man in exile in his own country. He had to change his location daily, often leaving in the middle of the night.[2]

Villa kept 50 bodyguards around him at all times and narrowly avoided assassination time and again.[3]

During the revolution, Villa would not have wasted his time meeting with two cowboy actors. Additionally, even though Tom was making westerns in Arizona during the time period of Villa's revolution, neither Tom nor Jack Hoxie was famous enough between 1910 to 1915 to warrant anything from Villa other than a firing squad. Additionally, both men were married with children by the time the Mexican Revolution was underway. It is not credible that they would risk being killed and leaving their wives and daughters destitute.

It is most probable that Tom and Jack Hoxie were able to visit Villa because, after the revolution ended, Villa was a vain man who missed the spotlight. He would often write scathing letters to inflame the Mexican body politic, ensuring that the press would once again cover his exploits. From 1915 to 1923, Villa lived like a fallen potentate, with harems of women in various haciendas and an entourage of hangers-on.[4]

Thus is it likely that Villa agreed to meet with the two famous Americans to boost his ego and rekindle his public profile.

Sadly, there are no pictures to confirm that this event occurred. This is troublesome, considering that both Tom and Villa were astute publicity seekers who knew enough to bring a camera or a photographer to such a summit. Hoxie was less adept at such things. This raises doubts about the veracity of the story because surely Tom or Pancho Villa would have had a picture taken of the meeting. If there was one taken, it is lost to history.

The single most important piece of evidence which tends to prove that Tom and Jack Hoxie met Villa was the saddle that Hoxie kept with him until his death. It is a Mexican charro saddle with the name Villa engraved on the saddle bags. Villa is a common name in Mexico, so it is possible the saddle belonged to any one of 100,000 Villas, but it is unlikely that Jack Hoxie, who was less of a bombast than Tom, would make up the story that Villa gave him the charro saddle and then haul that saddle around with him his entire life just to propagate a myth that he and Tom had met Villa. It defies logic. Hoxie's film career ended in 1933 and he went back on the wild west and circus trail, taking the saddle with him. Surely he would not have gone to such effort to preserve the saddle if it were not genuine.

11

As often happens in the film industry, external events often overtake an actor and affect the path of his career. By 1917, Tom's star began to rise just as Selig began to experience trouble with financing and distribution. Tom had been a steady moneymaker for William Selig's company and probably thought that his film career at Selig was somewhat secure.

Tom began 1917 thinking all was well at Selig, but a mere three pictures into his contract Tom could see that something was terribly wrong.

Tom started the year filming two one-reel quickies, *The Saddle Girth* and *The Luck that Jealousy Brought*. He followed it up with another major feature for Selig, *The Heart of Texas Ryan*, a five-reeler that would turn out to be Tom's last film at Selig.[1]

Money and distribution problems had begun to haunt the small studio company. Selig's films—with the exception of Tom's—were doing poorly at the box office. Vitagraph wanted out of the "the patent" because its movies were of a higher quality than the lesser-known studios. Lubin, a French studio, shut down. The top brass at Selig Polyscope reacted to the crisis by folding their cards. In short, the company crumbled under pressure, cut production and tried to hang on by hooking up with a distributor named George Kleine along with Essanay and Edison's company. In early 1917 the studio sent word down to Tom that he had to cut costs to keep making pictures. Tom's production unit was already running a bare bones operation and Tom just didn't see how he could cut costs, unless he fired some of his longtime friends like Sid Jordan. Tom enjoyed the collegial atmosphere of working with his cowboy friends and couldn't imagine pink-slipping his friends. Indeed, Olive said Tom considered himself and his crew as a team.[2]

"Before he began each picture he gathered the other actors and the production crew together for a kind of pre-filming pep talk to remind them that the Tom Mix films were by no means merely the product of the efforts of one individual," Olive said.[3]

The straw that broke the camel's back was when an efficiency expert was dispatched by Selig to evaluate Tom's operation. The expert infuriated Tom by suggesting that Tom not feed the horses on days the horses did not work on camera.

He also insisted that Tom fire several cowboys from the production unit and suggested that Tom pay board for his horses used in the production. Tom reacted like a bull to a matador's cape.[4]

He realized that he was at a crucial juncture in his film career. He could either hang on at Selig or find another studio.[5]

Tom decided to make two major changes in his life. He would go directly to Hollywood and find another studio to work for and he would divorce Olive. It is unknown if Tom had begun a relationship with Victoria Forde prior to divorcing Olive, but it is likely.

Victoria Forde was born on April 21, 1896 in New York City to a theatrical family. Her mother, Eugenie, was an actress, as was her father, Arthur Hanna Forde.

Tom and Victoria met in 1915, while Tom was on location in Arizona. Sid Jordan remembered that Tom was initially interested in Eugenie Forde, Victoria's mother, but then switched his attentions from the married Mrs. Forde to her 19-year-old daughter.[6]

Eugenie and Victoria both played roles in Tom's films beginning in 1915 and Victoria quickly became Tom's favorite leading lady in his last two years at Selig.

Olive was deeply hurt by Tom's interest in Victoria, whom Tom called "Vicky." Olive fought with Tom, chiding him for focusing his attentions on "a wild girl."[7]

By Christmas 1915, it was clear that Tom's marriage to Olive was ending.

In early 1916, Tom moved his production unit to Newhall, California, in part because the location was more visually striking, but also because it was remote from Hollywood and he could work—and carry on with Victoria—without incurring Olive's increasingly violent wrath. He and Victoria moved into a house at 24248 Walnut Street in Newhall.[8]

Indeed, Tom's relationship with Victoria was all too typical in the movie business. An unknown actor becomes famous and ends up divorcing his wife for a woman who is also in the movie business, usually another actor of equal stature. In short, the now-famous actor "trades up" to a more glamorous spouse. It is clear is that Tom and Victoria enjoyed each other's company and had moviemaking as a common vocation. By 1917, Victoria was becoming a popular movie star in her own right, thus she and Tom were at a similar career point.

What is interesting about their relationship is that Victoria Forde is by the far the most homely woman with whom Tom ever became romantically involved. She was not pretty, even by the standards of the day. She had an oversized mouth and large teeth. Her eyes are set wide apart and she had a prominent nose. The only photos of her which make her appear somewhat attractive were photos which were heavily retouched by Fox Studio's publicity photographers. What set Victoria apart was her vivaciousness. She had a personality that lit up a room—and a movie screen. She had the same pizzazz as modern-day star Liza Minnelli. Tom was absolutely smitten with Victoria. Indeed, he worshiped her.[9]

While Olive may have been violently upset at her breakup with Tom at the time, years later she recalled the event without rancor. "We decided on divorce simply because our life together couldn't be what we had so long wanted it to be—what is had started out to be. It was far too late for that. The incompatibility between us did not grow from within our house, but from the forces that beat upon it from the outside. Our separation was not one of bitterness, but one of deep sadness," Olive wrote. "He was the father of my child, and in the depth of his love for Ruth I found happiness."[10]

Olive's autobiography couches her breakup with Tom, and the years thereafter, with rosy flourishes. In truth, they would take each other to court often. Olive, who was earning between $700 to $900 a month from her oil well, was richer than Tom when they divorced. As a result, she got a pittance from him in their divorce and Tom was ordered to pay a paltry $50 per month in child support. Olive would later squander her wealth and hound Tom for money right up until his death.[11]

As the chaos at Selig grew worse, Tom informed William Selig that he was going to find another studio and then, in a gesture very few movie stars have ever made, paid his production team and company of actors out of his own pocket while he searched for a new studio home. Tom's employees responded by closing ranks around their leader. One of these devoted employees was Hank Bell, the cowboy-turned-stuntman whose handlebar mustache and bulbous nose were familiar to silent and early talkie western film audiences. Bell gave Tom the highest compliment any cowboy could want of another, when he said that Tom was "the kind of man any cowboy would want to ride the river with."[12]

To Tom's delight, Victoria offered to put up some of her own money to bankroll Tom's unit until a new studio could be found. This gesture brought the two even closer together.

Tom heard the Fox Studios was looking for a movie star to make highly profitable outdoor movies. He was determined to get a contract at Fox, one of the major studios in Hollywood.

William Fox remembered meeting Tom. "Every morning for a week this…figure was waiting always in different [cowboy] costume, each one louder than the last, until my curiosity was aroused. One day he approached me and said, 'My name is Tom Mix. I made up my mind I wouldn't work for any other company until I saw you, Mr. Fox.' He was very picturesque and I interviewed him and decided to engage him."[13]

Fox apparently screened several of Tom's Selig five-reelers and liked what he saw.

Director George Marshall, who would later direct Tom in a handful of films, said Fox liked that Tom did all of his own stunts. "It was the action things that attracted Mr. Fox," Marshall said. "…the horse falls, crashing through glass windows on horseback and so on."[14]

Tom struck a deal for himself, his horses and his unit of cowboys. Tom's personal salary would be $350 per week. All of his unit cowboys were put on salary and their horses were guaranteed board at Fox's expense.[15]

The deal was good for both Tom and Fox Studios. Fox saw something in Tom that Selig had also seen—that Tom Mix could produce exciting western movies on a tight budget that would bring in big profits. Fox needed big profits because his studio was ailing after a string of box office flops.

Tom moved his entire stock company and crew from Newhall, California to Fox's studio lot in Westwood, California, a suburb on the west side of Los Angeles. Fox would be Tom's studio home for 11 years.[16]

When Tom's contract began at Fox, the village of Hollywood was in its first major growth spurt. In 1910, there were roughly 5,000 people living in among the citrus groves which dotted the Los Angeles basin. By 1920, there were 36,000 people and 20,000 more were moving in every year. By 1930, Hollywood had nearly 250,000 people.[17]

Tom's deal with Fox was similar to his Selig arrangement, except that William Fox insisted on producing Tom's first films at Fox personally. Tom would eventually have his own production unit and would exercise considerable control over the films he produced, a feat he would accomplish by making his films as far away from the studio as possible.

Tom's first six films for Fox were similar to his Selig product. *Hearts and Saddles*, *A Roman Cowboy*, *Six Cylinder Love* and *A Soft Tenderfoot* were all one reel comedies that differed little from Tom's previous films at Selig. Tom made two western dramas for Fox in 1917 called *Durand of the Badlands* and *Tom and Jerry Mix*.

Durand of the Badlands was a Dustin Farnum movie, with Tom cast in a supporting role. To the surprise of studio bosses, Tom's charisma shined through and the die was cast. Tom Mix would be a major star for Fox Studios. Tom was given a $50 per week raise.[18]

With Fox's superior distribution to its chain of movie theaters across the country, Tom's Fox films played to a far wider audience than his Selig films. The audience reaction was immediate and positive. Tom was a box office draw.

At the end of 1917, Tom's future at Fox Studios appeared secure. Fox had decided to increase Tom's budgets to improve production values. Tom's wardrobe was improved. The studio even provided Tom with a western-style backlot of his own, a twelve acre production facility in Edendale, California which the studio dubbed "Mixville."[19]

The studio lot became Tom's home away from home. Elaborate western towns, complete with interior sets, were built. An Indian village was built nearby. Tom was provided with an inordinately large contingent of crew members, all of whom were placed at his disposal. Tom, who was often referred to as "the major," ran Mixville with a paternal air. He treated all of his actors and crew as his equal and won their cooperation with his good humor. Those who chose to argue or insult Tom were sent packing. One cook disliked Tom and made it known to all who would listen, referring to Tom as a "plutocrat cowboy." When the cook refused to cook breakfast for Tom's large crew, citing the earliness of the hour, Tom fired him on the spot. The cook reacted violently, swinging at Tom with a haymaker. Tom ducked the cook's heavy blows and the two men began brawling. The fight ended quickly after a tent collapsed on top of the two men. When the tent was lifted up, Tom was sitting on the prone form of the unconscious cook.[20]

Tom ran Mixville like a ramrod ran a ranch outfit. There was housing for the cowboys at the backlot, or nearby at apartments and cabins at Silver Lake. The men took their meals at a chuck wagon run by Tom's new "cookie," a feisty man named "Banty" Caldwell, who brooked no insubordination among Tom's cowboys. Caldwell took over the cooking duties after Tom's run-in with the prior cook.[21]

In 1918, Tom made six features and one short one-reeler for Fox. *Cupid's Roundup, Six-Shooter Andy, Western Blood*, which featured Buck Jones, Tom's old friend from the 101 Ranch, *Ace High, Mr. Logan U.S.A.*, and *Fame and Fortune*. These were all five-reel dramas and *Who Is Your Father?* was a two reel comedy. Each of these films further added luster to Tom's star, and by the end of 1918 Tom appeared poised to take the mantle of King of the Cowboys from William S. Hart.

Tragedy struck on January 29, 1919 when Tom's favorite horse, his blue roan, known as "Ol' Blue," stepped into a gopher hole in his corral at Mixville. Tom rushed to the scene, but it was clear that the horse had broken its leg. Tom was devastated. He had acquired Blue during his 101 Ranch days and had kept the horse for more than a decade and had ridden the horse in nearly all of his Selig films. Tom sobbed uncontrollably when the horse was euthanized and he was somber for days thereafter.

Tom rode many different horses in his movies, but he realized now that he'd have to start riding one of his other horses as his primary mount. Tom decided to use "Tony Boy," which he shortened to "Tony."

The legend of Tony is as muddled as any other mythology surrounding Tom Mix. Olive Mix recalled the most commonly repeated story that Tom's friend Pat Chrisman, who worked for Tom as one his cowboys, saw Tony as a colt walking behind a chicken wagon in Edendale, California.[22]

Chrisman bought the colt for $14 and raised and trained him and sold him to Tom for $600.[23]

Olive said Tony was black in color as a colt and that he as he grew he became sorrel in color.[24]

She also said that Tom was the only person to ride Tony from 1914 to 1932 which is incorrect.[25]

Tom came to value Tony so much that he bought Buster, a horse similar to Tony, to use as Tony's stunt double on particularly dangerous stunts. Buster did not have a white stripe on his nose like Tony, so the makeup artist would paint one on his nose before Buster went on camera.[26]

Tom had become so popular by 1919 that he began to get product endorsement contracts. One such product was the Renulife Violent Ray, an "ozone regulator" that purportedly cured sprains and bruises.

Tom made seven feature films for Fox in 1919. William Fox had nixed any more short one-reelers for Tom. Now that the studio was paying Tom $1,500 per week, and the budgets for Tom's films were increased further, the only profitable way to utilize Tom's talents was with five-reel western features.[27]

In 1919, Tom starred in *Treat 'em Rough, Hell Roaring Reform, Fighting for Gold, The Wilderness Trail, Rough Riding Romance* and *The Speed Maniac.*

The studio steadily increased Tom's budgets, even approving some location shooting in San Francisco for *Rough Riding Romance* (1919).

The Mix unit traveled to Flagstaff, Arizona for location filming of *The Wilderness Trail*. His heroine in the film was a lovely 16-year-old named Colleen Moore. She would later gain stardom as a "flapper" in a series of films epitomizing the glitz and glamour of the 1920s. Moore wrote in her 1968 autobiography, *Silent Star*, that when she met Tom she "completely lost my heart..."[28]

She recalled that Tom was "as real a he-man as they come. Not that he wasn't vain and proud of his looks. He was."[29]

Moore said Tom was "a tall, handsome man...," that Tom had a "slim, no-hips figure and a face tanned to leather by the sun. He had strong jaw lines, a large, slightly hooked nose, ebony black hair, and brown eyes so dark they were almost black."[30]

During the filming of *The Wilderness Trail*, Moore recalled that she developed an enormous crush on Tom. "In my love scenes with him I nearly swooned away," she wrote. "I was absolutely enchanted by him." Moore recalled that Tom seemed more interested in her mother, who was Tom's age.[31]

Tom was a snappy dresser, she said. He wore "some of the fanciest clothes I've ever seen."[32]

"All the wranglers, as the cowboys were called, took great pride in their appearance. No woman on the best-dressed list was ever as particular with her clothes fit as they were about theirs, and Tom Mix, who had his clothes custom made at Porter's in Prescott, Arizona—as every cowboy did who could afford it—was the best-dressed of them all. He even had Western style evening clothes. One I remember was a purple dinner suit, worn over black boots with a large black Stetson. But my favorite was his white tuxedo, so beautifully fitted to him he looked as he'd been born wearing it."[33]

Moore had done one western for D.W. Griffith prior to working with Tom. On that film she met Indian actor Monte Blue, who taught her how to ride horses.[34]

Moore liked working outdoors and found Tom, and his group of cowboys fascinating.

"The cowboys were real cowboys who found riding the range in Hollywood movies easier and better-paying than on the Lone Prairie," Moore recalled.[35]

"The cowboys were always doing stunts, even between scenes. They rode Cossack—the rider passing from one side of the horse under the horse's belly to the other side. They rode Roman—standing astride the horse's back going at a running pace. They also took some awful spills, which I suppose was why they'd never let me try either of those stunts."

In the truth-is-stranger-than-fiction department, during the location shooting for *The Wilderness Trail,* Moore was actually kidnaped by an amorous Indian. She was on her way to the location from Flagstaff, riding in a buckboard wagon with one of Tom's cowboys, who had been sent to bring Moore to the set. An Indian rode up to the wagon on horseback, grabbed Moore and rode off with her kicking and screaming. The cowboy gave chase in the buckboard. Somehow, Moore managed to spook the Indian's horse and, as the Indian fought to control of his mount, she fell off. The Indian fled and never bothered her again.[36]

In *Fighting for Gold* (1919), Tom plays a miner who tries to keep his gold claim from being stolen by a syndicate. Tom is first seen atop a rock with his pet bear. He is wearing a battered grey, high-peaked Stetson and the typical garb of a cowboy of that time. He wears a silver Colt Peacemaker on his right hip. Tom's shirt has ten pearl snaps and is a broad check pattern that Tom designed himself. He would design much of his wardrobe while at Fox.

The film opens with Tom running off claim jumpers headed by Sid Jordan. He then quarrels with his drunken partner. Tom comes to the aid of a pretty gal who's having trouble landing a big fish and then ropes her and hoists her up a cliff just to flirt with her.

Meanwhile, a bandit robs a local businessman. It is interesting to note that the bandit is riding Tony. In the next scene Tom is scene riding Tony. While Tom owned Tony for several years, he treated the horse as just another saddle horse before Blue's death. In this film, Tony does double duty, no doubt a budget conscious measure.

While making *The Speed Maniac*, a film with a title that is sadly insightful and prophetic, Tom was nearly killed while driving a race car on the Santa Monica racetrack. During a racing sequence shot at actual race speeds, Tom insisted on doing his own driving. Tom always insisted on doing his own stunts. As the speed of the race increased and the camera rolled, Tom took a curve too sharply and his primitive race car—a tube-like vehicle with no roll bars or other protection for a driver's exposed head—turned over and over in a rolling somersault. A crowd of onlookers brought in as extras screamed in horror and word spread throughout the grandstand that Tom was dead.

Surprisingly, Tom climbed out of the battered car and waved to the crowd. He had sustained only minor cuts and scratches in the crash.[37]

Tom not only raced automobiles for his movies, but he began racing as a hobby on the amateur circuit. A speed demon with a manic love for wild, high-speed driving, Tom entered the Pacific Coast Amateur Championship, which was scheduled to be held at Ascot Park in Los Angeles. Proceeds from the race were to be used for the Actor's Fund. On July 20, 1919, Tom arrived driving a Stutz Special, a high-powered roadster. A crowd of 15,000 watched the 25-mile race, which was a barnburner, and when the race was over Tom had won handily. Amazingly enough, Tom's car traversed the course at an average dizzying speed of 60 miles per hour—considered breakneck speed in 1919.[38]

In late 1919, Tom was before the cameras for Fox's *The Feud* and *The Cyclone*.

Tom's leading lady in *The Cyclone* was, again, Colleen Moore. Moore recalled in her book that the film was shot in Prescott, Arizona. "We went on location to

Prescott, whooping it up at the saloon on Saturday nights, guns and all, [which] was exactly what the local cowboys did."[39]

Moore remembered that Prescott was a frontier town just like the ones seen in Western movies. She recalled staying in a hotel that looked just like one would expect, a false-fronted hotel with a second story balcony over the plank sidewalk below. During her stay at the hotel, Moore and her mother witnessed an old-fashioned shootout on the street below.

"One Saturday night Mother and I were standing on the balcony just outside our bedroom when we saw two cowboys walk in opposite directions down the street, turn, take aim, and fire. And saw one of them fall dead," she wrote. "The most eerie thing about it—and the only thing not like the movies or television—was that nothing happened. No rushing of people out of the saloon. No sheriff and his posse saddling up to ride after the killer and hang him. Only the sound of honky-tonk music from the saloon as the man who was left got on his horse and rode away into the stillness of the night."[40]

Part of *The Cyclone* was filmed on a roundup at a ranch owned by one of Tom's friends. Moore recalled that the roundup sequences interspersed fantasy with reality as Tom and his cowboys assisted with the roundup, while camera caught the events. She remembered that after the bull calves were castrated the entire company of cowboys and the film crew feasted on Rocky Mountain oysters—bull testicles. "Afterward the cowboys would fight to see who got the 'fries,' as they called them. They would roast these small glands over the branding fire and eat them, the word being that the 'fries' gave them sexual powers."[41]

During the shooting of *The Cyclone*, Moore met Buck Jones, a friend of Tom's from the 101 Ranch days who would later become a big cowboy star in his own right. She said Jones taught her how to twirl a lariat and roll a cigarette with one hand.[42]

Moore recalled that her location work with Tom's film unit helped her to discover the American West, "when it was still really the old West, not long removed from pioneer days.". She remembered how the bright sunlit days gave way to ink-black nights. "In the desert there is no twilight. One moment the sky is brilliant with reds and purples, and almost the next totally black." She remembered telling Tom one night that the deep, darkness of the desert was "frightening." She said Tom's reply was both profound and comforting. "There's nothing about darkness to be frightened of. It's a covering that's saved many lives on the desert."[43]

Moore said that Tom showed her that the American West was "a colorful and romantic place." She said working with Tom was "one of the high spots of my life."[44]

When *The Feud* and *The Cyclone* were released on the same day, January 25, 1920, Tom's year started off with a bang. *The Feud* was a post–Civil War take on Romeo and Juliet and popular with movie audiences but *The Cyclone*, a saga centered on the Northwest Mounted Police, was an enormous hit, due in no small part to an amazing stunt in which Tom and Colleen Moore ride up Buster up several flights of stairs in a building, only to have the floors cave in beneath them one by one. The unique stunt was created using floors made of chicken wire and plaster. When Tom and Moore ride Buster onto the breakaway floor, the floors collapsed as they fell. Amazingly, neither Buster nor Tom and Moore were injured.[45]

Moore recalled the events in her autobiography. She confirmed that Tom used one of the many stunt doubles he had for Tony for the stunt. "Tony had at least five different doubles to perform his stunts for him. Tom wouldn't let Tony do them, for fear he might break his leg. It was a matter of practicality, I guess, as well as love. The way Tom looked at it, there were plenty of stars around and plenty of leading ladies, but a good horse is hard to find."[46]

In *The Dare-Devil*, Tom plays the son of a rancher who has become a bit of a dandy. After several blunders he is unable to prove his mettle, until he is given the job of railroad agent. Tom must stop train robbers from victimizing the railroad.

Tom's next film was *The Terror*, which he then followed up with *Three Gold Coins*, a shoot-em up filmed on location in Prescott, Arizona. In this film, Tom does some impressive stunts, such as swinging from one building to another on a rope before dropping into the saddle and riding off.

Tom enjoyed the movie-making part of the business. He loved being out on location, perpetuating the cowboy lifestyle he enjoyed so much. Victoria had given up being an actress and had taken on the role of Tom's in-house publicist. While Tom was busy cranking out films, Victoria traveled the country, meeting with film distributors and theater managers, pushing them to book Tom's films for extended runs, and pushing them to spend dollars promoting the movies. It was clear to all in Hollywood that Tom Mix was a personable star with wheelbarrows of talent and charisma, and ambitious. Vicky Mix was even more ambitious than her husband. Her business savvy did much to promote Tom's stardom.

By 1920, Tom Mix was the biggest western star in the world, surpassing the dour and melodramatic William S. Hart. Years later, singing cowboy Gene Autry summed up Hart's contribution to western film in 1978, when he wrote that

Hart created "the ritual of the two gun draw, shot from the hip. The other [contribution] was pure genius. The horse. Soon Fritz, his pinto, was as famous as Hart himself."[47]

Autry recalled that Tom overcame Hart's dour image with something Hart did not offer. "Then came Tom Mix...he came up with one trick Hart could never manage. A smile. The next thing anyone knew, Mix was getting fan mail."[48]

Not only did audiences like Tom's affability, his movies thrilled audiences with his amazing stunts, so much so that William Fox tapped Tom to stage and direct a chariot race in the studio's epic production of *The Queen of Sheba* (1921). Tom did a marvelous job, so much so that the April 23, 1921 Motion Picture News raved that Tom "deserves unbounded praise for the manner in which he has enlivened the scene and made it throb with vigorous action."[49]

Tom's devil-may-care attitude and self-deprecating machismo played well in movie theaters around the world. In the silent movie days, title cards could be written in any language with relative ease. Thus Tom Mix was as popular in Europe and South America as he was in the United States. And Tom, by turning out fast-paced action westerns, had found his niche. Much like modern day Jackie Chan movies, the emphasis was on tongue-in-cheek humor and breathtaking physical stunts. Indeed, no other movie star but Chan has combined the elements found in Tom's films, including doing his own stunts.

Hart had developed a screen persona that reflected his Victorian morals. Indeed, Hart's stern, good badman was somewhat unapproachable as a hero, while Tom's screen persona reflected his own devil-may-care attitude and his affable personality. In the end, Tom's persona outshone Hart's.

Audiences realized that, unlike many of the actors featured in westerns who had no cowboy skills, Tom was actually a real cowboy and former lawman. "Tom was the genuine article," Autry, who had to be taught how to ride and shoot for the movies, said candidly. "No part on screen could compete with the kind of life he lived." Legendary heavyweight boxing champion Jack Dempsey concurred. "[Tom] wasn't one of those fake cowboys...he was a helluva rider and he could handle a lasso," Dempsey said. The two men met in the mid-1920s and became friends and sparring partners and Tom later taught Dempsey how to ride a horse.[50]

Pioneer director D.W. Griffith, whose landmark films *Birth of A Nation* (1915) and *Intolerance* (1916) literally created modern feature-length film-making, spoke highly of Tom at the time. "Mix could burn a hole through a camera lens by merely staring at it if he wanted to. When he looked at you, you knew you were being looked at. He can't act but he can ride like hell and everybody loves him; I don't know why!"[51]

At the height of his fame Tom became a fixture on the Hollywood scene. He drove enormously expensive convertibles, including Rolls Royces, Dusenbergs and Cords which he kept in his seven-car garage. Hollywood was in the throes of its "Roaring '20s" excess. Sex in all forms was available without effort. Booze and all kinds of drugs flowed freely, and there was as much intrigue as could be found in any tiny kingdom. Tom was as famous as Douglas Fairbanks, Sr. and Mary Pickford, the king and queen of Hollywood stars; comic genius Charlie Chaplin, heartthrob Wallace Reid; and Italian love god Rudolph Valentino.

Tom attended Hollywood premieres and social events dressed in the finest custom made outfits, all designed in a western motif by Tom himself. He wore only diamond encrusted platinum jewelry and was so flashy and so glamorous that other Hollywood stars, such as Fairbanks and Pickford, could barely attract attention at any event where Tom was in attendance.

Tom even purchased a yacht, which he named "The Miss Mixit." The boat was launched on March 11, 1923 into Los Angeles Harbor after Ruth smashed several bottles of water from Tom's Arizona ranch against the hull.[52]

Screenwriter Adela Rogers St. John, who wrote two of Tom's films, *The Bronco Twister* (1927) and *Arizona Wildcat* (1927) during his heyday at Fox, recalled Tom in her autobiography, *The Honeycomb,* with obvious admiration. Tom and Victoria were often guests at star-studded dinner parties at St. John's Whittier ranch. St. John said such dinner parties were "wild with excitement."

Calling Tom "the most important star we have ever had," St. John described Tom as "the most attractive man I ever knew from every standpoint—physical, mental and spiritual—...Debonair. Brilliant. Brave."[53]

"I wish you could have seen Tom in dinner clothes," St. John continued. "The broad shoulders, the trim waist, flat hips and stomach, he had the figger (sic) to wear 'em. As I look back now, Tom was as elegant on a horse as Fred Astaire on a dance floor, and that's the elegantest there is."[54]

She insisted that Tom was a deep thinker, obsessed with the works of Ezra Pound and William Shakespeare and even the Biblical depictions of Jesus. She said Tom, even though he hadn't finished grammar school, gave readings of Shakespeare that were "brilliant." She remembered a conversation with Tom wherein Tom insisted that casting older actors to play Hamlet was absurd. Tom thought of Hamlet as a "millionaire juvenile delinquent" and he argued that when older actors played Hamlet that it strained credibility. He told St. John that if Hamlet was as old as thirty "it's a lousy play. [If a] [m]an that old took that long to make up his mind what to do about the blackguard that murdered his old man, stole his throne and seduced his mother, somebody ought to put him out of his misery like a horse that's got a busted leg."[55]

St. John's revelation—that Tom Mix was a lover of high drama and poetry—is backed up by singing cowboy Gene Autry, who remembered Tom giving memorable poetry readings. "He loved poetry," Autry recalled in his autobiography, "and he read it well, with a rich, deep voice that rumbled out of his throat like a train out of a tunnel."[56]

Tom's voice is not lost to time. Thankfully, he made a handful of sound films in the early 1930s. The best example of Tom's recorded voice is in *Rider of Death Valley* (1933).

During one conversation which St. John recalled at length, she asserted that Tom had a vision of Jesus that was far removed from the iconography of the time. "That country [Jesus] was in [was] like our Southern California," she quoted Tom as saying. "Jesus had to be weather-beaten, tanned, walking and sailing and fishing and climbing mountains all the time. Can't do that no way and stay the underside-of-a-fish color some painters make him. I looked it up quite a lot. At his age it's unlikely he wore a beard, or if he did it'd be a short trimmed one. Long straggly beards were on old men. We wasn't a little bitta guy either. Those Galilean fishermen were mostly five ten or maybe six feet. Had to be. He didn't wear his hair long, at least not that long, it'd have caught in the sails or the fishing lines and he slept outdoors, too."[57]

St. John recalled that Tom told her he'd discussed the life of Jesus at length with the aging Wyatt Earp after the two men had become close friends.[58]

Tom was so popular that he was a favorite guest of the richest players in Hollywood. Even billionaire newspaper publisher William Randolph Hearst was fond of Tom, according to St. John. She recalled one conversation in which Tom debated Shakespeare's writing style with Hearst. Hearst told Tom that newspapers had to have style as well and Tom replied that newspapers "gotta be sensational, too."[59]

St. John noted bluntly, however that Tom was not so suave when he was drinking. "If he left the firewater in the bottle, Mix was brilliant. If not, not."[60]

Autry's and St. John's reminiscences are unique. No other recollections of Tom Mix have ever portrayed him as a pseudointellectual. Tom was known for his humor, loyalty to friends, for being generous with his money and for being a down-to-earth cowboy. Tom sprinkled his conversation with western colloquialisms and was not known to put on any show of intellectualism or elitism. It is unclear if St. John's hero worship of Tom actually rose to the level of unrequited love. Clearly her recollections of Tom approach that level, especially when she stated that she hoped that when she died and went to heaven, she wanted to find Tom waiting for her there.

That said, Autry's recollections add considerable weight to those of St. John's. It is well known that Autry admired Tom because Tom welcomed the awkward singer from Tioga, Texas to the bastion of cowboy stardom, even though Autry's star was eclipsing Tom's. In short, Tom was kind to the man who replaced him as king of the cowboys.

Tom clearly thought of St. John as one of his closest "Hollywood friends," so much so that he gave her a prize Thoroughbred horse as a gift.[61]

Interestingly, St. John, while praising Tom, took time to disparage William S. Hart was a "second-rate Shakespearean actor" who was "scared to death of horses." Colleen Moore, who worked with Tom in *The Wilderness Trail* (1919) and *The Cyclone* (1920), echoed St. John's sentiments when she recalled Tom in a favorable light and also disparaged Hart as a cold man who was cruel to actress Winifred Westover during her brief marriage to Hart. She recalled an incident wherein Hart, who was 48 years old, actually physically abused Westover, who was barely 18-years-old, by cruelly pinching her one afternoon when Moore was visiting.[62]

Tom's success was due in large part to his incessant self-promotion. He instinctively using a technique called "branding," a tactic pioneered by Coca Cola. Tom promoted his brand, a TM set at an angle in a diamond shape, by having it embossed on everything from his clothes to his cars to his houses and yachts. Indeed, Tom made sure every movie fan and movie star in Hollywood knew where he lived by installing a neon TM on the roof of his $250,000 Beverly Hills home.

Tom's mansion was as ornate a castle as the home of any other big star in Hollywood. St. John, a frequent guest, described the home as a "fantastic domicile."[63]

During the 1920s many of the roads in Hollywood were still unpaved, so Tom had his TM brand imbedded in the treads of his car tires to that everywhere he went people could see that Tom Mix had passed by.

Tom Mix was the first movie star to understand the financial gain and the publicity value of what Hollywood calls "franchise." The *Star Wars* action figures and the myriad of other items sold to fans worldwide is a marketing phenomenon that began with Tom Mix.

During the mid-1920s, when Tom was absolute king of the cowboys, he made millions—and spent them as fast as he earned them. Olive recalled that Tom's tendency to extravagance was "almost a disease…the ultimate symbol of success achieved; and yet he was not completely happy amid all of the luxury."[64]

Tom both loved and hated the Hollywood lifestyle. Victoria loved it unabashedly, and Tom spent money like water to please her, but felt a little separated from all the glitz and glamour of his wealth. He told a reporter at the time that he felt lonely in the giant house.[65]

Indeed, Tom's children were fixtures on the junior Hollywood party scene. Newspaper society pages were filled with stories and photographs Ruth, and later Tom's younger daughter, Thomasina, at various parties. In the late 1920s, Thomasina was especially busy, attending parties at the homes of many of Hollywood's biggest celebrities. She had a Halloween party on November 11, 1925, attended a party at Harold Lloyd's mansion for his daughter Mildred on May 27, 1926, had her own birthday party that same month. In all of these society page stories, the children of the stars are portrayed as happy, glamorous little children. One markedly noticeable sour face is William S. Hart, Jr., the son of the western icon, who is seen scowling in all of the photos.[66] Hart's lack of a relationship with his son would haunt the younger Hart for his entire life.[67]

Less than two years into his contract at Fox, Tom was already chafing under the supervision of the Fox hierarchy. At Selig Polyscope, Tom had been in complete control of his production unit. As is often the case when movie stars are given complete control of their movies, these films, while popular, vary in quality. Selig could afford to indulge Tom because the studio was a smaller studio and Tom's films were shot quickly and on a low budget.

Fox was a major studio, and as such it had a complex bureaucracy and many people with specific job duties working in tandem to produce quality movies. Tom's films had a much higher budget at Fox and, in Hollywood, with added budgets come added oversight. William Fox was building Tom into a major money machine for the studio, and he wanted crisp, well-photographed westerns with exciting stunts and solid stories. The days of shooting one and two reel quickies were gone. Tom was now a major movie star and Fox wanted to make sure its Tom Mix product attracted repeat customers who appreciated the quality of Tom's films.

Tom realized quickly that the only way to get out from under the collective thumbs of Fox Studios brass was to take his production unit and shoot his films on location. When it came time to film *Three Gold Coins*, Tom pushed to shoot the action-packed film in Prescott, Arizona. It would give Tom a chance to visit his new 11,000 acre Arizona ranch and, in the days when telephones were few and far between in the desert southwest, it would put some distance between Tom and the studio.

On location, Tom made sure his film sets had the ambience of a camp during roundup. "The filming of a Tom Mix film usually went off without a hitch, and with a minimum of frayed nerves and an almost complete exclusion of temperament," Olive said.[68]

Tom loved that his locations felt like cow camps. A chuck wagon cook woke the cast and crew before dawn by banging an iron triangle with an iron peg.[69] Steaming coffee and a hot breakfast of bacon, eggs, beans and biscuits awaited the groggy cowboys, actors and crew members as they blinked the cobwebs from their eyes.[70]

The sunrise breakfasts were quiet events, as if in reverence to the beauty of the morning. Evenings were spent sitting around the campfire over coffee (and more times than not a little whiskey) enjoying sing-alongs and tall tales.[71]

Tom loved to sing Stephen Foster songs and would break out into an off-key version of the famed minstrel songs when the mood hit him.[72]

Each night, before Tom turned in for bed, he'd eat a handful of celery and down a glass of buttermilk. Olive called it a "nightly ritual."[73]

By the time the sun climbed above the horizon, the cast and crew had finished breakfast and preparations began for the day's filming. Tom would check on Tony and Buster, Tony's stunt double, who were usually groomed and cared for by Tom's favorite horse trainer, Pat Chrisman.

A quick production meeting would take place and the shooting would begin while the sun was low in the morning sky, providing the cinematographer with what is called "good light," a low angle of sunlight that casts shadows which provide for more three-dimensional images on film.

Tom had begun insisting that Fox allow Tom to produce films based upon his own story ideas, as he had done at Selig. The difference at Fox was Tom's ideas were then given to studio writers to polish, unlike at Selig where Tom's jotted down his own ideas and shot them on film, often that same day. Tom's initial films at Fox had been one or two-reelers, so Fox had let Tom continue as he had at Selig, but now that Tom was making feature length films he had to work as part of the writing team.

Tom wrote the stories for five-reelers such *Western Blood* (1918) and *The Terror* (1920).

In addition, Tom insisted that he be allowed to direct, as he had done at Selig. Tom directed and starred in *The Dare-Devil* (1920).

Tom finished up the fall of 1920 shooting *The Untamed*, which was written by legendary western novelist Max Brand, *The Texan* and *Prairie Trails*. In late 1920, Tom starred in *The Road Demon*, another western with an auto racing theme.

In late 1920 and throughout 1921, Tom starred in *The Road Demon, Hands Off, Big Town Round-up, After Your Own Heart, The Night Horseman, Trailin,'* and Tom wrote and starred in *A Ridin' Romeo* and *The Rough Diamond*. *The Road Demon* was shot in the desert in Victorville, California from September 27 until November 17, 1920, giving Tom a respite from working in the confines of the Fox studio lot. The film contains a breathtaking car race, including one sequence where Tom races his roadster across a railroad trestle.

Trailin' survives and is available on video and DVD. It is an action-packed film in which Tom plays an aristocrat who travels west to find out who killed his father in a duel. The story, by Max Brand and adapted by Lynn Reynolds, contains a funny recurring gag in which Sid Jordan, trailing Tom with plans to assassinate him, comes into contact with people who've encountered Tom. Each one says, "he may look like a tenderfoot and act like a tenderfoot, but he *ain't* no tenderfoot!" The film contains some breathtaking stunts. In one scene, Tom rides Tony (most likely a double) across a narrow bridge over a raging stream which collapses, sending Tom and his horse into the current. Later, Tom and heroine Eva Novak slide down a sheer cliff face to escape a posse. In one stunt, Tom leaps off of a six foot embankment and catches a tree limb, and vaults into up a tree. It in itself is an amazing feat of physical strength. *Trailin'* contains an interesting piece of trivia in that Tom does not once wear his trademark cowboy hat in the entire film.

In 1921 Tom was so popular that he was invited to visit President Warren G. Harding and Ms. Harding at White House. Tom brought along Tony and the White House press corps went wild.[74]

In the fall of 1921 Tom took his production unit to Arizona's Grand Canyon to shoot one of his biggest productions to date, a thrilling western entitled *Sky High*.

Sky High opens with a funny scene in which Tom arrests illegal Chinese immigrants trying to cross the U.S. border with Mexico. He is riding a black horse which looks to be Colt .45, one of Tom's first movie horses. The scene sets a light-hearted tone for the film. Tom is then sent to infiltrate a gang of smugglers who plan to bring a large group of illegal Chinese immigrants across the border at Calexico. Sid Jordan played "Bullet Bates," the thug heavy, who works for the mastermind of the smugglers and is operating out of a cantina on the border.

It is interesting to note that in the opening sequence that the smuggler is using a Model T Ford. Later, when Tom and Jordan head across the border, they climb into another Model T. Tom later hops aboard a biplane to guide a motorized posse to the smugglers' lair. The heavy usage of modern cars and planes in Tom's films set a pattern which B westerns would follow for another 30 years. The blending of the new west and the old west made the stories seem immediate and freed Tom and other cowboy stars from having to set all of their films in the Old West. Additionally, when singing cowboys became the rage, this device made it easy for the studios to set the stories in such modern environments as movie studios and radio programs, thus cross-marketing these warbling waddies.

In 1922, much of the American west was still traveled by horse and buggy. Dirt roads were the norm and rural electricity did not become commonplace until the Great Depression, when President Franklin D. Roosevelt signed into law the Rural Electrification Act. Thus, Tom's modernized westerns often mirrored life in the great southwestern deserts at that time.

In *Sky High*, Tom rescues Eva Novak, who is taken captive by bandits and then hides her in the cliffs of the canyon. He repels down the wall of the Grand Canyon with just a rope. Later in the film, he climbs back up the canyon wall using the same rope. Tom and the bad guys engage in a foot chase along narrow cliffs that is harrowing. Still later, Tom gallops his horse (not Tony) from the floor of the canyon up the narrow mule trails all the way up to the rim of the canyon, often barely avoiding disaster. In the climax of the film, Tom dives out of the airplane into the Colorado River grabs a white horse and chases after Sid Jordan. Sid runs down a sheer hillside on foot and Tom gives chase on the white horse. At the bottom of the steep grade, the white horse stumbles and somersaults. Tom is thrown hard onto the ground. At first glance, one wonders if Tom was using a "Running W," a device used by stunt men to make horses fall in a somersault, but clearly this is an accident. Despite the horrific fall, Tom simply leaps up, grabs the horse before it can run off, remounts and continues the chase. This unintentional stunt makes an already thrilling chase spellbinding. No western star before or since has ever taken such an accidental neck-breaking horse fall and simply continued with the scene. Modern actors don't even attempt such chase sequences without computer-assisted special effects and should a modern day actor happen to go down in a horse fall the location would shut down and the actor would be flown to a hospital.

Less than a month after *Sky High* opened to smash success Victoria gave birth to Tom's second daughter, Thomasina, born February 12, 1922.[75]

Tom followed *Sky High* up with such 1922 releases as *Chasing the Moon, Up and Going* (for which Tom wrote the story), *The Fighting Streak, For Big Stakes, Just Tony* (from a story by Max Brand), *Do and Dare, Tom Mix in Arabia* and *Catch My Smoke*. The films were all solid big budget westerns, except for *Tom Mix in Arabia*, which blended Tom's formula with a little plot homage to Rudolph Valentino, the Italian-born star whose *The Sheik* (1921) was a major hit with audiences that year. In *The Fighting Streak*, the 42-year-old Tom does some boxing, showing off his amazing physique, including his six-pack abs.

Just Tony was filmed as "Tom's tribute to Tony." It was also a shrewd marketing ploy to make the horse an even bigger household name. It is a fictional tale of how Tom found Tony, rescuing the horse from a vicious Mexican horse tamer. In the scene, in order to save Tony from a beating, Tom leaps over a six foot fence from a standing start, in itself a feat of great athleticism, and fights with the Mexican vaquero. The remainder of the film involves two plots, Tom's attempts to capture Tony, now living wild in the desert, and a subplot about the identity of a man who shot Tom in the leg years before for—of all things—playing the wrong song on a banjo. There is a terrific sequence wherein we see Tom actually riding a bucking horse. Again he does not use a stunt double.

Just Tony was a smash hit, and it added further luster to Tom's star power.

At the end of 1922, Tom must have felt that he was on top of the world. Wherever he went, he drew crowds of frenzied fans. Personal appearances at various Fox movie theaters always turned into major news events. Tom would ride Tony into the movie theater and up the stairs onto the stage, as the grand palace movie theaters of the Roaring '20s had stages for live performances. Tom would then put on a little show. The fans, most of them young boys, went wild, cheering and applauding their hero.

One newspaper editor called Tom "the idol of every American boy," a sobriquet that was proven correct time and time again as Tom made personal appearances with Tony at charity events all across the country. Many celebrities throughout the years have donated their time to charities, often with their participation contingent upon their expenses being paid. Tom unselfishly made himself available to many charities at no cost throughout his career, and he often brought his entire vaudeville act along as an added attraction. As a result, Tom raised thousands—maybe even millions—for charities.

Tom was so highly thought of that Los Angeles Police Chief Louis A. Oaks made Tom an honorary lieutenant of the LAPD on May 16, 1923.[76]

Tom's output of quality westerns continued in 1923 with *Romance Land*, a thrilling adventure in which Tom does battle with the villain while swaying in a cable car more than 100 feet above the ground. Tom leaps about—at his own obvious great peril—to rescue the heroine from kidnappers.

Tom's next film has been lost to time, unless some collector or library has a copy and doesn't realize its value. It is a shame, because *Three Jumps Ahead* contains the greatest stunt Tom ever did—jumping a horse over the Newhall Pass, also called the Newhall Cut. Located northwest of Los Angeles outside the town of Newhall, California, the "cut" is a deep, narrow crevice barely wide enough for a horse and wagon to pass through.

The director was John Ford, who would achieve legendary status with his Oscar-winning dramas such as *The Grapes of Wrath* and *How Green Was My Valley*—as well as a series of brilliant western epics which starred John Wayne. Ford had used the Newhall Pass in an early Harry Carey-Hoot Gibson western called *Straight Shooting* (1913). It is unknown who thought of the stunt, but it is likely Ford mentioned the Newhall Pass to Mix, who then decided to jump the pass on horseback. Ford later included the pass, also called Beale's Cut, in the climactic stagecoach chase in his epic *Stagecoach* (1939), the film which made John Wayne a major star.

One of the most famous photos of Tom Mix is the photo of him jumping over the Newhall Pass. It is also one of the most highly controversial stunts ever filmed.

Some revisionist historians insist that the jump was merely a camera trick. Others insist it was done by a stuntman named Ed Simpson, though their only source for this information is an interview with Judy Ishkanian, Simpson's great-niece, who was not present when the stunt was performed and claims simply that Simpson told her he did the stunt.[77]

Still others insist that the jump was actually done by Tom but that the Newhall Pass was made to look more dangerous by using a camera trick that, in essence, shrunk the size of Tom and his horse to make the gap seem larger. There were many in Hollywood—including Tom's crew—that insisted at the time that Tom performed the stunt. Ford said for years that Tom did the stunt.

An examination of the photo reveals that Tom has built a ramp, much like a partial bridge, which elevates his takeoff altitude, so that when the horse—Tony's stunt double—leaps, he is actually higher than the opposite side of the pass, allowing for the angle of descent to be such that the horse and rider actually make it to the other side. This lends considerable proof that the stunt was actually completed. Why would Tom have built a ramp if the jump were a camera trick? Indeed, Tony did not make the jump, as Tom had insured Tony for $20,000 and Tom loved the horse too much to risk its life.

If the jump did indeed occur, then surely Tom did it. Tom did not use a stunt double until 1935, during the making of *The Miracle Rider*, when he used Cliff Lyons. By then Tom was 55 and had only recently been seriously injured in two bad horse falls. Tom did all of his own stunts from the beginning of his film career in 1910 until 1933. Even at age 53, Tom did not use a stuntman, even on such dangerous gags as jumping Tony Jr. off of a train, over several high fences, and more. The assertion that he would use a stunt double on the Newhall Pass jump is implausible.

Further, cowboy Ted French, who worked on many Mix films, was emphatic on the subject. "Tom Mix wouldn't let nobody double him," French said flatly.[78]

Director George Marshall, who directed Tom in *Prairie Trails* (1920) and *Hands Off* (1921), said Tom did "all his own stunts—the horse falls, crashing through glass windows on horseback, and so on. There was no imitation glass during this period either and they didn't dig up the ground to spot a fall. Wherever they were shooting that's where you fell."[79]

An actress who appeared in *Treat 'Em Rough* (1919) with Tom, Jane Novak, was also emphatic about Tom's stunt work. "Tom always did his own stunts." Her sister, actress Eva Novak, who appeared with Tom in *The Speed Demon* (1919), *The Feud* (1920), *The Dare-Devil* (1920), *Chasing the Moon* (1922), and *No Man's Gold* (1926), agreed. "He had a double for Tony. But he never had a double for himself. He did all his stunts and they were something, let me tell you."[80]

Many revisionist historians have sought to claim that Tom did not do his own stunts, but none have ever produced a transcript or recording of an interview with a crew member or fellow actor to verify this claim. Most of Tom's stunts were shot with the camera close to the action so the audience could clearly see that it was Tom doing the stunt. Thus the claim that he did not do his own stunts is disproved by the film record. Tom did not use a stunt double until 1935 when, after several life-threatening injuries, the 55-year-old cowboy star occasionally used stunt double Cliff Lyons in his final serial, *The Miracle Rider*.

The Newhall Pass stunt was so famous that Will Rogers spoofed it in the film *Uncensored Movies* (1923). In that film, Rogers does a wickedly funny impersonation of Mix, including an obvious camera trick recreation of the Newhall Pass jump in which Rogers, imitating Tom, riding "Tony" does flips while completing the jump. There is also a hysterical sequence in which Rogers walks up and mounts "Tony." It is funny because Rogers makes a face that is a dead-on likeness of Tom, and fascinating because Rogers literally mounts the horse without using his hands, an athletic feat in itself.

Sadly, *Three Jumps Ahead* is lost. There is some evidence that a print of it might exist in the Czech film archives, but that film has not been located and reproduced. If it is ever recovered, as many "lost" Tom Mix films have been discovered in the past decade, then perhaps the controversy will be put to rest and another great film will be preserved for future audiences.

Tom's next film, *Stepping Fast*, was shot in the ruins of an ancient Indian cliff-dwelling in Arizona and on location in Victorville, California. From there he finished *North of Hudson Bay*, again directed by John Ford, *The Lone Star Ranger*, *Mile-A-Minute Rodeo* (written by Max Brand) and *Eyes of the Forest*.

On November 10, 1923, Tom and Tony were nearly killed during the making of *Eyes of the Forest*. The stunt called for Tom, a forest ranger on the trail of thieves, to ride Tony at breakneck speed. Unbeknownst to Ranger Tom the trail has been mined with a huge explosive charge. The script called for Tom and Tony to ride by the explosives, which were supposed to detonate about two to three seconds after they passed. Someone missed the cue and the explosion occurred right as Tom and Tony passed by. The explosion was massive, sending sharp rocks and other debris in all directions with tremendous force. The film crew stood in shock as Tom and Tony were thrown 50 feet, landing in sickening thuds as their unconscious bodies hit the ground. Tony sustained a large gash in his side. Tony woke and staggered to his feet, dazed. Tom regained consciousness a minute or so later, disoriented and in shock. His back was torn to shreds, as if he had been hit with a blast of rock salt from a shotgun.[81]

When Tom saw the extent of Tony's injuries, he shook away the cobwebs, sent for a first aid kit and spent the next hour cleaning and meticulously sewing Tony's wound closed. Tom accomplished this despite the fact that his own back was torn to shreds with tiny shrapnel wounds from dozens of rocks blown by the explosion. Tom refused medical attention until Tony had been attended to.[82]

Olive recounted the story differently in her memoir, though it is likely based on hearsay as she was not present at the time as she and Tom were divorced by that time. Olive stated that Tom and Tony were actually partially buried by rocks after the blast and that a veterinarian—and not Tom—sewed Tony's wounds closed.[83]

12

In 1924 Tom starred in only six movies, got into a nasty spat with the 101 Ranch and was shot by his wife.

The year began with Tom waiting for Fox to notify him that the studio was renewing his contract. Tom had fulfilled his commitment to the studio by starring in *Ladies to Board, The Trouble Shooter, The Heart Buster, The Last of the Duanes* (from a story by western icon Zane Grey), *Oh, You Tony!, Teeth* and *The Deadwood Coach,* from a story by *Hopalong Cassidy* creator Clarence E. Mulford.

Once again, Tom did his dead level best to film at locations as far away as possible from the studio, taking his production unit all the way to Zion National Park and Cedar City, Utah in July and August of 1924 for *The Deadwood Coach*.[1]

After Paramount had a smash hit with the epic, *The Covered Wagon* (1923), all of the studios began to view westerns as a good investment. Fox had consistently increased the budgets of Tom's films, so much so that the front office began planning fewer and fewer Tom Mix films for each year. Fox was also pushing the running times of Tom's films up from five reels to six. The studio also charged higher theatrical rents on Tom's films.[2]

Despite his obvious value to the studio, Fox executives began to view Tom's salary as too expensive. By the eighth year of his contract he was making an enormous $17,500 per week, more money in five days than most people in the United States made in three years.[3]

After months of silence from Fox, Tom began negotiating with the Miller Brothers 101 Ranch and Wild West Show to spend the summer circus season touring with the show. Tom and Zack Miller agreed that Tom would star in the summer tour. His salary with the 101 show would be about $6,000 per week, roughly 1/3 of his movie salary. Tom looked forward to hitting the sawdust trail. The thought that he could spend the summer performing for the fans and escape the confines of Hollywood filled him with enthusiasm.

Fox Studios got wind that Tom was planning to hit the trail and, realizing their goose that laid the golden egg was about to leave town, suddenly informed Tom that the studio was renewing his contract. Tom was in a box. He was overcommitted. He couldn't honor his contract with the 101 without angering Fox and he couldn't honor his contract with Fox without angering the Miller brothers. Fox paid three times what Tom would make on the 101 tour and, pressed by the enormous financial obligations of his movie star lifestyle—and Victoria's out of control spending—Tom chose to honor his movie contract and risk the ire of Zack Miller.[4]

Zack, a contrarian and obdurate businessman, sued Tom for breach of contract and lost profits. It wasn't the first time the Zack used the courts to try and control, and profit from, Tom—he had previously trumped up a horse stealing charge—and it wouldn't be the last.

Tom returned to work at Fox and his lawyers negotiated a settlement to the 101 lawsuit. Tom would divide his time that summer between his work at Fox and the 101 Ranch show. Tom agreed to appear in five major cities: Kansas City, Missouri; Chicago, Illinois; Cincinnati, Ohio and New York City.[5]

Tom discovered during these performances with the 101 Ranch show that he enjoyed performing for live audiences more than he enjoyed making movies. He realized that he could not have become a movie star had it not been for his wild west show days, but he knew that his celebrity and financial success came directly from his movie work. One thing was certain, if his movie career ended for whatever reason, Tom knew he could return to the sawdust trail and perform for live audiences.

During the 1924 San Bernardino State Fair and Rodeo, Tom appeared with a contingent of movie cowboys, including fellow 101 Ranch alumni Hoot Gibson and Buck Jones. Ken Maynard and movie cowboy Art Accord were also there. Tom was dressed all in white and attracted considerable attention at the event. During the rodeo, Iron Eyes Cody, the Indian actor, and actress Bertha "Birdie" Darkcloud were to be married on horseback during a break in the performances.[6]

The wedding party was drinking and whooping it up during the rodeo and, when it came time to mount their horses for the ceremony, Hoot offered to help Darkcloud mount her horse. As he did so, he said, jokingly, "okay, squaw lady, up you go." It was meant affectionately, but Darkcloud took offense and kicked Hoot in the forehead so hard he was knocked unconscious. Cowboy star Tim McCoy, another real-life cowboy and former cavalry officer, was best man. He bent over Hoot and began to revive him.

"Don't worry, he's been kicked in the head by horses, he'll be all right," McCoy joked. Cody and Darkcloud called off the wedding, but were married in an Indian-style ceremony shortly thereafter.[7]

Tom's Hollywood life had, by this time, taken on a surreal tone. He worked at the studio risking his life to make thrilling movies and earning as much—and often much more—than the greatest movie stars in town. Victoria, still in her late 20s, spent money like crazy trying to fit into the upper echelon of Tinseltown society. While Tom enjoyed socializing with friends in Hollywood, he viewed the upper crust as elitists who spent their time swathed in diamonds and furs and looking down on the average joe. "There's probably more summer, winter, spring and fall ermine coats in Hollywood than any other place in the world," Tom said in 1927. "I know picture women who bought ermine coats when they didn't have anything to wear under them—not that they wear much under them now." Tom despised the haughty nature of the social elite who "sit around with a bored air that is supposed to indicate social manners."

Tom summed up his attitude toward the Hollywood elite: "I like who I like here in Hollywood. Them that I don't like can go square to hell."[8]

In an event which could only have been scripted by a Hollywood mystery writer, Tom's dislike for the Tinseltown elite nearly caused his own death. In March 1924, during one of Victoria's social engagements, Tom was nearly murdered by his own wife. As often happens in a world where booze flows freely and guns are present, violence erupted during an argument. Tom was severely injured when Victoria picked up a gun and shot Tom in his arm and back. This amazing story of domestic violence occurred when Tom came home from a hard day at the studio to find Victoria entertaining "friends" from Beverly Hills. As Tom was introduced, one of the house guests made a derisive comment about Tom's work and Tom took offense, ordering all of Victoria's elitist friends to leave his house.[9]

Victoria had been drinking and she angrily picked up one of Tom's loaded revolvers and in a rage fired all five shots in the cylinder at Tom.[10]

As Tom dove for cover, Victoria shot him in the left arm and in the back, where the bullet lodged near Tom's spine. Amazingly, Victoria missed hitting any of Tom's vital organs, but he was bleeding profusely. An ambulance was summoned and Tom was rushed to the hospital, where Fox Studios public relations men went into damage control mode, insisting that the shooting be listed as an accident.[11]

"She shot and hit me in the arm," Tom said in 1933. "She shot five times. One bullet lodged in the chair and I don't know where the others went."[12]

Victoria claimed Tom was a mean drunk and that she acted in self-defense.[13]

It is ironic that Tom was nearly killed by Victoria, a woman who struck Colleen Moore as a "fragile" woman.[13]

Amazingly, Tom and Victoria would remain married for another four years.

13

Tom Mix's movie career had hit its peak at the beginning of the decade in 1920 and began its decline as the decade came to a close. Along the way Tom had become the biggest western star in the world.

Chafing at the bit to try some new story ideas and to make movies free from the interference of the studio brass, Tom was growing restless.

The studio agreed to a change of pace production and in late 1924 produced *Dick Turpin*, which cast Tom as the notorious British bandit. The story was basically a Tom Mix western set in merry old England, but it gave Tom some new, fresh plot twists. Predictably, audiences were lukewarm to the film, which had Tom jumping around in silks and large, feathered hats.

Dick Turpin is actually a good film. It opens with Tom as the notorious highwayman who robs the rich to aid the poor, a la Robin Hood. Tom rides a big, black horse called "Black Bess." Throughout the film Tom scales parapets, roofs, high walls and crashes around in the fashion of Douglas Fairbanks, the leading swashbuckler of the cinema at that time. Tom equates himself well in the light-hearted actioner, but he is no Fairbanks. He doesn't possess that light-hearted savoir faire that made Fairbanks such a movie favorite. Tom's limitations as an actor show through in the scene where his horse is shot out from under him. He simply drops his head so that his hair falls in his face to show he is grief-stricken. And yet, the image of him holding his dying horse's head is striking and evokes sadness.

Tom followed up Dick Turpin with perhaps his most famous movie, *Riders of the Purple Sage*. Filmed in the high desert of Lone Pine, California in November and December of 1924, the movie was based on the epic western novel by Zane Grey. Tom plays Lassiter, the gunman all dressed in black who is bent on saving a woman rancher from the wiles of a vicious gang of rustlers.

The movie contains the film image of Tom Mix which is perhaps best remembered through the ages. Tom is wearing a tall, black, high-crowned, wide-brimmed "Tom Mix Stetson," a black silk shirt with white western piping, black pants and ornate black boots and two six guns held in a custom-made buscadero gun-belt. This is the first time on film that Tom appears on celluloid wearing the circus-style western outfit that he wore at personal appearance.

Tom's reputation for gaudy clothing has been overstated throughout the years. On film he generally wore less flashy attire, while his wardrobe for "on the town" or for circus performances was quite gaudy. Tom was famous for purple crushed velvet suits and diamond studded belt buckles when he was dining out, and brightly-colored western clothes for live performances. As his fame grew, Tom began designing his film wardrobe. The western yokes and piping on both shirts and pants—creations of Tom's fertile imagination—became de rigeur for movie cowboys from Ken Maynard and Gene Autry and the scores of other cowboy stars—and much later country music singers—to follow. Outfits that today are often called "Roy Rogers outfits" actually got their start from Tom Mix.[1]

Tom had his hats custom made by John B. Stetson and his boots custom made as well. Many craftsmen of western-style clothing became famous because Tom Mix wore their products.

Ed Bohlin, who would become famous as an artisan with silver and leather, including boots, saddles and gunbelts, got his first brush with fame after a chance encounter with Tom. At the time, Bohlin was working as a circus and vaudeville performer, doing intricate tricks with a lariat. His act was similar to many rope spinners of the day, including Tom and Will Rogers. Bohlin and Tom were appearing in the same show at a Los Angeles vaudeville theater. During Bohlin's act, Tom stood in the wings watching Bohlin work. What had caught Tom's eye wasn't the act itself, rather it was Bohlin's finely crafted leather coat. Bohlin took the coat off for part of the performance, but noticed Tom was taking an unusual interest in the garment. Bohlin became convinced that Tom was going to purloin the coat, during his performance. This distraction caused Bohlin to miss some intricate rope tricks. "When I finished my part of the act I walked over to him and asked 'What do you want?' Bohlin recalled. "I want to buy that coat," Tom replied. He offered Bohlin $35 for the coat. Bohlin said Tom wrote out a check and handed it to Bohlin. The check had Tom's name and picture on it.

The next day Bohlin visited Tom at Fox Studios. Bohlin showed Tom a fine, hand-tooled leather bag and Tom was impressed. Looking down at Bohlin's feet, Tom commented on Bohlin's alligator skin cowboy boots. Tom asked Bohlin if he had made the boots and Bohlin said that he had. The boots were flamboyant, the way Tom liked them. He asked Bohlin if he could try them on and Bohlin agreed. Tom put on the boots and loved them. Just then, silent movie great Dustin Farnum, who had starred in Cecil B. DeMille's classic western *The Squaw Man* (1913), dropped by and he and Tom walked off to discuss some business.

After waiting patiently, Bohlin—still bootless—walked over to Tom's studio office to retrieve his boots. When he arrived, Theodora "Teddy" Eason, Tom's secretary, told Bohlin that Tom had left to go on location. "But he has my boots on!" Bohlin exclaimed. Teddy smiled and told Bohlin that it was okay, whereupon she handed him a check from Tom for $250 for the boots and the leather bag. It was more money than Bohlin had seen in his life.[2]

After that Tom used Bohlin extensively and promoted him to his friends. By 1937 Bohlin had a thriving custom saddle and silver store located in the heart of Hollywood at 5760 Sunset Boulevard. Bohlin became a millionaire leathersmith, saddle-maker and silver craftsman, catering to the needs of the various flamboyantly dressed cowboy stars who rushed to copy Tom's style of dress.

After appearing in *Riders of the Purple Sage* in his circus-style garb, Tom would forever spruce up his wardrobe on and off film with brightly colored, flashy outfits.

Riders of the Purple Sage is an important film. More so than any other film Tom had done before, he was now presented as more than a western hero. He was a western icon. The affable, tongue-in-cheek humor is gone. Tom plays Lassiter straight, without humor. Shot on location in the snow-capped High Sierras, the movie has breathtaking vistas and crystal clear cinematography. The Zane Grey story is stripped of its anti-Mormon preoccupation with polygamy and is boiled down to a fast-paced action film. It is, without question, one of the finest silent Western movies made. Lyrical and dramatic, *Riders of the Purple Sage* stands the test of time perhaps better than any of Tom's movies.

The climax has Tom and the heroine, played by Beatrice Burnham, scaling a cliff face and sending a boulder down into a ravine, sealing themselves off from the rest of the world forever.

In addition to Beatrice Burnham, the film features Warner Oland as the chief villain. Oland would go on to great fame in the early 1930s as the legendary Asian detective in the *Charlie Chan* films.

Riders of the Purple Sage was such a massive hit that Fox immediately rushed Tom into a sequel entitled *The Rainbow Trail*, which Tom insisted be shot on location in Arizona, far from the stress of the studio. Tom then went on to film *The Lucky Horseshoe*, *The Everlasting Whisper*, *The Best Bad Man* and *The Yankee Señor*, which contained some sequences shot in the still-experimental Technicolor process.

The Lucky Horseshoe is notable because it contains some fantasy dream sequences in which Tom is dressed up like a dashing swordsman. Frank Cooper, a young cowboy from Montana who was working as an extra that day, said at the time that the sequence seemed to be a Robin Hood vignette. As Cooper watched Tom film the scene he turned to a crewman and remarked that he didn't think

Tom was a very good actor. "He's good enough to make $17,000 a week," the crew man replied.[3]

That same extra also rode as part of the posse in Tom's Fox production of *Riders of the Purple Sage* and would later change his name to Gary Cooper and become a major star in his own right.

One of the most intriguing—and completely forgotten—pieces of trivia about Tom comes from 1924, when Tom's friend John Ford directed his first truly epic western, a saga called *The Iron Horse* (1924). For years rumors have persisted that Tom wanted to play the lead in the film, but Ford chose athletic George O'Brien, a young actor who had worked on Tom's production unit for several years. O'Brien would go on to western stardom and work in Ford pictures for another 30 years. This author recently viewed *The Iron Horse* and discovered—in a mob scene where the Irish railroad workers protest their working conditions—a quick closeup of a disgruntled, unshaven worker and it is, undoubtedly, Tom Mix. His face is obscured by a heavy beard stubble—clearly charcoal beard makeup—but it is Tom. This author posits that Tom was visiting O'Brien and Ford on the set and decided to jump into a scene for hell of it.

After *The Iron Horse* became a smash hit, Ford went to William Fox with the idea of starring Tom, George O'Brien and Buck Jones in a western called *Three Bad Men*. The story is a tale of revenge for a woman wronged, but the heroes die by the final fade out of the film. Fox eventually shot down the idea of Tom and Buck Jones starring in the film, not wanting to make a film which had the studios three favorite cowboy stars dying. Ford finally made the film, with O'Brien, Tom Santschi, Frank Campeau and J. Farrell McDonald.

Tom finished the winter 1924-25 shooting schedule in time to leave for a tour of Europe.

Tom's popularity was such that other studios began trying to cash in on the western bonanza. Tom's old pal, Hoot Gibson, had become a major star in his own right, and his salary of $14,500 per week at Universal Studios rivaled Tom's.[4]

One studio tried to cash in on Tom's name without Tom when it hired an actor named George Kesterson and renamed him Art Mix. Fox Studios sued Kesterson, claiming that the actor was trading on their famous star's name, but the court ruled for Kesterson.[5]

Tom's popularity extended worldwide. Because silent movie title cards could be written in any language, Tom was as big a hero in Europe and South America as he was at home. To build on his popularity, Tom and Fox Studios decided that Tom should make a tour of Europe.

Tom was such a big star by this time that Thomas Kellogg, the United States Secretary of State, wrote a letter on March 12, 1935 giving Tom a letter of introduction to carry to American diplomats should he need official government assistance while abroad.[6]

George Holmes, the chief of the Los Angeles Police Department, wrote a letter of introduction for Tom to present to Scotland Yard, the English police. "Tom is not only a screen celebrity, but a regular fellow, as well...He is a very close friend of mine and is much interested in police work."[7]

On March 28, 1925 Tom, Victoria and Thomasina boarded a cross country train to New York. Their itinerary was to meet the ocean liner *Aquitania* in New York and depart April 8 for South Hampton, England. Tom brought along Tony and Pat Chrisman to care for the horse. Victoria brought along her mother to help care for Thomasina. When the train arrived in the Big Apple, an enormous crowd descended on the railroad station and New York City police had to help Tom unload his family and Tony safely. The police invited Tom to keep Tony at the city's stables along with the mounted police horses. Tom accepted, knowing that Tony couldn't be safer than in a police stable.

When the time had come to board the ocean liner, Tom arrived with his family and made a big publicity splash when he rode Tony up the gangplank and onto the *Aquitania* in front of Fox Movietone news cameras and newspaper photographers from across the country.

The crew of the *Aquitania* was very hospitable to Tom and his party, even going so far as to construct a stall below decks for Tony that was designed by Tom to keep the horse safe. To keep Tony in shape, Tom exercised the horse daily on the passenger deck, to the delight of the rest of the passengers. During one formal dinner, Tom rode Tony into the dining room and up a grand staircase. The applause was thunderous.[8]

The *Aquitania* arrived at South Hampton harbor to find a throng of fans and reporters awaiting the arrival of America's famous cowboy star. Tom brought Tony onto the passenger deck and rode down the gangplank to the cheers of the welcoming crowd. Dignitaries such as the mayors of Brighton and Howe and the deputy mayor of South Hampton greeted Tom and Tony as if they were visiting royalty. Edward, the Prince of Wales, sent an emissary inviting Tom to board Tony at Tattersalls, a royal stable.[9]

After securing Tony at Tattersalls, Tom met up with Victoria and Thomasina at the Savoy Hotel.

The next day Tom put on his fanciest outfit and headed to Tattersalls, where he saddled Tony and rode him through Hyde Park. Hyde Park is an enormous, beautifully manicured park located in the most expensive part of London. In 1925 the most elite of London's rich would take horseback rides along a 90-foot wide avenue called King's Way. Before Tom had ridden far a crowd began to gather. Soon thousands of children and adults had lined King's Way and Tom put on an impromptu show. He galloped Tony down the path, doing some fancy trick riding. He then rode Tony Roman-style, standing on the horse's back as he galloped along. The crowd cheered.[10]

At one point Tom had to cross a crowded street in heavy traffic. The teeming mass of cars and double-decker buses came to a screeching halt as Tom stopped Tony in the middle of the intersection, stood on Tony's back and put his hand to his forehead as if he were scouting a trail. An enterprising photographer took a picture of Tom and the photo was published the next day in the London papers.[11]

Tom took London like a conquering hero. Everywhere he went Londoners cheered him, greeted him warmly, and expressed great admiration for his films and his willingness to be a role model for young children.[12]

English men admired Tom's machismo, and horseman from the Emerald Isle were especially respectful of Tom. He was given guided tours of polo fields and toured the stables used by polo teams. Tom later said, "I was great and beyond my dreams and expectations that the American cowboy was so popular throughout England."[13]

On April 17, 1925, Tom visited the Royal National Orthopaedic Hospital for the Care of Crippled Children in London. His appearance buoyed the spirits of the patients and the hospital staff, who were further overwhelmed when Tom made a financial contribution to the hospital.

Arl Meyers, the director of the hospital, wrote Tom a warm letter of thanks the following day. "Dear Mr. Mix, I have great pleasure in enclosing herewith a receipt for the very generous donation you gave us yesterday when you called here. It was very good of you to come and your visit gave much pleasure to our little patients as well as providing some extremely useful publicity for our "Buttercup Day" as I must thank you for your sympathy and support."[14]

After several days of creating pandemonium in London, Tom and his entourage took the train to Dover and then crossed the English Channel to France, arriving in Paris on April 18, 1925. Tom's arrival created a sensation. He was immediately deluged with requests to appear at various charity functions. He accepted most of them. He appeared with Tony before a crowd of 6,000 spectators at Trocadero Hall at a benefit for the Children's Welfare League. Tom rode into the audience and up and down the aisles, even into the balcony. The crowd cheered as boys and girls reached out to touch Tom and Tony and shake Tom's hand. Tom never worried about riding Tony into a crowd of children. Tony seemed to enjoy the crowds as much as Tom did and he never spooked or kicked at the children, even when they ran underneath his belly and between his legs, something that would terrify many horses. The chairman of the benefit was so overwhelmed with gratitude to Tom that he tearfully kissed Tom on both cheeks in the traditional French manner and presented him with a silver medal from the French Association for the Protection of Horses. Tom took off his hat and bowed his head to receive the medal and the audience erupted in thunderous applause.[15]

Tony was stabled in the famous Maison Lafitte, a racing stable, alongside Epinard, a famous French racehorse and Tom spent several days visiting hospitals and charity events. One afternoon Tom dropped in at a Boy Scout camp to visit with the scouts and donate much needed equipment.[16]

Tom's entourage boarded a train to Brussels, Belgium, where crowds of fans awaited at each station along the way to cheer the famous cowboy.

In Brussels, Tom and company boarded the Amsterdam Express to Berlin, Germany. Germany was still recovering from the devastation and economic ruin of World War I, but Germans turned out by the thousands to see Tom's arrival. Germans were big fans of American western books, so much so that actor Eric Rosenthal took the name Billy Jenkins and became known as the "German Buffalo Bill." Germans loved western movies and Tom Mix was their favorite movie cowboy.

Tom realized that the German fans wanted to get a good look at him so he saddled Tony and, much like he had done in London's Hyde Park, rode down the famous Unter den Linden, a wide park lane lined with linden trees. Children and adults flocked to the park as word spread that Tom was there and Tom put on an impromptu performance for the crowd.[17]

After safely stabling Tony, Tom met up with his family at the Adlon Hotel, where dignitaries and fans came to pay their respects.

By mid-July Tom was tired of Europe and longed to return to the United States. He left Tony in Pat Chrisman's care and boarded the *Mauritania* for New York. Pat took Tony to meet up with the *Aquitania* so that Tony could make the Atlantic voyage in the safety of Tom's specially built stall.

Tom arrived in New York on July 5, 1925, several days ahead of the scheduled arrival of the *Aquitania*, so he spent those days visiting hospitals throughout New England. Tom's support for the humane treatment of animals had endeared him to the Humane Society, which made certain that Tom's arrival in a town was greeted by animal lovers and members of the society's various chapters.[18]

Tom traveled on to Canada, where he attended a luncheon at the King Edward Hotel in Toronto. He was then a guest of the Canadian Parliament and met many prominent Canadian politicians at a reception in his honor. The next day Tom visited the Royal Canadian Dragoons, a mounted military unit.[19]

Tom returned to New York to meet up with Pat and Tony. They caught a train to Washington, D.C., where Tom appeared with Tony at the National Horse Show. On a lark, Tom took Tony through the jumping course and thrilled audiences when Tony cleared the highest hurdle.[20]

President Calvin Coolidge invited Tom to be a guest at the White House. On May 21, 1925, Tom arrived at the White House aboard Tony and his arrival made the newspapers all across the country. Victoria accompanied Tom as well. Tom sat with President and Mrs. Coolidge during a performance in honor of the Disabled American Veterans. Tom and Tony then entertained the crowd on the White House lawn.[21]

The pictures of the event are remarkable. President Coolidge is dressed in a light-colored suit and is wearing a straw topper. Mrs. Coolidge is dressed in a loose-fitting dress and a necklace of large, black beads. She is wearing a wide-brimmed straw bonnet. Tom is wearing a black, western-cut suit and a bow tie—and a dazzling white Tom Mix Stetson. His pants are tucked into brightly colored, hand-tooled boots. In one photo, Tom rides Tony in front of the West Wing of the White House, doffing his hat for the cameras.

From Washington Tom went on a personal appearance tour set up by the Fox publicity department.

During a stopover in Philadelphia, Tom was welcomed by Mayor W. Freeland Kendrick. As the two men rode through the streets of the city in the mayor's car, Tom's young fans swarmed over the vehicle scratching the paint.

Kendrick joked about it in a letter to Tom. "No damage was done to my car by the children except for a few scratches which amount to nothing. Your popularity with the children was really an inspiration to me, and indicates your great influence over the coming generation."[22]

Tom put on an abbreviated version of his vaudeville act in Buffalo, New York before going on to Detroit, Michigan where he stayed at the Book-Cadillac Hotel, causing pandemonium at the hotel once fans learned that he was registered there. Tom then traveled to St. Louis, Missouri and Denver, Colorado. From there Tom returned to Los Angeles where he was met by a parade made up of cowboys, Indians and six stagecoaches, all sent over by Fox Studios to herald Tom's arrival.[23]

14

By 1925, Tom was growing irritable under the strain of his responsibilities and the supervision by Fox executives. He began to drink more heavily and, when drinking, became surly and difficult.

It is likely that Tom resented the pressure of the Fox machine and he missed the wide open spaces he had so cherished as a young man. He missed the camaraderie of the cowboys on the trail and the fellowship of his fellow wild west performers. His life had once been an endless, rootless ride from ranch to ranch, from town to town, working as a cowboy or small town sheriff or performing his trick shooting, roping and riding and then spending his evenings drinking and carousing with his friends. Now his life was regimented by the demands of the studio and the ever-present realization that each frame of film he created had to please his millions of fans worldwide. And his box office grosses had to please an increasingly unfriendly studio.

Tom felt he had to get out from under that regimentation and get back the energy and enthusiasm he felt in his early film-making days at Selig Polyscope. He insisted that his films were shot in distant locations, so distant and remote that the cast and crew had to live in tents and eat food cooked by an old-fashioned chuck wagon cook.

Tom simply could not adjust to the studio meddling in his films. He wanted to be independent and shoot his movies away from brass and their spies. He wanted to return to that world he had known where he was a man of the rugged outdoors, making movies alongside his saddle pals.

"You'd never believe some of the scripts those white-collared screen writers handed me. Some of the scenes were plumb ridiculous. The motion picture studio conferences were a big joke. All those dude writers ever did was to increase the overhead of five-reel pictures," Tom told writer Walt Coburn years later. "Any conference lasting less than three hours ain't no good. Not that anything is decided upon that gets in the picture but it fills in the day until time to go out and shoot a few holes of golf, the latter bein' a by-product of the movin' pictures business. At these here story conferences all of 'em talk and talk and talk, but none of them says anything. They seem to get nowhere. Any suggestions that I may make an me a'knowin' the west, is properly squelched as bein' out of order.

Anytime I talk I am speaking out of turn." Tom said he would often simply fall asleep in the production meetings, "leaving them to themselves and their vacuum."[1]

Olive said that Tom was a low-key guy on the movie set and wanted his film sets to feel like a family venture. Tom got tense whenever Fox's number two man, Winfield Sheehan, or his cronies came down from the front office at Fox to spy on Tom and see what he was up to. Tom distrusted them and often bristled under their supervision.

Tom's relationship with William Fox had grown strained. Fox once derisively said that he controlled Tom's rancor by treating him like a recalcitrant horse. "I'd pull his bridle off and swat [him] on the rump and away he went, putting his heart and soul into his work."[2]

It was at about this time that Tom met a young, strapping Iowan who played football at the University of Southern California. The kid was named Marion Morrison, called "Duke" by his friends. Duke Morrison had come with a fellow teammate to Fox Studios to meet Tom and ask him for a summer job. The meeting was set up by USC Head Football Coach Howard Jones. Tom greeted the handsome Morrison and his teammate warmly and took him on a tour of the studio.[3]

There are various versions of the events that occurred thereafter, including several different versions told by Morrison after he became famous as John Wayne. One story is that the three men then went to a nearby bar and got drunk together. Morrison remembered that Tom promised him a job as Tom's personal trainer and as an extra in Tom's next movie.

The second version told by Wayne was that he met Mix at Mix's private boxing gym and talked after Tom had finished sparring with another boxer.

When Duke Morrison arrived at the Fox Studios gate to go to work, he was assigned a job as a prop man.[4]

When Morrison saw Tom on the studio lot several days later, he went to complain to the star about his job. Tom allegedly gave Morrison the cold shoulder.

One time, Wayne claimed that Tom was only nice to him long enough to wrangle some special box seats for USC football games, and then cold-shouldered him after that.

Another time, Wayne once said that Tom promised to give him a part in the upcoming *Great K & A Train Robbery* and that Wayne went to Colorado with Mix's unit and acted a propman on the film and that Mix snubbed him the entire shoot.[5] This is likely not true as there are numerous photos of the Mix unit taken during production of the film and the very recognizable Duke Morrison is not visible in any of the photos of the crew.

Years later, Duke Morrison, re-christened John Wayne and now a major Hollywood star, would often tell people, including interviewers, that Tom had treated him unkindly. It is an odd situation for several reasons. Firstly, it is entirely outside of the character of Tom Mix to have promised a studio job and not deliver it. Tom was responsible for the employment of literally dozens of cowboys and roustabouts at the studio. Indeed, the studio often pressured Tom to fire some of his cadre of cowboys, complaining that Tom's Mixville production unit was constantly over budget due to his largess. Secondly, Tom never cold-shouldered people. He was renown for his affability, and even in the dark times when he was drinking heavily, he reserved his temper for those who disrespected him. When disrespected or insulted Tom turned to stone.

Tom never commented on the incident because he died within a year after John Wayne became a major movie star in 1939 with the release of *Stagecoach* and Wayne didn't relate the story until years later. What likely happened is that Tom liked Morrison or, as a favor to USC Coach Howard Jones, Tom got Morrison the only job he could find for him at the studio at that time. Morrison felt he'd been insulted and that he had been given a job beneath his status as a glorified USC football player. Indeed, if Morrison went to Tom to complain that Tom didn't get him a good enough job, Tom most probably cold-shouldered the young football player. Tom was a man of the plains, a cowboy who kept his word and was loyal to his friends. He would have viewed such an attitude as ingratitude and the worst of all insults.

The facts are undeniably this: Tom Mix used his influence in 1926 to get Fox Studios to give a young college student a job for $35 a week at a time when that salary was more than a living wage.[6]

Had not Tom Mix obtained that job for Duke Morrison, there would likely never have been a John Wayne, because it was at Fox that Duke Morrison encountered directors John Ford and Raoul Walsh, who became his mentors and propelled him to movie stardom.[7]

What is certain about these tales about Tom's cold shoulder is that John Wayne was the only one who told them, and he did so long after Tom's death. Ironically, Wayne's closest professional mentor was Ford, who was a close friend of Tom's. Whether Wayne was jealous of Tom's friendship with Ford is unknown.

Since John Wayne's death there have been increasingly revealing books about Wayne's persona, including depictions of an ego and pettiness that have been previously unreported. It is possible that Wayne's tale is more revealing about Wayne than Tom.

Tom took his production unit on location in late 1925, where he starred in *My Own Pal, Tony Runs Wild, Hard Boiled, No Man's Gold, The Great K&A Train Robbery* and *The Canyon of Light*, all of which were released in 1926.

The Great K&A Train Robbery is one of Tom's best films. Filmed along the old narrow gauge railways in the Royal Gorge in Colorado, it is a saga of a railroad detective trying to find the identity of an insider who is tipping off train robbers as to when the trains contain shipments of large sums of money. The movie opens with bandits plotting a train robbery, unaware that Tom is suspended 100 feet above the floor of the gorge by a rope, eavesdropping on the gang and overhearing its plan. Tom then slides effortlessly down the rope and lands perfectly in the saddle and gallops off on Tony. He then races alongside the train and leaps aboard the speeding iron horse without skipping a beat. In another scene Tom rides Tony across a narrow wooden bridge suspended over the raging Colorado River.

Tom rescues a hobo who is trapped under a speeding train in a breathtaking stunt in which Tom ropes the ankles of the hobo and jerks him out from under the train while the train is moving. The hobo, a long lost friend, joins Tom on his mission. At one point the two men are riding Tony double through the mansion of the railroad tycoon. They are cornered by body guards and Tom jumps Buster, who is doubling for Tony, off of a balcony into a swimming pool with both men aboard. The scene is simply thrilling.

The Great K & A Train Robbery is a fantastic example of a Tom Mix film from a period when Tom was at the peak of his powers. The film made a huge profit for the studio and Tom felt that his success would keep his business relationship with Fox on sound footing.

Sadly, William Fox had begun to loathe his top star, mostly because Tom was too famous and quickly becoming too rich. Rumors began circulating at Fox Studios that Tom Mix was getting too expensive and difficult to keep happy. Despite the fact that all of Fox's studio profits were generated by Tom's films, he had become too costly. Executives began debating about whether or not it was more profitable to build a stable of imitators to fill Tom's boots and make films more cheaply, thus garnering profits against smaller overhead.[8]

Fox began grooming Buck Jones (the former Chuck Gephardt) who had worked with Tom at the 101 Ranch, as well as others as potential replacements. Buck Jones' films became quite popular, due in no small part to Buck's reputation as a war hero and former cowboy. Indeed, many of the exploits Tom used to pad his public relations biography had been lifted from Buck's tales of his own true-life adventures. Fox was pleased with Buck's films because the studio spent less money on an entire budget of a Buck Jones film than it did just on Tom's salary alone.[9]

Indeed, the studio remade Tom's *Durand of the Badlands* (1917) in 1925, this time starring Buck Jones.

Realizing that the studio was developing Buck to take his place, Tom said, darkly, "Apparently I'm a prune in the motion picture game."[10]

Other studios had built up cowboy stars who were nipping at Tom's heels, such as former minister Fred Thomson, whose films were virtual copies of Tom's, with thrilling stunts and tongue-in-cheek humor.[11]

Even worse, theater managers who were paying inflated rentals for Tom's films had begun to complain about the quality of some of Tom's films, including hits such as *Hello Cheyenne* and *Riders of the Purple Sage*, which were decried as "a poor story" and "a disappointment" respectively.[12]

While Tom's films did generally well at the box office and Tom's popularity was at an all-time high, theater owners had begun to notice that some of the storylines of Tom's films were getting simplistic and repetitive and the fear was that Tom would begin to lose popularity. Reviewers had begun to use words like "hokum" and "average" and "typical" when discussing Tom's movies.[13]

Tom made seven films in 1927, including *The Last Trail*, *The Bronco Twister*, *The Circus Ace*, *Tumbling River*, *Outlaws of Red River*, *Silver Valley* and the *Arizona Wildcat*. *The Last Trail* was taken from a story by Zane Grey and *The Bronco Twister* and *The Arizona Wildcat* were both from stories written by Adela Rogers St. John, who would gain considerable fame during the heyday of MGM Studios in the 1930s as a top notch writer.

The Last Trail is a thrilling adventure which showcases Tom at the height of his powers. The movie opens with Tom rescuing a damsel in distress from Indians and then evolves into a tale of stolen gold shipments and stagecoach robberies. There is a spectacular stagecoach robbery and chase, the elements of which would be reused in 1939 by John Ford for his classic sound western *Stagecoach*.

Tom is dressed in a brilliant white "Tom Mix Stetson," his trademark hat, and a white western shirt with Tom's trademark arrow pockets. In the film Tom adopts his dying friend's son, adding the familiar element of a young boy into the story for boys in the theater audience to identify with. There is even a basset hound for comic relief.

The action, in addition to the stagecoach robbery, is simply breathtaking. Tom and Tommy, the young boy, survive a firebomb attack on their cabin by robbers by crawling down a tunnel beneath the floor only seconds before the cabin explodes. Tom is ambushed by a bandit and turns the tables on him, then falls asleep from exhaustion. He awakes late in the morning and must ride hell-for-leather to make it to a stagecoach race in time to enter the race. Tom races Tony down several sheer embankments—no small feat for the most experienced rider—and gallops Tony full speed to the starting line of the stagecoach race. The footage of Tom racing Tony across the flat land at a full gallop is awe-inspiring. Tom sits atop Tony as he thunders across the flat prairie with the grace of a ballet dancer and he is clearly a man born to the saddle.

During the stagecoach race, Tom does all of his own driving, racing the top-heavy, unwieldy coach at top speeds across rough terrain. A bandit has cut through Tom's reins and Tom must tie them back together without losing the race. We see Tom, not a stuntman, leap off the driver's seat onto the traces, where he then slides under the horses to retrieve the reins. The thundering hooves of the horses miss Tom's head by inches. This stunt became commonplace in the westerns of the 1930s because stuntman Yakima Canutt performed it often on film, but Tom Mix was the only cowboy star to do it himself—and he did it first.

In the most thrilling sequence, Tom's stagecoach overturns—and again it's Tom doing the stunt. Tom breaks the front axle off the stagecoach and jumps aboard, continuing the race in Roman chariot style. We see Tom racing the horses flat out, a feat no actor has ever performed on film before or since. Tom does so with ease. The sequence predates the famous chariot race in *Ben Hur* (1959).

Tom grew restless around mid-1927 and took little solace in his enormous wealth. The trappings of his fame seemed to close in around him. He spent little time on his new yacht, the "Miss Mixit," a 69-foot motor yacht outfitted with twin 200-horsepower LM-6 Hall Scott motors and mahogany and teak decks. Victoria loved the boat so much that when she and Tom divorced she demanded and received it as part of her divorce settlement.

Victoria left Hollywood—and Tom—for Paris on May 12, 1927. She planned to catch the cruise liner "City of Paris" when it departed from New York City on May 14, 1927. Thomasina went with her mother, as did Victoria's mother, Eugenie Ford, and director Lynn Reynolds' wife. They planned an extended tour of Paris, France; Italy, Spain, England and the rest of Northern Europe—all at Tom's expense.[14]

Tom was finishing up his production work for the year when, on November 29, 1927, word reached him that his father was dead. Edwin Mix died at the age of 73 back home in Pennsylvania.

Tom had learned all he knew about horses from his father. The two men looked a lot alike, and the gift they had when it came to understanding what motivated and controlled horses was passed down from father to son. Tom did not speak openly about his feelings at the time, but those around him could tell that he mourned the loss of his father and his grief weighed heavily on him.

Saddened by the death of his father, the strain of his marriage to Victoria—and her outrageous spending—and the increasing pressure from the studio, Tom's drinking increased, as did his irascibility. Additionally, Tom began to suffer from bouts of a deep depression that would overwhelm him.[15]

While such diagnosis didn't exist at the time, Tom's symptoms mirror those of manic-depression.

Tom's mood deteriorated and his temper flared more often. Director George Marshall said Tom's work became erratic. "Tom was temperamental, but it ran in streaks. Every once in a while this would come to the surface, particularly if he was drinking. One picture would sail along with not a problem; the next would be full of them and he would be sullen and unapproachable."[16]

Raymond "Colorado Cotton" Smith, a cowboy who worked on Tom's films added, "When you start a Mix picture, you'd best leave your right mind hanging on the gate post."[17]

Sometime in late 1927, Tom simply disappeared. The most famous cowboy movie star in the world—a man instantly recognizable the world over—simply vanished. The studio and Tom's family and friends were distraught. Rumors that Tom had been kidnaped or killed began to circulate around Hollywood. Tom finally called the studio and told his longtime secretary, Theodora "Teddy" Eason, that he was "going out of town."[18]

The studio brass panicked. Stars disappearing in the middle of a production can cost studios a fortune in down time as the remainder of the cast and crew of a film end up sitting around—on the clock—waiting for the star to return. Worse yet, such inexplicable behavior often meant some scandal lurked that would make headlines around the world and could ruin Tom's career.

Days later, Tom called Olive at home. Though the two had been divorced for 10 years, Olive knew just from the sound of Tom's voice that something was terribly wrong.

Tom told Olive he was hiding in Lake Arrowhead and he asked if Ruth, now a teenager, could come spend some time with him. Olive agreed immediately and

Ruth was driven up to meet her father. When she arrived, she found him in a rented cabin sitting in near darkness. Ruth asked Tom if he was sick and Tom touched his chest.

"I'm just sick right here, Ruthie," Tom said softly. At Ruth's insistence, Tom tried to explain how he felt. "I really don't know what's the matter, Ruthie. All of a sudden I got fed up on everything. I didn't want to see anybody. I just wanted to forget that I was Tom Mix—famous movie star—and just be all by myself and have a chance to think."[19]

As she would do often in the last years of Tom's life, Ruth buoyed his spirits and motivated him to go back to work.[20]

Ironically, after calling Olive and Ruth in his time of dark despair, in November 1927 Tom sued Olive for custody of Ruth, claiming that Olive was gallivanting around the country leaving Ruth with strangers. The suit was quickly settled.[21]

Ruth had, by this time, become a kindred spirit to her father. She was much like him. Her manner was as daring and cavalier as her father's. She would later run off and elope with her first husband before she was of age and would spend her early life on the wild west show circuit and in the movie business. Ruth had even inherited the Mix gift with horses. Just like her grandfather, Ed, and her father, Tom, Ruth was a natural equestrian. At age 15, Ruth was unstoppable with horses. During the warm afternoon hours of November 4, 1927, Ruth caused a great scare that left Tom shaken. Ruth was riding a young horse while on location at Tom's ranch in Prescott, Arizona, where her father was filming a movie. Ruth's horse suddenly went out of control and began running away with her. Rather than panic, Ruth calmly rode the horse, gradually gaining control of it. Dan Clark, one of Tom's most trusted friends and his cameraman for more than a decade, was present. He recalled that Ruth's calm under pressure was much like her father's. Clark said Ruth sat the runaway horse with the same posture and manner of her father, bringing the horse to a safe stop. Tom saw the entire incident and was so rattled by it that his hands shook visibly as he tried to light a cigarette.[22]

Ruth exclaimed after the heart-stopping incident, "Gee, but she can run!"[23]

Victoria and her entourage returned to New York City from her seven-month long tour Europe on December 4, 1927 aboard the "Ile de France."[24]

Tom's popularity was at an all-time high, so much so that he was invited to enshrine himself in the Hollywood tradition. On December 12, 1927, Tom put his signature, hand prints and Tony's hoofprints in cement at the entrance of Sid Grauman's famous Chinese Theater in the heart of Hollywood.[25]

The cement slab still exists in the courtyard of the theater, now called Mann's Chinese Theater, and is seen by hundreds of thousands of tourists annually.

Around this time period Tom appeared in a Fox Movietone News short which may be the first time Tom spoke on film. A historian only recently discovered the newsreel, which is dated January 27, 1928. In a story entitled "Dedication of Park Row," Tom is seen talking with an actor portraying Communist revolutionary Leon Trotsky in a production being directed by Raoul Walsh. Historian Dan Streible notes that the appearance of the idol of every American boy talking with what appears to be a notorious Communist is striking in its absurdity.[26]

Tom made only four pictures in 1928 for Fox. *Daredevil's Reward, Horseman of the Plains, Hello, Cheyenne* and *Painted Post*. Ironically, all four films made Fox a great deal of profit, but Tom had become too expensive. Fox Studios had discovered that there were plenty of cowboy actors who could ride and shoot well and didn't cost nearly as much per week as Tom's $17,500 weekly salary.

The Hollywood studio system was in its infancy. The big studios employed actors on a small salary and paid them whether they worked on film or not—though most were worked to death on a dizzying array of projects. The studio system even permeated the lower echelon of studios known as Poverty Row. It would be perfected in the late 1930s when Poverty Row studios Mascot, Consolidated Film Laboratories and Lone Star Pictures merged to form Republic Studios. Studio head Herbert J. Yates put all of his cowboy "stars" on the same $75 per week contract. When Gene Autry and Roy Rogers rose to the top of the pack of all of the singing cowboys and their pictures were grossing millions of dollars, both men were still paid a paltry $75 per week. Yates made it clear that there would be no Tom Mix-size salaries at his studio. At Yates' rates, he could afford to have 233 cowboy stars working per week for the price of one Tom Mix.

Fox Studios unceremoniously dumped Tom in March 1928. After a couple of days of black despair, Tom put out the word that he was returning to the sawdust trail while his agent shopped around for a new studio home.[27]

An eternal optimist, Tom began to think of his departure from Fox as an opportunity for getting out of Hollywood and seeing the fans.

Having been run in circles by the Fox studio hierarchy about stories and production values, Tom began looking for a studio that would let him make his movies without interference.

To his chagrin, the movie studios weren't showing much interest. Tom couldn't figure it out. How could he go from being the highest paid and most profitable movie star of the 1920s suddenly to a persona non grata in Hollywood?

The answer was sound.

Movies were no longer silent. When vaudeville star Al Jolson had turned to the audience in the 1927 Warner Brother's film, *The Jazz Singer*, and said aloud "You ain't heard nothin' yet!" the world was stunned and Hollywood was stunned as well.

Movies that could talk were first thought of as a fad. Studio executives thought audiences would hate them. Many of these studios owned their own chains of movie theaters and the thought of having to equip them with projectors that had sound systems was daunting.

They believed that the public would return to silent films with open arms after the hype had worn off. Tom thought as they did. Will Rogers, who was making $2,500 a week in the silent era while Tom was making $17,500 per week, initially hated the idea of sound films, calling them "the noisies." He changed his mind when Fox Studios offered him an unheard-of salary of $600,000 on June 1, 1929 to make four talking pictures. He would sign another contract in October 1930 for $1.12 million to make another six pictures. Will was a humorist known for his verbal wit, and sound films made him even more popular. By the time of his death in 1935, Will Rogers was the highest paid movie actor in Hollywood.[28]

The survival of silent film was not to be. Audiences loved hearing their heroes speak—at least the ones that could speak.

Silent movie stars, many of them Eastern European Jews who had come to Hollywood and carefully crafted exotic names and resumes, were suddenly out of work. Other silent movie actors were hicks from the sticks who had created exotic personas that their speaking voices would belie. The jig was up. Audiences caught on quickly. Silent movie icon John Gilbert, one of the most dashing and handsome of the screen's red-hot sex symbols, found his career in tatters after one of his first sound films was released. Gilbert's voice sounded shrill and high-pitched and audiences, used to accepting him as the macho lover, burst into peals of derisive laughter when Gilbert spoke.

Gilbert's speaking voice—or lack of it—was big news, the subject of coffee table conversation and newspaper speculation throughout the country. Gilbert was washed up overnight.

Tragically, Gilbert did not have a poor speaking voice. His voice—and his career—was merely the victim of the fledgling technology. Film speed need only be increased by a few frames per second to turn the speaking voice of an actor on that film into *Alvin and the Chipmunks*. Some film historians have posited that the studio boss, Louis B. Mayer, deliberately sabotaged Gilbert's career after the two men quarreled at Gilbert's wedding to screen goddess Greta Garbo. Garbo jilted Gilbert at the altar and Gilbert, drunk and furious about it afterward, told

Mayer that "all women are whores." Mayer took offense and the two men scrapped. When their scuffle was over Gilbert won the fight and lost the war. Mayer allegedly tampered with Gilbert's movie and ruined him by making sure Gilbert's speaking voice was altered.

Tom Mix was rapidly becoming a victim of the changeover to sound movies. He wore false teeth that clicked embarrassingly when he talked, something that was not a problem when film was silent. Tom hated speaking in front of crowds—and the camera—for that reason.[29]

Will Rogers joked with Tom that he needn't worry, because even though he didn't speak well, Tony "could at least snort." Rogers was already prospering in the new sound medium, and derided silent films because all he did "was run around barns and lose my pants."[30]

Now that technology had advanced to the point that he had to speak on film, Tom hoped that sound movies would fade quickly and silent films would return.

"Well, I'm not going to say much because the fans know me as one full of action and without much to say. Besides, I don't like to talk about this new innovation because I can say a number of things that wouldn't please my old pals back on the movie lots," Tom said.[31]

Tom wanted to make more silent movies, and he had to find a studio that had not converted to sound production—and fast.

15

Tom's pursuit of a silent movie studio dragged on and he began looking for ways to bring in big bucks—and fast. He had a movie star lifestyle—and a spendaholic wife—to support.

Tom decided that since the studios were balking at offering him a new contract he would go on the road with an abbreviated version of his wild west show. He traveled to Denver where he joined the Orpheum vaudeville circuit. For ten weeks Tom played to packed theaters all across the country.[1]

As popular with fans as ever, Tom made headlines in every city in which he toured.[2]

He chafed at the limitations on his act, mainly because he could only do a few rope and shooting tricks. The vaudeville circuit was not the same thing as a circus or wild west show. Tom was often limited by the sheer size of the stage and was frustrated by the lack of space to put Tony through his paces. Tony was often left to just stand on stage. Occasionally Tom rode into the audience, when the theater permitted.

Tom lost his temper—and deservedly so—toward the end of the vaudeville tour when a spectator walked up and, for no apparent reason, slapped Tony between the eyes. Tom later related the event to a friend:

"One night after the performance was over a man from the audience walked backstage. He walked up to Tony and said, 'Hello, old boy,' and gave him a quick, hard slap between the eyes. Tony, as you would expect, threw back his head and shied away from him, at which the man turned to me and said, 'That's a fool horse you have there. Can't a person get near him?'"

Tom said he leapt up and punched the man right in the nose, "giving him what he had given Tony." The man cried out in pain and covered his nose with his hands and Tom read the man the riot act about treating horses with respect and gentleness.[3]

Tom returned to Los Angeles, determined to find another studio at which to make silent movies.

To his surprise, a small and struggling studio partially owned by a Massachusetts rum-runner named Joseph B. Kennedy made Tom an offer to do silent movies at the studio. Kennedy was making a fortune running whiskey illegally during prohibition and had expanded his financial holdings to include movie studios. It was well known around Hollywood that Kennedy, a married Catholic, was having an affair with silent screen goddess Gloria Swanson.

Tom signed on with Film Booking Office, a.k.a. FBO, the studio that would later become RKO Radio Pictures. Kennedy would go on to become a diplomat and one son, Jack, would become president of the United States and another son, Ted, would have a notable career in the United States Senate.

Tom's first film for FBO was *Sons of the Golden West*. Production began on July 11, 1928.[4]

The film has some noticeable differences from Tom's films at Fox. For example, Tom appears in the period western in an untypical low-brimmed hat, as if to send a message to movie audiences that he was back but doing some things differently.[5]

When production was completed on July 31, Tom was in good spirits.

Tom next began production on *King Cowboy* on August 9, 1928. Shooting continued until August 25, 1928. The film was a further departure from any formula and reminiscent of *Tom Mix in Arabia* (1922). Tom and a band of cowboys go to Africa to search for their missing boss, where they encounter an evil emir.[6]

Tom began shooting his next FBO film, *Outlawed*, on September 7, 1928 and wrapped up shooting 22 days later.[7]

On October 1, 1928, *Sons of the Golden West* was released nationwide. Reviews were mixed. The September 29, 1928 *Motion Picture News* was enthusiastic. "If there is anyone in the western field who knows how to pay the part of the dashing cowboy hero, it's Tom Mix, seen here in a whooping, whirlwind western, which gallops along at a hot pace, has all the necessary embellishment and is a good picture of its kind...Yes, you can say that this western comes home with a bang."[8]

Harrison's Reports, in its October 6, 1928 issue, was more critical. "If Tom Mix (or FBO, whoever is responsible for this picture), cannot make better pictures than 'Sons of the Golden West,' he had better give up producing to save himself from killing his reputation...it is a tame affair at best."[9]

Tom kept up with the mixed reviews and moderate box office of *Sons of the Golden West* while he began work on his fourth FBO film, *The Drifter*, which began production on October 15, 1928. The film took 31 days to complete shooting, and wrapped up production ten days before the release of *King Cowboy*.[10]

While Tom was hard at work on his FBO films, Victoria packed her bags and took Thomasina on another extended European "vacation." Hollywood wags began to speculate that she would divorce Tom while she was overseas. Tom was upset that Victoria had taken his young daughter so far away, and he was further distressed when he did not hear from her or Thomasina for months on end. He wrote a steady stream of letters to them, but received no reply.

"I haven't heard a word from her in some time," Tom told a reporter. "I write every week to her and our daughter but strangely I do not hear from them." Tom added that he did not want a divorce, but that he was dismayed at Victoria's silence.[11]

Tom spent Thanksgiving 1928 alone and lonely, taking solace in the good reviews for *King Cowboy*.

King Cowboy opened during the Thanksgiving holiday weekend, on November 26, 1928. Critics were more enthusiastic. The December 26, 1928 *Variety* raved, calling *King Cowboy* "one of the best westerns seen recently and above the average Mix quality."[12]

Audiences flocked to see *King Cowboy*, but the film didn't make money on the scale of Tom's Fox Studios productions, mostly because FBO did not have the extensive distribution that Fox had.

Buoyed by the good reviews and brisk box office of *King Cowboy*, Tom nevertheless looked at returning to work at FBO with unease. The studio was poorly run and he felt as if he was working beneath his capacity. The sets were run down and the wardrobe and props were second rate.[13] The film used by the studio was cheap and the images captured by the cameramen were of poorer quality than his Fox films.

Production began *The Big Diamond Robbery* on December 10. Work continued through the holidays, except for Christmas and New Years, and the film was completed on January 10, 1929.[14]

By then, Tom had little enthusiasm for the production, which had a confusing script and lackluster production values.

Weary of the shoddy operation at FBO and worried that the studio might damage his reputation, Tom contemplated a return to performing live before audiences. He was surprised to receive a letter from Zack Miller inviting Tom to sign up as a featured act with the 101 Ranch and Wild West Show. Since the 1924 lawsuit, Tom and Zack had barely spoken and the two men eyed each other warily. Zack rather condescendingly asserted to Tom that his movie stardom days were over, and implied that Tom would be better off signing on as a performer with the Miller show. "You have reached the age, the same as all movie picture stars must at some time, where you cannot expect to make the money out of the game you have in the past," Zack wrote. It was typical of the impresario to address Tom with a tone of condescension. He had done so throughout the history of their relationship, something which always kept the two men from becoming close friends. Tom worked for the Millers, made money for and with them, but was never allowed to get personally close to any of the Miller brothers. It was always a boss to employee relationship. Even when Tom's motion picture salary exceeded the entire gross of the 101 show, Tom was never treated as an equal.

Miller continued: "…and this is your opportunity to go on for years to come and put you before the public in a manner worthy of your drawing power. There is no question in my mind but that this show can go out and make a half million dollars every year."[15]

Miller went so far as to offer Tom an ownership interest in the show, and even offered to let Tom buy him out.[16]

What Zack Miller did not tell Tom was that in April 1928 he had screwed up and turned down an offer from the American Circus Corporation, owner of the Sells-Floto and Ringling Brothers, Barnum and Bailey Circuses, to buy the 101 Ranch Wild West Show. Since that time the 101 Ranch show had begun losing money. Further, Zack's brother, George, had taken over the management of the far-flung 101 operation and he had heavily leveraged the Millers' assets to invest in highly speculative oil well projects.[17]

Had Tom remained at Fox, it is likely that he would have rebuffed Miller's letter. No longer making $17,500 per week, Tom was now drawing about $10,000 per week from FBO. This nearly 50 percent reduction in his income made Tom uneasy about meeting his enormous financial obligations. As it is, Tom sent noncommital a telegram to Zack that he would consider Zack's offer.[18]

Three days after shooting on *The Big Diamond Robbery* was finished, Tom got a call that Wyatt Earp had died of chronic cystitis and the flu. Earp, who had tamed the frontier towns of Dodge City and Abilene, Kansas and shot it out with the Clanton gang in the famous gunfight at the O.K. Corral in Tombstone, Arizona, was by then an octogenarian living quietly on the fringe of Los Angeles with his wife, Josephine. He had befriended many of Hollywood's elite western stars, including Tom, William S. Hart, and Harry Carey. Directors John Ford and Raoul Walsh had both become friends with Earp as well. Tom had gotten to know—and become close friends with—the aging frontier marshal. Tom used to take Earp to bet on the horse races as Santa Anita.[19]

The two men had become kindred spirits, often sitting up late into the night discussing literature and poetry and the Bible.[20]

Tom and Hart were pallbearers at Earp's funeral, and screenwriter Adela Rogers St. John, who was also present, said Tom was visibly upset and wept openly during the funeral. "I found it brave that he cried all the time he was carrying his old friend's casket," she recalled.[21]

Singing cowboy star Gene Autry recalled that Tom wore his emotions close to the surface. "Mix was a sentimental man, as cowboys often are. He was the kind of man who could weep at a picture on a bordello wall," Autry said without sarcasm.[22]

Outlawed was released the following week, on January 21, 1929, to poor reviews. *Variety*'s February 13, 1929 issue called the film "painfully slow" and took great pains to criticize Sally Blane, the heroine, calling her "a very blase' little creature."[23]

A month later, *The Drifter* was released on March 19, 1929 to mixed reviews. The March 20, 1929 issue of *Variety* called the film "particularly well done." The film contained some terrific airplane stunts, including Tom diving off the wing of an airplane in flight to grab a hold of the villain, who is wearing a parachute. The men struggle as they plummet to the ground.[24]

Despite the thrilling stunts and all of the elements audiences came to expect in a Tom Mix movie, critics began to pan Tom as old hat. Children went to the theaters in droves, but adult fans read the mixed reviews and stayed away.

Tom's final film, *The Big Diamond Robbery*, was released on May 13, 1929 to unexpectedly bad audience reaction and poor reviews. The action sequences were so over-staged that audiences laughed in unintended places. Tom's stunts were so extreme that they lacked credibility. When Tom jumped from roof to roof over entire streets, audiences didn't buy it and chuckled. When he roped a chimney three stories up, audiences guffawed in disbelief. The April 24, 1929 *Variety* derided the film as "very thin" and dismissed it as "cowboy burlesque."[25]

By the time *The Big Diamond Robbery* was released, Tom saw the handwriting on the wall at FBO. The struggling studio was not the right place for him. Weak story ideas, low budgets, skimpy production values, including cheaper film stock which resulted in grainier-looking final films, were all serving to send a message to the world that Tom Mix was losing his touch. Tom had been a stickler for top quality stories, sets, production values and film stock with highly stylized cinematography while he was at Fox. He insisted that the lighting designers use backlighting to give his films a radiance that enhanced his larger-than-life image. He demanded that his films look and feel as top quality as those of silent movie god Douglas Fairbanks, the star of *The Mark of Zorro* and *Arabian Nights*.

At FBO, Tom felt as if he was back in the Selig days, when production values gave way to expediency. Despite the fact that Tom, at 49, was in the best shape of his life, he looked older and more tired than ever. Part of the problem was the cheaper makeup used by FBO's makeup department, which caked on Tom's face and accentuated the lines and wrinkles caused by decades in the broiling southwestern sun.

Unbeknownst to Tom, one film director was trying to engineer his return to Fox Studios—and in a big way. Director Raoul Walsh was planning an epic sound film called *The Big Trail*. The film was to be shot in 70mm widescreen, an enormous format that was unheard of prior to this time. The movie, a saga of a wagon train crossing the hostile plains, featured as its hero a plainsman who is hired to guide the settlers through Indian country. Walsh wanted a quintessential westerner to play the role and he wanted Tom Mix.[26]

It is not known whether William Fox approved of Tom's possible return to the studio. Some accounts record that Walsh was told by the studio that Tom was working on another film or for another studio and was not available. Clearly Tom was gone from Fox by 1929, so historians who claim that Tom was working on another film for the studio at the time have it wrong. Tom was making films at FBO until January 1929 but he was indeed available after that.

In any event, Tom was not asked to play the lead in *The Big Trail* and Walsh, after trying to lure a young star named Gary Cooper from Goldwyn Studios, settled on Duke Morrison, rechristened John Wayne, as his star.

There is some evidence that this story might be a fabrication. One of those who told reporters that John Wayne was chosen over Tom Mix for the role was John Wayne himself, who told a reporter in 1930 when the film was released that he had been given the role because both Tom Mix and Gary Cooper were unavailable for it. During this interview Wayne also recounted his tale of being snubbed by Tom in 1926.[27]

The Big Trail bombed at the box office, mostly because the Great Depression was crippling the nation's economy and movie theater owners were still trying to convert to sound projection and there was no money to add the 70mm projection equipment as well.

Tom did not make another film in 1929 and Hollywood wags were already predicting his untimely demise. He was, however, not ready to be put out to pasture.

16

Tom left his short tenure at FBO and hit the vaudeville trail. His one man act, which featured Tom, Tony and some shooting and roping tricks, was highly profitable because Tom traveled lightly. His entourage was usually another cowboy to watch after Tony and a helper to assist Tom with the trunks that contained his props. For Tom, vaudeville was easy money. He had little overhead and was drawing hefty sums for his appearances.

Zack Miller was determined to lure Tom into touring with the 101 Ranch show, which had been losing money for the past four years under pressure from the American Circus Corporation, which operated the Hagenbeck-Wallace Circus, the Sells-Floto Circus and the gargantuan Ringling Brothers, Barnum and Bailey Circus. Zack had missed an opportunity to sell the 101 show at a profit to American Circus the year before and now he was unable to compete with them.[1]

To make things worse for Zack his older brother, George, had died when his neck was broken in an automobile accident on an icy Oklahoma country road on February 2, 1929.[2]

Ironically, Tom would die of a broken neck in a car crash 11 years later.

After George's death, Zack was unable to run the Miller empire by himself and he was getting desperate to raise large sums of money to pay off the $700,000 in debt with which George had saddled the 101 for his oil schemes.[3]

Zack wired Tom again, but Tom's only reply was that he was booked up until May 23.[4]

Growing frantic, Zack decided to go see Tom personally. He traveled to Philadelphia, where Tom was performing at the Earle Theater. He arrived the afternoon of April 6, 1929, where he met Tom at his hotel. The two men had a cordial dinner and discussed the terms of Zack's offer. Zack tagged along to the theater and watched Tom perform to an enthusiastic audience, no doubt envisioning such audience response for the 101 show if Tom signed on.[5]

When Zack left the next morning, he was confident that he and Tom had reached a handshake deal that Tom would tour with the 101. Zack returned to the train station in Philadelphia and wired the Associated Press office in Oklahoma and issued a press release announcing that Tom would tour the balance of the 1929 circus season as a featured act with the 101 show beginning on May 23.[6]

Zack traveled to Chicago the next day, where he received a telegram from Tom telling Zack to "hold everything" until Tom had time to discuss the deal further. Tom's telegram was sent from New York City, Tom's next stop on the tour, where Tom was negotiating with another circus. On April 15, Tom sent a wire to Zack, advising him that he would not be touring with the 101 Ranch show. On April 17, Tom signed with the 101's main competitor, the American Circus Corporation, agreeing to tour with the Sells-Floto Circus for the about half of the same salary he made during his reign at Fox Studios.[7]

Zack went ballistic. He immediately hired a team of lawyers to go after Tom in court. In June 1929, Zack filed a $50,000 breach of contract suit against Tom, filing the case in Natchez, Mississippi, an odd jurisdiction indeed considering the alleged contract was agreed to in Philadelphia. Not content to file his $50,000 lawsuit, Zack filed a $325,000 lawsuit against Tom in Erie, Pennsylvania, the town where Zack's lawyers had offices. Zack then dropped his ill-advised breach of contract suit in Natchez, Mississippi and re-filed it as a libel lawsuit, claiming that Tom libeled him during an interview in Natchez in which Tom said Zack's version of the contract dispute was "a nightmare of Zack's." The cases were set for trial, but would not come to court until 1931.[8]

Tom was deeply upset that Zack had sued him. He spoke openly about how he'd always appreciated Zack's sense of humor, noting that Zack was always ready with "laughs and pranks."[9]

But this was no joke, and Zack was trying to take money from Tom's pocket, money that Tom could not afford to pay. As Tom put it to his close friend, western writer Walt Coburn, Zack was trying to "stomp my guts out."[10]

17

For most Americans, the boom of the 1920s seemed as if it could never end. Money was plentiful, jobs were easy to find, the cost of living was down and wages were up.

Despite the unwise passage of Prohibition, which did little to stop the drinking of alcohol but did much for the establishment of smugglers and organized crime, life seemed an endless opportunity for making money and having fun. Much of the moneymaking was accomplished through investing in corporate stocks which were traded on the exchanges housed on Wall Street in New York City.

When the prices of stocks plummeted and the stock market crashed in October 1929, the wealth of many Americans evaporated.

Tom Mix was included in that group. He went from a movie star worth about $5 million to a former movie star worth about $150,000 in the span of a week.

He had spent the past nine years spending money like water, investing in enterprises solely on the advice of friends. He bankrolled business schemes concocted by friends that could never have profited. He bankrolled a wildcat oil exploration venture and lost $500,000 on that one transaction. He had invested millions in real estate and stocks, all of which were worthless when the market crashed.[1]

Tom did not just spend his fortunes on the trappings of wealth. Olive recalled that when Tom was rich, he donated "astronomical" sums of money to charities.[2]

Tom had always managed to bounce back from the setbacks which came from these risky investments. He replenished his wealth solely by working at a feverish pace. Like many movie stars, including John Wayne and Clint Eastwood some 40 years later, Tom Mix had to continue to work not only to support his own movie star lifestyle, but also to keep food on the table for all of his employees who counted on him making movies for their livelihood.

Tom had gone from the highest paid movie star at a major studio to the star of low budget movies at a studio with no prestige, to circus star. To make Tom's financial condition worse, his friends and employees were as badly hit by the depression as Tom. Not knowing what to do, he doled out "loans" to friends who were destitute, knowing that he'd never see the money again. Tom's loyalty to his friends would cost him tens of thousands of dollars, but, in Tom's mind, he was responsible for their well-being.[3]

Just the year before Tom was making between $17,500 per week at Fox Studios. Now he was 48 years old and had overnight lost nearly all of his worldly holdings.[4] Thankfully, his earnings with the circus were a healthy $10,000 per week.

Tom was a resilient man, but he sank into a black despair. Victoria had gone to Europe, taking Thomasina with her, and was on a wild spending spree. Ruth was living with Olive and Tom was paying support for Ruth. Tom was having to constantly bail out Olive, who had squandered her oil fortune and was repeatedly hounding Tom for money.

Ruth was now making appearances in movies in which producers were billing her as a "chip off the old block." The "old block" part galled Tom.[5] He didn't feel old.

Even though he was only two years away from his 50th birthday, he was in the best shape of his life. He could still ride and rope and shoot as well as—and usually better than—anyone in the movies. He was at the top of his game, and despite competition from Buck Jones, Ken Maynard, Tim McCoy and Hoot Gibson, he was still the most famous Hollywood cowboy. The others cowboy stars may have been working steadily and were younger than Tom, they still worked for a lot less money than Tom and their box office receipts were lower than even Tom's FBO films. But times had changed and the world was embracing the iconography of the modern 20th Century.

Charles Lindbergh had crossed the Atlantic Ocean in an airplane and had become—and deservedly so—a national hero. Pilots and airplanes were the rage, cowboys were seemingly going out of style. Suddenly Hollywood was making "aeroplane" movies. Stars strapped on pilots' helmets and climbed into cockpits in front of process screens and pretended to be daring bush pilots. What westerns that were being made often contained subplots involving airplanes. Tim McCoy was making westerns in which he was both a cowboy *and* a pilot. Tom couldn't believe that audiences were willing to reject his real-life stunts and derring do and embrace actors on a soundstage in front of a process screen pretending to be pilots. He wondered aloud if the era of the cowboy hero had passed. The thought chilled him.

Tom was always a fidgety person, unable to sit still. He'd pace, sit down and jump up and walk around while talking. He often had a piece of rope in his hands, which he would twirl and fiddle with to keep his hands busy.[6]

Olive noticed that Tom's fidgetiness had become unease. Tom had become "nervous" and that his inability to sit still had become anxious pacing.[7]

Tom had again been lucky. The Sells-Floto Circus, the same circus at which William F. "Buffalo Bill" Cody had finished his lengthy career, had hired Tom as a headliner six months prior to the beginning of the Great Depression. Tom had taken a look at his options and had realized that when he compared Zack Miller's offer to the Sells-Floto offer, appearing with Sell-Floto was a better deal. Not only that, Tom would be returning to the sawdust trail he loved so much.

Sells-Floto agreed to pay Tom roughly half of the salary he had been making at Fox—$10,000 per week. In addition, the circus offered to provide Tom with a private railroad car for the tour. Equally important to Tom, Sells-Floto agreed to hire much of Tom's company of cowboys.[8]

Tom had rejected Zack's offer and, on April 17, 1929, signed with Sells-Floto. He began touring with the show in May 1929. He ended up staying through 1931.

Olive said later that she thought that leaving movies for the circus was Tom's "big mistake."[9] She felt that Tom was secure in Hollywood and that circuses were a risky business, and felt a "premonition of disaster."[10]

Tom was delighted to be back on the sawdust trail and was thrilled with the response of the audiences from the very beginning of the tour. Whenever Tom rode into the circus tent to the blare of the music of the circus band, the cheers of the audience were deafening. Olive described these moments as "a rosy dream."[11]

At each performance Tom made a grand entry riding Tony around the entire circumference of the arena, dressed in his circus finery. Tony was decked out in Tom's best silver-studded saddle and bridle. Olive recalled that the cheering often lasted for an entire five minutes as Tom rode around the ring, flashing his dazzling smile as if he were a conquering gladiator. Tom would then spur Tony to a gallop and do the same trick riding act he'd done in his twenties. Tom would then draw his six guns and, in an act reminiscent of Buffalo Bill Cody's mounted shooting act, shoot targets while riding at a full gallop.[12]

Audiences didn't see Tom Mix, aged 50, riding into the sunset. To their great joy the Tom Mix who appeared before them had somehow defied time. Fathers who'd thrilled to Tom's silent films at Selig and Fox brought their sons and daughters, who had also watched Tom's later films from Fox and FBO and these two generations of fans would cheer heartily as their hero rode by, literally glowing in the bright, white light of the spotlights.

To the people who attended the Sells-Floto Circus, Tom Mix was still the greatest hero of their time.

Tom felt the same thrill he'd felt in the early days when he toured with the 101 Ranch. He insisted on each show being as good as, or better than, the show before it.

"We've got to be just a little better today than we were yesterday," Tom often told his fellow performers. "All of us—because we've got more to give today than we had yesterday."[13]

Tom returned the love of his audiences in kind. He spent hours after every performance signing autographs. He took time to visit every children's hospital, crippled children's wards, and orphanage at each stop on the tour. He donated money to charities in each town the circus played.[14]

Olive recalled that Tom lived in a private train car but that he ate and socialized with the rest of the circus crew and performers.[15]

After seven months of spending Tom's money lavishly and living it up in Europe Victoria returned to the United States in July 1929, two months after Tom left to go on tour. She and Thomasina joined up with Tom and spent a week on tour with him, but left to return to Hollywood, saying that touring with Tom "was too much of a strain on myself and my daughter to remain with him." Little did Tom know that upon her return Victoria would began planning to leave Tom and divorce him.[16] Tom had given up on Victoria.

There were unconfirmed rumors at the time that Tom was trying to court 32-year-old aviatrix Vera Dawn, that he had even proposed marriage to her and that Dawn had turned him down. He was often seen in the company of circus aerialist Mabel Ward.

Tom kept up a grueling tour schedule in the face of mounting legal problems and even serious physical injury.

Zack Miller's breach of contract suit against Tom was dragging on, and Tom was constantly worried about the rising legal costs and the potential damage to his financial and public status.

In October 1929, around the time of the stock market crash, Tom was galloping a horse across the arena in Dallas, Texas, when the horse stumbled and went down hard. Tom tumbled with the horse, landing on his shoulder with such force that it shattered. Tom was rushed to the hospital for surgery, where doctors wired his shoulder together. Tom returned to the show a couple of days later and continued to perform, but the pain became so great that he had to return to the hospital for additional surgery. The doctors rewired the shoulder again and Tom was back in the saddle within a week. Tom toured throughout the next 13 months despite great pain.[17] He turned increasingly to liquor to numb the pain so he could perform and sleep.

While Tom was enduring the tremendous pain of his injured shoulder as he toured the nation, he was dealing with mounting legal problems.

To Tom's great distress, shortly after he joined the Sells-Floto Circus, a federal grand jury in Los Angeles, California, issued an indictment charging him with income tax evasion. Tom was accused of overstating his deductions for 1925 through 1927, specifically that Tom allegedly claimed to have paid his brother-in-law, Eugene J. Forde, $12,000 to be Tom's business manager, when no such money was actually paid.[18]

Tom was performing with the circus in Minneapolis, Minnesota when the news hit the press. A visibly stunned Tom told reporters he knew nothing about the tax returns as he turned his finances over to his accountant. "I thought I was paying the right amount of tax," Tom said.

"This is all a mistake," Tom said during an interview. "I've never tried to beat the government out of any taxes, and if there has been any mistake it is up to the expert I employed to look after the matter."[19]

"I'm just an honest working man and I don't know anything about taxes...I would not think of defrauding any person or the government and if I do owe the government anything I want to pay it," Tom added.[20]

While Tom continued touring, his lawyers began negotiating a settlement of the charges. The accusation gnawed at Tom's insides. He knew that there was a possibility of jail time and he worried that his status as an army deserter might come to light, exposing him to even more jail time and potentially ruining his career. The thought of Tom Mix, the idol of every American boy, finishing life as Tom Mix, the tax-dodging Army deserter, sent him into a black despair.

To avoid Tom's arrest, Ivon Parker, Tom's lawyer, posted $10,000 in Liberty Bonds as bail on May 11, 1929.[21]

An investigation revealed that Marjorie Berger, Tom's accountant, had failed to properly fill out Tom's tax returns. On March 5, 1930, Tom appeared in federal court in Los Angeles and pleaded guilty to filing a falsified tax return. He was ordered to pay $175,000 in back taxes and penalties and the minimum fine of $3,000. Tom appeared in court in a brown custom-made suit and fancy cowboy boots. He stood solemnly, hat in hand, during the hearing, in which U.S. Attorney Samuel McNabb told the court that Tom should receive the minimum punishment. Tom paid the taxes, penalties and the fine and never trusted an accountant again. He was furious—and embarrassed—that his reputation as a cinema good guy had been tarnished by the improprieties of an accountant.[22]

Tom's legal problems continued. In June 1930, daughter Ruth decided to elope with her boyfriend, a small-time actor named Douglas Gilmore, who had appeared in *Hell's Angels,* a movie financed by billionaire Howard Hughes. Ruth was only 17 and Gilmore was 27, thus Tom was frantic to prevent the marriage. He learned the couple was headed to Yuma, Arizona for the elopement, so he sent a telegram to the Yuma County sheriff's office to head the lovestruck couple off at the pass, but officials arrived too late to stop the ceremony. Tom had been paying Ruth an allowance of $225 a month for 13 years and, to punish her for her rush to the altar, he cut off the funds. Ruth was incensed at her father and hired lawyers and filed a lawsuit against her father, seeking a reinstatement of the allowance. Ruth told the court that Tom had agreed to pay her the money and help her promote her budding cinema career until she was 21 years old. Ruth added that she'd purchased a $13,000 house and was counting on the allowance to make the payments. On July 5, 1930, the court ruled that Ruth had emancipated herself by marrying Gilmore and ordered that Tom did not have to pay the allowance.[23]

Tom and Ruth's relationship was strained for months and the estrangement made Tom irritable and depressed. He loved Ruth dearly. As often happens in father-daughter relationships, Ruth had, at times, mothered Tom as he entered middle age. It was as if Doug Gilmore had stolen his little girl right out from under his wing. Tom despised Gilmore, and brooded over the loss of his "Ruthie."

When the Sells-Floto season ended, Tom returned to Los Angeles on November 1, 1930. Victoria made it plain to Tom that he wasn't welcome at home, so Tom moved into the famed Hollywood Roosevelt Hotel. Exhausted and in great pain, he began looking for a doctor and on November 7 went to Dr. R. Nicholas Smith, who admitted Tom for surgery and operated on him removing the wiring from Tom's shoulder. After Tom regained consciousness, Smith informed Tom that he was developing arthritis in his back. Tom told Smith to keep the arthritis a secret.[24]

On November 20, 1930, Tom went to his Beverly Hills mansion to visit Thomasina, who was sick. Tom had not been allowed to see Thomasina for weeks, so he spent some time visiting with her by her bedside. As he prepared to leave, he and Victoria began arguing. Victoria would later claim that Tom had threatened her with a gun during the argument.[25]

On November 26, 1930, Victoria went to court and obtained a court order granting her a legal separation from Tom. Despite the fact that she had once shot Tom in the arm and back during an argument at their Beverly Hills home—a nearly fatal incident of domestic violence that was hushed up by Fox Studio brass—Victoria told the court that Tom had deserted her and subjected her to mental cruelty. Victoria told the court that Tom abused her by spinning a loaded revolver and threatening her. Tom could not believe Victoria's gall. Despite the Great Depression, Victoria had continued spending and living the high life in the Beverly Hills house with Thomasina and Victoria's father, Arthur Hanna-Forde; and with two servants, Virginia Mantino and Fred B. Borchardt, to attend to their every need—and all of it was paid for by Tom.[26]

Screenwriter Adela Rogers St. John, a devoted friend of Tom's, recalled that Tom and Victoria Mix were a mismatch. "Tom wanted always to be himself and Vicky wanted to be somebody else."[27]

St. John saw that Victoria had changed since the early days of her relationship with Tom. "Vicky had been a cowgirl and Mix's leading lady, now she kept her diamonds spilling out of a gilt casket when she didn't wear them to breakfast..."[28]

Colleen Moore, in her autobiography, concurred with St. John's assessment of Victoria Mix. "Victoria Forde [was] a beautiful, fragile girl who loved diamonds as much as [Tom] loved to shower her with them..."[29]

She recalled that Tom "loved his horse Tony more than he loved anyone, even, I'm afraid, his wife."[30]

Tom filed an answer with the divorce court denying the accusations and the case was set for trial.

Tom became enveloped in a deep depression, as evidenced by his comments to a reporter on December 13, 1930. "I was a very poor cowpuncher. I was in love with this girl. When I got my first movie job, I was bewildered. I didn't know what it was all about. We were married. That was 12 years ago. I became an extremely rich man. But I have never been anything but a plain man and a cowpuncher," Tom said sadly. "All I ever wanted was a suit of clothes, a bed and a horse. I don't claim to be intelligent. I don't claim to be a great actor. But I can bulldog a steer and ride a horse as well as any man alive."[31]

Tom spent the Thanksgiving and Christmas holidays of 1930 as he had spent them the year before—without his family and facing the trial of his divorce from Victoria and the lawsuit with Zack Miller right after the New Year.

The Natchez libel trial began in January 1931, and Tom was represented by American Circus' lawyer John M. Kelley.

Zack took the position that he and Tom had a verbal contract based upon their handshake that Tom would work for Miller's show for $10,000 per week. He said that initially he'd offered Tom $6,000 per week, then $7,000 per week and then the two men had agreed orally on $10,000 net. Zack said he was willing to pay Tom so much because the 101 show had paid bronc riding champion Jess Willard $6,000 per week and Tom had "more drawing power..."[32]

Zack said that he and Tom had entered into a verbal contract.[33]

Olive Mix, who had been on cordial terms with Tom until she squandered her oil fortune and Tom cut off Ruth's allowance, appeared in court and, now embittered toward Tom, stabbed him in the back. She testified on behalf of Zack Miller that Tom had told her that he had agreed to appear with the 101 show for $10,000 per week. Olive testified that Tom had told her of the deal backstage at the Earle Theater after Tom's show, telling her that he didn't insist on a written agreement. "Hell, no, I do not need a contract with Zack. We shook hands on it and I have started in with him," Olive quoted Tom as saying. She said that Tom told her that Zack had agreed to give Tom top billing.[34]

Olive's testimony was erratic and her words contained considerable vitriol. She testified that Tom paid her $4,000 or $5,000 alimony when they divorced. She said she used some of Ruth's child support to support herself. Olive sourly noted that Tom initially had to pay child support of $50 per month, but that it had been increased to $225 per month when Tom became wealthy.[35]

Olive testified that "Tom never paid a grocery bill in his life," an obvious falsehood, and said, further, that at one time she had been independently wealthy from her oil well.[36]

Olive also testified that Tom was not her first husband. She would later recall in her autobiography, published in 1957, that Tom was her first love and that she was a virginal girl when they first wed. In her testimony at the Natchez trial, she admitted to being married prior to Tom; that, when she was 18, she married a man whose last name was Brown.[37]

Tom took the position that there was no contract, only some negotiations. He testified that he had no contract with Zack Miller and that he did not have a conversation with Olive about the contract backstage at the Earle Theater.

Tom testified that he demanded that Zack Miller provide him with a written contract and a performance bond, that he told Zack that he was no longer an itinerant cowboy but a businessman who insisted on written contracts.[38]

He added that several days after his meeting with Zack he signed a written contract with the Sells-Floto Circus and that they had provided him with a performance bond.[39]

Tom disputed Olive's testimony in an attempt to show her bias against him. He said that Olive made "continuous demands" for money. His testimony mirrored Olive's when it came to her squandered oil fortune. Tom said, "One time I gave her a thousand and one time two thousand dollars...one other time she came and said the creditors were after her, and I said figure out what you owe...and she had amounting to $1,500.00, and I said, 'Here is a check for two thousand; now settle it and do not go into debt again.'"[40]

Tom estimated that he'd given Olive "between fifty and seventy thousand dollars" since their divorce.[41]

During Tom's testimony, Zack Miller's lawyers tried to make Tom out to be a drunk. They repeatedly insinuated that Tom was unable to hold his liquor, which Tom denied repeatedly. Tom broke up the courtroom during one cross examination. Zack's lawyer asked Tom if he'd ever been under the influence of alcohol. Tom quipped, "I don't think a man is under the influence of liquor until he has to hold onto the grass to keep from falling down."[42]

Years later, crooner Dean Martin would become famous for a similar saying, when he joked, "You're not drunk if you can lay on the floor without holding on."

Zack Miller's assertion that he had an oral contract with Tom flies in the face of logic. The two men had once been close, but their relationship had been rocky since Zack had falsely accused Tom of horse-stealing; and Zack had sued Tom in 1924 for breach of contract when Tom had agreed to appear with the 101 Ranch show during a break in filming for Fox Studios. To believe that he and Tom would trust each other enough to engage in a verbal contract was just not credible.

An examination of Olive's testimony is most revealing. She openly showed her bias against Tom, referring to him as a drunk and implying that he was a deadbeat dad, and candidly admitted that she squandered her oil fortune. She was likely lying under oath during her testimony about being in Philadelphia when Tom met with Zack Miller and she denied that Zack had paid her $1,000 for her testimony. Both Tom and Zack stated in and out of court that that Zack had left after Tom's show and Tom had departed for his next stop on the vaudeville tour. It would have been impossible for Olive to have discussed the "contract" with Tom backstage because both men left town immediately after the show.

The transcripts of the Natchez trial reveal that Circuit Judge R. W. Cutrer, the trial judge, admitted a considerable amount of irrelevant evidence. Amazingly, the jury returned a verdict in Tom's favor, finding him not guilty of libeling Zack Miller and denying Miller's demand for $50,000 in damages.

Only a week later, Tom was in Erie, Pennsylvania, where the entire trial was rehashed again. This time Tom faced a $325,000 loss if Miller won, and the trial was hard fought. Tom was represented again by Kelley, who had ringmaster

Johnny Agee testify, incredulous as it may seem, that Tom was a terrible circus performer and that he wasn't worth $10,000 a week but $300.[43]

The tactic backfired. The jurors knew that Tom Mix was a famous movie star and circus performer and they knew of his enormous salary both in films and on the sawdust trail. For Kelley to posit that Tom was not worth the exorbitant sum he was receiving—at the height of the Great Depression—was a boneheaded tactic. Not only did the jury have good cause to resent Tom's wealth, it now had good cause to disbelieve Tom's version of the events and issues in controversy. After all, if Tom had people lying for him that he wasn't worth the inflated salary he was receiving, what else would Tom lie about? Additionally, Olive again testified against Tom, making a strong impression on the jury.

At the close of the evidence, the jury ruled for Zack Miller, awarding him $90,000 for Tom's breach of contract. Shockingly, shortly after the trial it was learned that Zack Miller had rewarded each juror with complimentary dinners and tickets to the 101 show, a blatant violation of the law.[44]

Tom reacted to the verdict publicly by saying, "I think the jury just wanted to help out an old circus man in that verdict. They probably figured I had the money and Miller needed it."[45] With the tactic Tom's lawyer took at trial, there is no doubt of the accuracy of Tom's assertion.

Tom appealed the verdict and was granted a new trial.

As Tom's lawyers filed his appeal of the Zack Miller verdict, Tom took a quick vacation to Florida, where he swam with Olympic swimming champion Johnny Weismuller, who was about to begin his career as the movies' most popular Tarzan.[46]

During the ensuing months, the 101 show became mired deeper and deeper in debt, despite strong ticket sales. Zack Miller, unable to control costs and maintain profitability, had unrealistically counted on the money from his lawsuit against Tom to keep the show afloat. By appealing the verdict, Tom suspended having to make any payment to Zack until the ruling of the appeals court, thus depriving Zack of funds. By August 1931, the 101 Ranch was unable to meet its payroll and closed permanently. The 101 show was teetering toward insolvency as well.

Before risking the entire 101 Ranch fortune on dicey oil schemes, George Miller had been, in Tom's words, the "astute, careful and watchful businessman."[47]

Now that George was dead, Zack was in over his head and saddled with the debt left by his brother, and the creditors were closing in for the kill.

Tom began preparations for the 1931 season with Sells-Floto. He was anxious to begin touring again. Never able to sit still for long, Tom was growing restless. He was suddenly legally separated from Victoria—who was keeping Tom away from Thomasina—and he was estranged from Ruth, who was now trying to start her own life with her new husband.

Tom was spending time with Mabel Ward and he surrounded himself with his cowboy cronies from the Fox Studios days and from his years on the wild west show circuit. He was grateful to begin the new season and threw himself into the schedule with gusto.

The 1931 circus was a gigantic production. In Ring Two, "Gypsy Joe" Bowers performed with his mules, Stanley Ross performed his comedic riding act, Grover McCabe performed with his mules, acrobats Vittorio and Georgetto amazed the crowds with their feats and The Billy Rice Trio did comedic acrobatics. Also in Ring Two, Lillian Burslem's monkeys performed their dancing and prancing act, and Irene Ledgett and Lorette Tucker displayed their trained respective elephants. Five different acrobatic acts then took over Ring Two after the elephants, including Jessie Goodenough's Cloud Swing, Ernest White's balancing act, the Kelleys, Agnes Doss, Dearo the contortionist and two acrobatic troupes which performed on swinging ladders. After the introduction of the Sells-Floto clowns, Ring Two was then taken over by the equestrian acts, including The Hodginis and their bareback riding act, the Schwartz Trio of European riders, and The Hobsons.

Tom's girlfriend, aerialist Mabel Ward also performed.

Then, as the audience grew restless from the flurry of acts, the Fire Cracker Dummy, a new clown act, rushed onto the stage and, before the laughter settled, the announcer shouted in his booming voice, "Ladies and Gentlemen, presenting Tom Mix, the world's most popular star, and his contingent of cowboys and cowgirls direct from the Mix Ranch in Arizona!" Tom would then ride into the ring at a gallop and dazzle the crowd with his rope tricks and trick shooting.[48]

Life on the road was not without drama. While traveling on the circus' train through Portsmouth, New Hampshire on June 20, 1929, Tom's suitcase was stolen by a train porter named Cai Freydendahl, a Danish national. Tom had $75,000 in cash in the bag. When the Freydendahl was arrested by city marshal George H. Ducker and Patrolman Dennis Kelley, Freydendahl had spent $4,200 of Tom's money. The remaining $70,800 was recovered, to Tom's relief.[49]

The depression had turned the national—and global—economy to mush. People had little money to spend, especially on entertainment, but they came to see Tom perform, and Tom's finances were solidly in the black.

Now that the 101 show had closed permanently, Zack Miller wanted blood money from Tom because he felt that had Tom toured with the 101 show, the 101's fortunes would have been different. Tom felt he would be vindicated in the long run, but the legal fight was expensive and the strain of it was constantly in the back of his mind. He was making an enormous salary at the height of the Great Depression. He wasn't about to give a huge chunk of his earnings to Zack Miller. He knew that to win the legal case he'd have to continue spending a fortune in lawyer's fees fighting Zack's lawsuit.

Despite the legal problems and the strain of touring during the economic desperation of the depression, the Sells-Floto show was heaven for Tom. He loved the crowds, the adulation, the easy pace of life on the sawdust trail. He didn't have to keep coming up with newer and more dangerous stunts to please his fans. He only needed to show up, do his time-honored rope and shooting tricks, and ride around the ring to thunderous applause. In short, Tom only had to show up and be Tom Mix.

He was still popular enough that corporations sought him to endorse their products. In October 1931, Tom signed to endorse Barbasol shaving cream. The ads contained a disingenuous notation that "Barbasol testimonials are not paid for."

To his great joy, he began to hear from Ruth, who began writing to him. Doug Gilmore turned out to be a terrible husband, and less than a year after her elopement, Ruth began reestablishing her relationship with her father. Tom was so delighted that by mid-1931 he had arranged for her to join the Sells-Floto show and tour with him. Ruth was again billed—to Tom's chagrin—as the "chip off the old block."

Ruth was now 19, and was a terrific horsewoman and roper. She was just like her father—a crack shot with a gun, an expert with a lariat and she rode as if she were born to the saddle. Tom took great pride in Ruth, though he was a bit chagrined that Ruth was an adult and a sort-of-married woman who attracted the attention of male admirers.

Since Tom's divorce from Olive, he had made great efforts to maintain his relationship with Ruth. From 1931 to 1938, Ruth toured with her father and their relationship would grow stronger and deeper even as Tom's health—and his fortunes—declined.

18

Tom's popularity on the sawdust trail was not lost on Hollywood. Audiences packed out Tom's performances and wherever he went there were throngs of cheering people. By the end of the 1931 season, the Sells-Floto Circus had traveled 14,891 miles, performing 177 shows, mostly to packed houses. Unfortunately, the depression had so weakened the national economy that the Sells-Floto Circus' days were numbered.[1]

Tom began planning a triumphant return to the movies, and to his surprise a major studio wanted him.

A widespread story from the time was that Will Hays, the stiff moralist hired by Hollywood as an in-house censor, pleaded with Tom to return to film to bring decent, family entertainment to the screen. This is most likely hokum. What is certain is that Tom met with Carl Laemmle, Sr., the head of Universal Studios and the two inked a deal for Tom to star in a series of westerns for $30,000 per picture.[2]

While the salary was half of what Tom was earning in his heyday at Fox, he was still being paid more than double what MGM was paying movie icon Clark Gable.

Universal felt it had scored a coup. The studio would be the first to make sound films starring Tom Mix. In October 1931 Tom began pre-production for *Destry Rides Again*. He was fit and happy and excited about his return to the screen.[3]

He arrived on the set in high spirits and looking better than ever. Singing cowboy Gene Autry recalled that Tom was in terrific shape. "He was no longer young when I met him, but he drove cars that were custom built and he wore lavish western outfits. [He] was a handsome specimin (sic), even in his late 50s, and was quite vain about his hair. He had a head full of it, straight as a string, and he dyed it so black it was almost blue." Autry recalled asking Tom about his appearance and Tom was philosophical about it. "'W'al, you know Gene, the L'ard was good to me. He presa'rved my h'ar, I can damned sure keep it black for him.'"[4]

Tom began working with producer Stanley Bergerman on the plots for the various films. Bergerman remembered that Tom was enthusiastic about the projects. Tom was also pleased that Universal had allotted budgets for Tom's films that were five times higher than Columbia was budgeting for Buck Jones' films at the rival studio.

"Tom sat in on story conferences and had many suggestions, especially with regard to the action sequences. He was an expert, very knowledgeable in his field, and had many helpful ideas. He wanted to make good pictures," Bergerman said.[5]

Tom was particularly enthusiastic about working with Daniel Clark, the ace cameraman who shot all of Tom's best Fox pictures, and with director Ben Stoloff, who directed Tom in some of his more inventive Fox films. Stoloff directed Tom in *The Canyon of Light*, a World War I combat film, the big top adventure *The Circus Ace*, and two more traditional westerns, *Silver Valley*, and *A Horseman of the Plains* at Fox.

One afternoon in late November, Tom finished a meeting with Bergerman and was walking across the Universal backlot when he suddenly grabbed his right side and grimaced. He shrugged off the concerns of bystanders and went home. Several days later Tom was in the hospital fighting for his life. Tom's appendix had burst and the seepage had leaked into his abdomen. He was stricken with peritonitis, a fatal condition in 1931. The same condition had killed movie icon Rudolph Valentino. Tom knew that another blood infection—tetanus—had killed fellow cowboy star, and Tom's chief box office rival, Fred Thompson in 1928. Tom was rushed to Hollywood Hospital where Dr. R. Nichol Smith performed emergency surgery to remove Tom's appendix.[6]

Word of Tom's grave condition spread like a wildfire and the world began a death watch. Four thousand letters and 1,500 telegrams poured into the hospital from well-wishers as Tom lay at death's door.

Silent movie comedian Harold Lloyd was in San Francisco when news of Tom's illness reached him. He sent a telegram to Tom on November 24, 1931. "Dear Tom, Just read about your operation and will be pulling for you all the way to recovery which I hope will be hurried and complete. Stop. All the best of luck in your fight. Harold Lloyd."[7]

Heavyweight boxing champ Jack Dempsey was in El Paso, Texas when he heard of Tom's grave illness and at 10:35 a.m. on November 25, 1931 he sent a telegram to Tom at the hospital which read: "Dear Tom, am en route to Phoenix just learned of your being confined to the hospital. Brace up old pal. My every wish for your speedy recovery. Kindest wishes, Jack Dempsey."[8]

Babe Ruth, the baseball legend, sent his well wishes the same day. In Chicago when he learned of Tom's plight, the bambino sent a telegram to Tom at 9:58

a.m.: "Extremely sorry to hear of your illness. My sincere wishes for a speedy recovery. Babe Ruth."[9]

That same day, Wednesday, November 25, 1931, Tom was given a bacteriophage to combat the infection but his condition worsened. Doctors took blood cultures from Tom's infection and sent them to Stanford University, where researchers worked to create an experimental antibacterial serum. Tom was given the serum on Thursday, November 26, but doctors held out little hope.

"I do not want to appear gloomy about Mr. Mix's condition," Dr. Nichols told a press conference. "He is in a precarious state and only time can tell. We are doing everything possible for him, and he has shown great courage and the value of this cannot be underestimated. He has a great constitution and a tendency to win, so we can still look forward to the best."[10]

Messages of hope and concern continued to pour in from Tom's friends. Old flame Lucille Mulhall and her family sent a telegram from their ranch in Mulhall, Oklahoma on November 27, 1931 at 9:18 a.m. "Sorry to hear your illness fight. Hope have a speedy recovery. Lucille Mulhall, Charley Mulhall, Mildred Carmichael, Owen Acton."[11]

Old pal Will Rogers was out of the country, but his wife sent a wire to Tom on November 26, 1931. "Will is on his way to China. We will be glad to know you are better. We are all holding a good thought for you and know you will be well soon. Betty Rogers."[12]

Western star George O'Brien, who got his start in movies working as a crew member on Tom's Fox Studios unit, sent a telegram on November 28, 1931. "Keep up the old fight, Tom. Best of luck always. Leo sends regards, George O'Brien."[13]

Terrified that his friend might die, Leo Carillo, the suave Mexican actor who became famous as Pancho, the sidekick to the Cisco Kid, sent Tom a flurry of telegrams. On November 24, 1931, he sent a brief message: "Ride 'em cowboy. Don't weaken. We all love you and you can't lose." On November 27, he sent another. "They've got you hogtied old pal but they can't slap the brand on you. My prayers are for your quick recovery. Leo Carillo." On November 29, he sent another. "What did I tell you. Give you a loose rein and let you have your head. You are good for a long tide. You soon will be sun fishing. Scratch 'em cowboy. Love and quick recovery, Leo Carillo."[14]

Director John Ford and his wife, Mary, sent a telegram to Tom from their vacation in Honolulu, Hawaii. "Ride 'em cowboy. Get well. Recuperate with us in Hawaii. Much love, Jack and Mary [Ford]."[15]

By November 28, Tom's condition began to stabilize, giving friends and fans some hope that Tom might survive.

Ironically, Tom's family didn't rush to his side. Daughter Ruth sent a telegram on November 29, 1931 from New York City which read: "Daddy Darling—Glad or Happy can't say what I feel I was so worried I wanted to be near you. Seemed so helpless here. Soon as I heard I called house but could find out nothing. I've written you home. Write again tonite. Be very careful dearest. All my love, Ruth."[16]

Tom's aging mother sent a brief note to her son on November 28, 1931. "Thank God you are better. My best love, Mother."[17]

Amazingly, Tom began to pull through. His condition improved such that on December 2, 1931, he was able to drink liquids. Two days later Tom was photographed sitting up in bed, alert and smiling and pointing to a newspaper.

Leo Carillo was so overwhelmed to hear of his friends recovery that on December 4, 1931, he sent a lengthy, heartfelt telegram to Tom. "Dear Tom, I am happy over your comeback. I am up on the Tevis Ranch riding and roping, having a great time. You had me worried, kid, but you kicked loose the hobble. I suppose the nurse has to flank to dress the band. See you next week. Leo Carillo."[18]

Director Raoul Walsh sent his well wishes on December 11, 1931, saying, "wishing you even greater health and happiness."[19]

Tom was discharged from the hospital only to learn that his prize Stutz sportscar had been parked in the same place since he was admitted to the hospital, at the intersection of Vermont Avenue and Sunset Boulevard. The car had been there so long Tom had gotten a parking ticket for violating section 28, issued on December 12, 1931 by Officer Earl G. Reed, Badge 207, Hollywood Division.[20]

For the third year in a row, Tom spent the holidays in poor health and poor spirits.

Ironically, while Tom was death's door, Victoria's lawyers were working to take Tom to the cleaners in divorce court. On January 4, 1932, a mere month after Tom began his recovery from a near-fatal bout with peritonitis, Victoria obtained her divorce decree. The ink was barely dry on the divorce decree when, a week later, Victoria married an Argentinian attachè named Don Manuel A. DeOlzabal. DeOlzabal was assigned to the Argentinian embassy in Washington, D.C.[21]

She would harass Tom with post-divorce litigation for years—even after his death.

After New Years, Tom returned home to his Beverly Hills mansion to recuperate. The publicity department of Universal was insistent on photographing Tom's recovery to protect the studio's investment. On January 6, 1932, Tom's 52nd birthday, he was photographed sitting in a lounge chair on the back lawn of his Beverly Hills mansion with Tony Jr. The horse is decked out in Tom's finest silver-laden saddle and bridle. The photograph was seen around the country and Universal used it to show that Tom was on the mend. What the studio didn't divulge was that Tom was so weak he could not stand without the aid of two canes.[22]

On January 25, Tom was back in the saddle and before the cameras. The film was given a generous budget by B-western standards of the time—$108,300. The film went slightly over budget by nearly $1,200 when production wrapped.[23]

Filming progressed at a steady pace over 17 days and completed on February 12, 1932. Each day, Tom arrived on the set knowing his lines and ready to speak on camera. At first, he had difficulty speaking his lines naturally when the camera was rolling, mostly because he was nervous about speaking at all. Tom had worn dentures for years, having lost most of his teeth in the rough and tumble worlds of cowboying, law enforcement, wild west shows and then the movies. He was painfully aware of the clicking his dentures made when he talked, and was fearful that his fans would notice the odd sound. (Tom was also fearful that he'd lose his lucrative contract as a spokesperson for the toothpaste Pepsodent, which credited Tom's brilliant smile to the use of the product!)

"By then his false teeth troubled him constantly," Gene Autry recalled. "Every few sentences he would reach up and click those teeth back into place with his thumbs."[24] An examination of Tom's existing film work shows that in any scene in which he is eating, Tom always eats a piece of cake, with his hands, just like it's a sandwich. Clearly this was designed to eliminate any denture problems while on camera.

Because of this problem with his false teeth, Tom was terrified of dialogue. He did not feel that he could speak long lines without problems and his lines were shortened. His had grown subconscious about speaking and thus his speech pattern had become, as Autry termed it, "deliberate."[25]

Tom had joked for years that he didn't know how to act. During the silent era, he'd simply ask a director whether he should have his happy or sad face during a scene. Ironically, Tom's way with dialogue is no worse than any of the other big cowboy stars of the day. Even young John Wayne, barely into his mid-20s and already becoming a major cowboy star in low-budget matinee westerns at Mascot, Lone Star, Monogram and Columbia, delivered his dialogue in a halting manner—a speaking style that would become one of Wayne's trademarks. Indeed, Mix's speaking voice is eerily similar to John Wayne's voice in later life. Wayne was born Marion Robert Morrison (later changed to Marion Michael Morrison) in 1907 in Winterset, Iowa. Mix lived his formative years in Oklahoma. Thus each man's persona was deeply infused with Midwestern mannerisms and speech patterns.

What is most noticeable about Tom's speaking is his gravelly voice—a somewhat nasal, buzzing, growling voice that is short on nuance but powerful and direct. His inflection is decidedly Midwestern, and he refers to his horse Tony as "Taw-nee."

As one watches *Destry Rides Again*, it is simply astounding to realize that only a month before filming began that Tom had undergone surgery for appendicitis and been at death's door from peritonitis. Tom did his own stunts in the film, including a breathtaking opening sequence in which Tom charges down a steep slope aboard Tony Jr. and then jumps a high fence. He later engages in a rough and tumble fist fight with the villain that is visually striking and even later in the film jumps Tony, Jr. on and off a train's flat car.

As Tom awaited the release of his first sound film, tragedy struck at the 101 Ranch. Bill Pickett, the black cowboy who created the sport of bulldogging, died on April 2, 1932 when a horse kicked him in the head. Picket was 62 years old at the time and was still employed by the ranch to break horses.[26]

Will Rogers announced Pickett's death on radio that day. History does not record Tom's reaction to the news, but it is likely that the news hit him hard. He had spent considerable time with Picket between 1905 and 1909.

When *Destry Rides Again* was released on April 17, 1932, the press took notice. Since the ad campaign for the movie highlighted the fact that it was Tom's first sound film, reviewers all commented on Tom's speaking voice. The April 16, 1932 issue of *Harrison's Reports* said, "The fears of some persons had lest Mr. Mix' voice should not record well will be dissipated by this picture, for the reproduction of it is excellent," and added that while the production was "very good," it panned Ben Stoloff's direction and heroine Claudia Dell's acting.[27]

Three days after completing shooting of *Destry Rides Again*, Tom made his clandestine relationship with circus aerialist Mabel Ward official. On February 15 he and Mabel were married in a brief ceremony in Yuma, Arizona, officiated by Judge Earl A. Freeman. Some accounts report that the marriage took place at Lute's Gretna Green Wedding Chapel, while others say the ceremony took place in front of the Yuma County Courthouse. Tom's best man was western actor

Monte Blue. Blue's wife came along and Tom's daughter, Thomasina, age 9, also attended.

Tom told reporters at the time that the wedding was Thomasina's idea. She remembered if differently in a 1969 interview. She also remembered that her father got drunk during the honeymoon in Mexico and then got into a fight in a cantina.

"He got drunk one night and got in a bar room brawl and cracked his dentures," Thomasina recalled. "He spent the rest of the trip in his hotel, embarrassed to be seen without his teeth."[28]

Another version of Tom and Mabel's wedding is that they were married in Mexico and then went to Yuma to make it legal in the U.S. This account has not be substantiated.

Tom returned to work on March 4 to begin his second Universal film. The film was supposed to be a sequel to *Destry Rides Again*, but before shooting began the decision was made to change Tom's character's name to Tom Rigby and the title was changed from *Destry of Death Valley* to *The Rider of Death Valley*. The film was an ambitious project, to which Universal committed a hefty $104,670 budget. The director, Al Rogell, wanted to shoot the drama in the Mojave Desert and capture the brutal nature of the scorching desert. As a result, the film went $25,000 over budget and shooting lasted 7 days longer than the allotted 15 days.[29] The story was darker than the run of the mill matinee western. There are strong images of Tom and others suffering from heat and dehydration, and a dark plot element dealing with the evil nature of greed.

The Rider of Death Valley was released on May 26, 1932 to good box office and good reviews. The July 1932 issue of *Photoplay* raved that the film harkened back to Tom's "good old days" at Fox and asked, "Who can do that grand old hokum better than Tom and Tony? No one, we'll say!" The May, 28, 1932 issue of *Harrison's Reports* raved that *The Rider of Death Valley* was "a good western; it holds one's interest to the very end...exciting."[30]

The Rider of Death Valley is perhaps the best made of all of Tom's films. It is strikingly dramatic, with a mature plot line about greed and man's inhumanity to man. Tom turns in the best performance of his career. Fit and confident, he delivers his lines with ease and a natural grace that elude him on his other sound films. Tom is charismatic and every bit the hero. The film contains terse dialog, stark black and white photography of the blistering Mojave Desert, and some exhilarating shots of Tom on Tony, Jr. There is a breathtaking scene where Tom rescues Lois Wilson from a runaway buckboard. Tom gallops after Wilson, pulling her onto Tony, Jr. just before the wagon plummets off a high cliff. Shot up close, the camera catches both Tom and Lois Wilson actually doing the stunt, giving it greater impact. In another scene, Tom and his ranch hands ride at full tilt across the shifting sands. Tony, Jr. stumbles and falls and Tom takes the fall with him then jumps back on to continue riding. In the finale, Tom gallops Tony, Jr., up to rescue Lois Wilson in the nick of time from being blown to bits by dynamite. As they ride away, there is an enormous explosion, showering them with sand. It is quite a good stunt.

Fred Kohler turns in a spectacular performance as a thug driven mad by thirst in the desert, and Willard Robertson is very good as the miner who is murdered for his gold.

On April 19, 1932, Tom immediately jumped from the wrap of *The Rider of Death Valley* into production of *The Texas Bad Man*, a solid western about Tom infiltrating a gang of robbers lead by a bandit (Willard Robertson, again) with a Napoleonic complex. Universal tried to increase its profits on Tom's films by allocating a lower budget of only $98,880 for the production—a full $10,000 less than the budget on *Destry Rides Again*, Tom's first Universal picture. The lower budget was unrealistic, but thanks to Tom being prepared and doing his own stunts, when production was completed on May 5, 1932, the film had run only slightly over budget, coming in at $99,257.05.[31]

Despite the lower budget, the film is an exciting, credible western and Tom is quite good in it. *The Texas Bad Man* tries to blend a thrilling western action story with some of Tom's trademark humor, which is provided via an odd segment in which Tom disguises himself as a Mexican. Having Tom dress up as a Mexican adds nothing to the story, and Tom equates himself well in the comic segment, but his Mexican accent is simply terrible. Tom does some exciting stunts, most notably jumping Tony, Jr. over some boards being carried across a street by two carpenters.

Overall the film is better than the average B-western. The advances in film technology created a deeper, more detailed film image, which heightened shadows and textures. Tom looks terrific. Tom is captured on this improved film, aged 52, a man in his prime. There are some dramatic shots, such as Tom riding across the desert in silhouette.

The Texas Bad Man was released on June 30, 1932 to good reviews. The October 1, 1932 *Harrison's Reports* called the film "fast-moving" and "exciting."[32]

What is ironic about the film is the back-story. Tom hated working with the director, Edward Laemmle, nephew of studio boss Carl Laemmle. Tom felt like he was being given a weak director out of nepotism. Ed Laemmle had a lengthy resume' in silent movies but little experience in sound production. Indeed, the studio had to order two extra days of shooting for May 12 and 13 to repair some dialogue sequences, which were directed by dialogue supervisor Gene Lewis.

Faced with Edward Laemmle's ineptness as a sound film director, Tom hit the roof. He demanded that the studio give him good directors who understood how to make solid, action westerns. Unfortunately, he was bucking the wrong tiger. Carl Laemmle owned the studio and Edward Laemmle was his nephew. Worst yet, Tom's producer, Stanley Bergerman, was Carl Laemmle's son-in-law. Tom was basically working at the Laemmle family business and his complaints had no chain of command to take advantage of. In late May, Tom went public with the dispute when he told *Daily Variety*, the Hollywood trade paper, that he didn't want to work with any "Laemmle relatives" who, Tom said, were inexperienced.[33]

The issue was resolved when the studio capitulated and agreed that Tom would not have to work with any directors with the last name of Laemmle. Bergerman convinced Tom to sign a contract extension and production began on one of Tom's best Universal films, *My Pal the King*.[34]

With a budget of $95,521 and 12 production days scheduled, *My Pal the King* began production on May 17, 1932 and completed production 14 days later on June 2, 1932, coming in over budget at $107,126.01.[35]

My Pal the King is one of the finest examples of image-building movie-making. The story is about a child king (a youthful Mickey Rooney) who is beset by palace intrigue. Tom arrives in the mythical kingdom of Alvonia to put on his wild west show and encounters the young king during a parade which the tiny monarch is viewing incognito. Tom picks the child up off of the ground and hoists him into the saddle to ride along with him on Tony, Jr. The boy introduces himself as "King Charles of Alvonia." Tom jokes that he knows a King by the name of Charles back in Texas. The joke ties the real-life Tom and the real-life Charles King of the King Ranch in Texas to the mythical story. It is a nice touch, blending the fictional Tom and the factual Tom.

The young king invites Tom to his castle and Tom reciprocates by inviting the young monarch to his wild west show, which is actually the Tom Mix Circus captured on film. Tom even violates the unwritten law of film and "breaks the fourth wall," looking into the camera to address the audience in the movie theater. As a result, the audience becomes a part of the audience of the wild west show. The device works, involving the viewer in the story of the film and in the wild west show.

This film captures for all time rare footage of Tom's circus. Were it not for this, there would be no motion picture documentation of this part of circus history.

We see Tom doing some trick riding and trick roping, as well as some excellent trick shooting.

The climax of the film is a rescue by Tom and his circus cowboys, who storm a castle to rescue the young king from the murderous Count De Mar. The sequence contains a remarkable stunt in which Tom rides up to the castle on Tony, Jr., ropes a parapet, dallies his lariat on the saddle horn and shimmies up the rope and over the castle wall. Few young stuntmen, much less a 52-year-old cowboy star, could do this stunt easily.

When *My Pal the King* was released on August 4, 1932, the film was a smash success. The July 9, 1932 Motion Picture Herald called the film "another sweet box office surprise..." and added that it was "good, clean wholesome entertainment without a vestige of anything that could stir objections from anyone."[36]

Tom was pleased with the film and pleased that he could show off his wild west show in it. One of the first celebrities to intuitively understand the concept of branding and cross-marketing, Tom used his films to promote his circus and retail products while using his circus and retail products to promote his films. In short, Tom was the first celebrity to cross-market himself.

Other studios used the concept of *My Pal the King* to promote their cowboy stars. Republic Studios promoted Gene Autry and Roy Rogers with films which cemented their personas such as *King of the Cowboys* and *Public Cowboy #1*. Autry and Rogers would carry the cross-marketing even further. Both would use the entirety of their names, in essence playing themselves, in their films. Tom would usually change his last name on film to Tom Miller, or Tom Rigby, etc. Even John Wayne used this marketing effort, playing literally dozens of characters on film named either John or "Duke," which was Wayne's nickname.

Tom's next film was *The Fourth Horseman*, an interesting film about a gang of thieves who take over a ghost town belonging to a young woman and turn it into a tawdry boom town. Universal trimmed the budget to $92,000 to make up for the overage on Tom's prior productions. The film began production on June 20, 1932 and was shot quickly. Instead of the usual 15 days, the film was shot in 10 days. That haste worked against the production. Nine days of extensive retakes had to be shot on August 4-9, August 20, August 27, September 3 and September 10, 1932.[37]

The result was a mishmash of footage and entire sequences were left out during editing. As a result, in the horse stampede scene, Tom is wearing a different shirt in one shot than he is in another. Despite that, the film is a taut, exciting film and Tom does some exciting stunts, including jumping Tony Jr. over a high fence.

The final budget for *The Fourth Horseman*, after the retakes, was $107,078.21 amounting to a nearly $16,000 increase.[38]

The Fourth Horseman was released on September 29, 1932 and again the reviews were favorable. "TOM MIX GOES OVER BIG…IN FAST MOVING DRAMA THAT HAS THE STUFF," the headline raved in all caps in the February 9, 1933 Film Daily.[39]

In *Riders of Death Valley*, *The Texas Bad Man* and *The Fourth Horseman*, Tom crosses six-guns with Fred Kohler, a terrific character actor with a deformed hand. Kohler was missing several fingers and the thumb on his right hand, and often used his deformity to enhance his characters by proclaiming that his fingers had been shot off in a gunfight. Kohler specialized in the type of villain called the "thug heavy." B-westerns usually had a mastermind villain who was dressed in nice clothes. These were called "dress heavies." The thug heavy did the dirty work for the dress heavy, who masterminded the criminal enterprises.

On film, Kohler was a good match for Tom. They were both gravelly-voiced, rough and tumble men, and their encounters on screen created sparks.

With the success of cops and robbers movies such as *The Big House* (1930) starring Wallace Beery and *The Public Enemy* (1931) with Jimmy Cagney, and the buzz over the upcoming prison drama *The Last Mile* (1932) starring Preston Foster, Universal decided Tom's next film should cash in on the sudden popularity of prison melodramas by making a similar film.

Tom began production on *Hidden Gold* on August 15, 1932. Universal again trimmed the budget to $87,000—a ridiculously low figure even for a B-western, considering that Tom was being paid $30,000 of that budget. The production bogged down when director Arthur Rosson fell ill and had to be replaced by director Ray Taylor. Filming ran four days over the projected 16 day schedule and the film came in over budget at $89,660.39.[40]

Hidden Gold is an odd film, a sort of pseudo-western with Tom sent to prison undercover to get some convicted bank robbers to reveal where they've hidden the loot from a bank holdup. It plays more as a depression era cops and robbers movie more so than a western, but Tom turns in a solid performance, showing off the boxing skills he honed while sparring with such heavyweights as boxing champ Jack Dempsey back in the 1920s.

While production was underway on *Hidden Gold*, Tom learned that Victoria—who had moved with her new husband to San Francisco, taking 10-year-old

Thomasina with her—was planning on putting Thomasina in a Catholic boarding school. A Pennsylvania Dutch protestant, Tom was furious. He told friends that he was aching to spend time with his daughter and it appeared to him that Victoria was trying to cast Thomasina aside so she could enjoy her new life as a diplomat's wife. Tom called his lawyers.

On August 18, 1932, Tom filed a petition in court seeking full custody of Thomasina. The case was set for a hearing on September 7, 1932. Before the case was tried, Tom and Victoria entered into a settlement wherein Thomasina would not be sent to any boarding school. She would also get to spend her summers with her father.[41]

When *Hidden Gold* was released on November 3, 1932, reviews were favorable, but not as strong as the prior Universal films. The Film Daily reported on March 22, 1933 that *Hidden Gold* was a "different western…with plenty of action, fights and thrill stuff."[42]

Tom's final three Universal pictures were *Terror Trail*, *Flaming Guns* and *Rustler's Roundup*. Production records are lost for these films.

During the filming of *Terror Trail*, on October 22, 1932, Tom was badly injured when Tony, Jr. fell and rolled over onto him. Tom was galloping the horse down a five-foot embankment when the horse stumbled, fell sideways, and rolled down the hill on top of Tom. Tom was knocked unconscious. For several agonizing minutes, the crew watched and waited for Tom to awake. When he regained consciousness, there was a collective sigh of relief. Tom was dazed and injured. His right leg was badly bruised and his right side hurt so badly that it appeared his ribs were broken. A quick trip to the hospital revealed no broken bones, but Tom was in pain for weeks thereafter.[43]

Tom not only suffered physical pain in 1933, he suffered the emotional strain of the ongoing breach of contract lawsuit with Zack Miller, which was set for a new trial after the appeal courts had overturned the first verdict. The second trial began on January 16, 1933 in Erie, Pennsylvania. It was basically a rehash of the Natchez trial and the first trial in Erie. As they had in the prior two trials, Zack's lawyers attacked Tom's credibility by attacking his talents. They educed ridiculously irrelevant testimony from Tom, asking Tom to admit that he was not the best horseman in Hollywood. They insisted that Tom admit that he, now aged 53, did not still do all of his own stunts. Olive, once again, testified that Tom had told her he had a verbal contract with Zack.[44]

By this time, Ruth had patched up her relationship with Tom and when the retrial in Erie took place, Ruth came to court to defend her father, calling Olive "a liar who has been paid to commit perjury."[45]

Olive's testimony was damaging to Tom at the second Erie trial. Oddly, she would recant her testimony in November 1933 during a deposition in California.[46]

Two weeks after the trial began, the jury, overwhelmed by the highly prejudicial and irrelevant information, handed down a verdict of $90,000 for Zack Miller. The judge reduced the judgment to $66,000 against Tom for breach of contract. Tom refused to give in and pay the judgment and filed another appeal. He decided to drag the case out until hell froze over rather than pay Zack a dime.[47]

Zack, more than $700,000 in debt, crowed to friends that his verdict against Tom was a harbinger of good things to come. "With the winning of the Mix case I seem to have had a break and think things are going to come my way a little better now."[48]

Tom was sick of being sued by people he did business with. He had even been sued in August 1932 by his attorney, Maurice Judd, for $10,000. Judd claimed Tom owed the money to him for tax preparations.[49]

Despite his personal and legal problems, Tom was still riding high on screen.

Terror Trail was released on February 2, 1933 to strong box office but mild reviews. The February 18, 1933 *New York Motion Picture Herald* said the film was "...a western film cut to a pattern by no means new."[50]

Such a blase' review is hardly warranted. In *Terror Trail*, Tom plays a former U.S. marshal brought in to track down a gang of bandits known as "the paint horse gang" because they ride pinto horses during their holdups. The film is a solid matinee western, with some touches of Tom's humor. In one scene, Tom is given a hotel room directly above a saloon, only to have character actor Raymond Hatton rouse him from his sleep by firing drunkenly into the ceiling of the saloon—and into Tom's room. Tom rushes downstairs and disarms Hatton, only to discover that in his haste he's forgotten to put on his pants. The scene is funny and well crafted, and is marred only slightly by Tom reverting to a little silent movie-style mugging.

Flaming Guns fared better with reviewers when it was released in June 1933. The June 17, 1933 *Film Daily* said the film was a "very good western with plenty of comedy...Good fun for everyone."[51]

Tom's final Universal film was *Rustler's Roundup*, which was released in September 1933 to solid reviews and good box office. The September 16, 1933 *Film Daily* said the movie was "formula without any signs originality, but it has been handled with a snap and punch."[52]

After finishing production on *Rustler's Roundup*, Tom declined to renew his Universal contract, telling reporters he wanted to stay in the circus to be "closer to the people."

It is unknown why Tom really wanted to leave movies. Perhaps he wanted to get out from under the constraints of working in the movies and get back on the sawdust trail, where he could be close to fans and where he needn't perform daring stunts. He only needed to show up, gallop around the arena and then perform his rope tricks and shooting tricks. Tom's circus performance did not involve tremendous physical strain or risk, unless a horse tripped and fell on him. Tom was getting older and the aches and pains from his injuries were plaguing him. The arthritis in his back was worsening and having to do strenuous stunts on film was ruining his health. Additionally, it was a matter of economics. Tom could earn $10,000 per week for performing about 30 minutes each day, and that sure beat the hell out of working from sunup to sundown on a movie for $15,000 per week.

Perhaps he and his aerialist wife, Mabel, felt more at home and connected to each other on the road.

On film, Tom was still in his prime. Despite his age, he made a good showing at the box office, but it is likely he knew that Universal would cultivate younger heroes, all of whom would copy his circus attire and derring do, with the help of stuntmen.

Cowboy star Gene Autry recalled that when Tom ended his contract with Universal there was a feeling in Hollywood that "Tom couldn't make it in the talkies."[53]

Tom decided to go back to the circus and tour extensively.

In 1933, Tom signed perhaps the most unique deal in the history of modern entertainment. He agreed to be paid by Ralston Purina to endorse the company's cereals and to "appear" in a radio program about his exploits. No doubt stung by the lawsuit which came from Zack's claim that he and Tom had a verbal contract, Tom insisted on a written contract. Ralston executives who negotiated the offer with Tom jotted the contract down on the back on an envelope.[54]

What is unique about the deal is that Tom would never once step in front of a microphone. Various actors, including Artelis Dickson, Russell Thorson, Jack Holden and Joe "Curley" Bradley were hired to "be Tom" on the radio. The five-year deal would net Tom $5,000 per year for five years and would be so successful that Tom renewed the deal in 1938. His estate would renew the contract in 1943 and again in 1948 and would benefit from the contract for a decade after Tom's death. The show would outlive Tom, lasting from September 1933 until

June 1950. Tom's name still lives in the national consciousness in large part to the success of the radio show.⁵⁵

Additionally, Tom licensed his image for books and comic books and numerous other toys, a concept that was very new in 1933 and continues today.

19

After he finished his commitment to Universal, Tom formed a circus act called the Tom Mix Roundup and signed on with the Sam B. Dill Circus out of Dallas, Texas on January 1, 1934. The troupe consisted of Tom's wild west cowboys and rodeo clowns. Part of Tom's compensation for appearing with the circus was the gift of what would now be called a tour bus or RV. General Motors had specially built the bus-like home on wheels, outfitting it in much the same way modern motor homes are constructed. The private coach cost $3,400—a princely sum in the depths of the depression.[1]

The Tom Mix Roundup gave its first performance on April 20, 1934 in Hot Springs, Arkansas and was a smash hit. Tom's show consisted of Tom and Tony, Jr. doing Tom's time-honored trick riding, trick roping and trick shooting as well as trick riding by Boots Sallee, Frank and Ruth Gusky, Herman Nolan, Ralph Clark and Augie Gomez. The circus consisted of Helen Ford's monkey's riding dogs; the Flying Arbaughs and the Flying Jordans, acrobats; the Bell Brothers and Wanda, acrobats; the Hobson Family horse-riding act; clowns; Herbert Beeson on the high wire; and trained seals.[2]

Tom had negotiated a piece of the action and he appreciated Sam Dill's circus management expertise, which maximized the quality of the show and the attendance figures. The show had capacity crowds in Tennessee, Kentucky and Ohio. Sam Dill could see that the main draw was Tom Mix and Tony and he ordered all of the show's publicity to feature Tom and Tony (actually Tony, Jr.) more prominently than the name of the circus. The success of the season astounded everyone, even Sam Dill, who used the profits to upgrade the show. He bought 24 new Ford trucks with powerful V-8 engines to transport the show.[3]

As was common for circuses and wild west shows, luck played a large part in the attendance of paying customers. One sold out show in Indiana was forced to close by the political maneuvering of a fundamentalist preacher who raised hell that the show was slated for a Sunday afternoon. When the show went on to Illinois it encountered even worse luck. What started as a rainy day turned into a terrible thunderstorm which spawned a tornado that zeroed in on the tent that contained the menagerie acts. The menagerie tent blew down on top of magician W.E. DeBarrie; Ada Moore's snake act; mentalist Norma Estelle; Mrs. DeBarrie's birds; the Perkins Company Dancers; Hillbilly Harold Riley; Marie Martino and Dorothy Voss, fan dancers; the Regan and Company Minstrels; and lecturer Rex Omar.[4]

As soon as the tornado was over, Tom rushed in with the crew to rescue the performers and to their relief found that there were no injuries. In the tradition of "the show must go on," the show opened the next day on schedule.[5]

Bad luck struck the show again on August 11, 1934 when one of the circus trucks plunged off a mountain road en route from Bristol, Tennessee to its next engagement in Kingsport, Tennessee. Two crewmen were killed and four others were badly injured. The show buried its dead in Kingsport and prepared to put on the show.[6]

To make matters worse, in May 1934, the Pennsylvania Supreme Court upheld Zack Miller's verdict of $66,000. Zack had become obsessed with collecting the judgment against Tom. He hired investigators to seek out and find all of Tom's assets. Tom was reputedly worth millions, and Zack needed the money. The 101 Ranch, a vast enterprise that had once equaled the famous King Ranch in Texas, was about to go on the auction block for repayment of debts. Zack was trying to raise $700,000 to appease creditors and he felt that Tom's $66,000 would help. "I never needed the money so badly in my life," Zack said at the time.[7]

The investigators reported back to Zack that Tom was virtually broke, that his enormous assets were encumbered by enormous debts. In short, Tom was living on financial borrowed time, and only stayed afloat because he worked constantly and kept his cash flow moving.

Zack didn't believe it. He began stalking Tom's circus, following it from town to town and filing collection lawsuits at each stop seeking payment. He became obsessed with trying to estimate Tom's gross receipts for each performance and then filing local lawsuits after each performance trying to attach Tom's box office receipts. The tactic caused Tom considerable aggravation, and his health—and his demeanor—began to sour, but he soldiered on. Zack and his lawyer, E.G. Moseley, seemed to enjoy dogging Tom's trail. Moseley wrote Zack on April 12, 1934 that "we made it very embarrassing for Mr. Mix in [Dallas] when we filed suit, since all the newspapers readily ate up the story and printed all the matters…and this irked him considerably."[8]

On the advice of his lawyers, Tom began threatening to file bankruptcy, which would have wiped out his unsecured debt to Zack and his other creditors. Tom could not actually do so, as to do so would have forced the sale of his assets to pay his secured debts—debts secured by collateral—but Zack was held at bay by Tom's threat.

Calgary Stampede promoter Guy Weadick, who disliked Tom ever since their controversy 22 years earlier, was pessimistic about Zack getting any of Tom's money. "I expect by the time you boys had got through the lawyers will have most of Mixes (sic) bankroll." Weadick incorrectly predicted that Tom was "through both as to outside show business as well as in the flickers."[9]

Indeed, three weeks later Weadick sent another letter to Zack in which he further maligned Tom, saying that Zack's lawsuits had "killed [Tom] for ever being popular like he was. He may have been able to draw money once, but I know in vaudeville he packed the house the first time around, but he was never able to repeat from what I have been told by many in the vaudeville business that hired him."[10]

With the deadline to repay his creditors approaching, a desperate Zack wrote Tom on June 27, 1934 and offered to take a settlement of $15,000 in cash, plus payments of $1,000 per month for 25 months with interest at six percent.[11]

Tom agreed to meet Zack when the show arrived in Amarillo in September for its final big stand of the season.

Unbeknownst to Tom, Zack was planning to ambush Tom even while he offered an olive branch. On July 23, 1934, Zack tried to hire the prestigious Los Angeles law firm of O'Melveny, Tuller and Myers to try and seize Tom's assets. The firm turned Zack down in a letter on July 30, 1934 because Zack did not have the financial resources to hire the firm.[12]

In September 1934, the two men met face to face at the Herring Hotel in Amarillo, Texas. The atmosphere was tense, a mixture of animosity over the $66,000 in dispute and the drama of a once amicable relationship between the two plainsmen now shattered by a dispute over money and honor. Despite a lengthy earnest attempt to resolve their differences, the meeting was a failure and Tom left without reaching an agreement with Zack.[13]

The show wound up the season in Amarillo, where it played for nine weeks at the Amarillo Fair and made an enormous profit.

In late October, Tom and Sam Dill had a disagreement about wintering the show. Sam wanted to keep the show in Texas and winter where the season had ended. Tom wanted to continue west and winter the show in California. The season was all but over and Sam didn't think crowds would come in great numbers to see the circus. Tom was insistent. He wanted to make a movie during the off—season.[14]

Why Tom didn't take his motor home and go to California without the entire circus is unknown. Tom's business acumen was often overridden by his stubbornness. It may also be that Tom was trying to whittle down the profit margin to avoid having to pay money to Zack Miller.

The trip to California would prove costly. The show headed west in November, hoping to play to big crowds in New Mexico, Arizona and perhaps Southern California. The crowds did not come and the show bled red ink all the way across the Great Southwest. Arizona officials shook down the show when it entered the state, insisting that all of the vehicles buy license plates from the state.[15]

When the show finally reached its winter grounds at the Oil Exposition Company in Compton, California, it had finished a 33-week tour across 16 states, traveling 12,895 miles. Tom was tired, but exhilarated by the adulation of the crowd. He was still Tom Mix, the famous cowboy movie star. And after 222 performances with the show his share of the profits totaled $65,000. This amount was in addition to his salary of $330,000—a hefty income for 1934.[16]

Even more good news reached Tom when, on December 21, 1934, Tom's lawyers reached a settlement with Zack Miller's lawyers on the breach of contract suit. Tom only had to pay Zack $22,000, instead of the $66,000 awarded in the judgment. Tom felt as if the clouds had lifted and he was hitting his stride once again. He was also happy that Zack was unhappy with the settlement because it had come too little too late and the 101 Ranch had been sold at auction to pay debts. The late George Miller's foolish oil speculation had ruined one of the greatest ranches in the history of the west. Without his brother, George, Zack had been unable to run the day-to-day ranch operation, much less the far-flung other investments held by the Miller family business. Additionally, Zack's obsession with chasing down Tom and collecting on a $66,000 judgment—when Zack owed $700,000 to his creditors—gives ample evidence of his lack of business sense. Even if Zack had collected all $66,000 owed, he would have still owed his creditors another $634,000. Had Zack remained at the ranch, rather than running around the country chasing down Tom, he could have sold off assets, subdivided the ranch into smaller holdings and sold them off. Instead, his vanity won out and he frittered away two years chasing down Tom's money. As a result, his two-year battle netted him $22,000—a paltry $11,000 per year, or, to put it another way, the equivalent of one week of Tom's salary with the Sells-Floto show.

20

With $65,000 in profits from the 1934 season in his pockets in cash, Tom decided that not only did he want to continue touring with a circus, he wanted to own one. As early as 1909, when he had founded his own short-lived wild west show in Seattle, Washington, Tom had harbored a dream of owning his own wild west show. He once stated that performing before a circus audience was his "first love." Now that his legal troubles seemed to be finally over, perhaps now was the time.

Fate stepped in when Sam Dill died of lung cancer shortly after the show set up winter quarters. In December 1934, just days after settling the lawsuit with Zack Miller, Tom sank $400,000 of his own money into purchasing Sam Dill's circus.[1]

Tom's "rosy dream" may have clouded his business judgment. He could have put that nearly half-million dollars into a secure investment and retired in comfort, but Tom was not one to sit still. He bought the circus and ran it as a sole proprietor, a risky move in any business because the owner's personal assets are at risk to creditors. Four years later, Tom's creditors would descend like vultures and carry off all of Tom's circus assets and Tom would spend the next two years working to pay off his debts.

Tom was 54 years old and he had built up his net worth large enough that he could have retired in comfort, as William S. Hart had done. Hart had been conservative with his money and, upon retiring from motion pictures in 1925 had rested comfortably at his ranch in Saugus, California. The thought of retirement terrified Tom because he equated retirement with old age and impending death.

To Tom, he had only one option. He had to be Tom Mix, even if it put him out on a limb.

"Tom was the sole owner of the circus," circus clown "Gypsy Joe" Bowers, who toured with the show, recalled. "There were no promoters or investors, although it would have been better for Tom if he'd incorporated."[2]

Olive Mix remembered her ex-husband's enthusiasm for the venture, but she saw dark clouds looming.

"He chose a particularly bad time to make this move, however, for the country was in the depths of the Great Depression," she recalled. Olive knew that Tom's cowboy friends were all hurting from the poor economy, and she knew that Tom would do what he always did—he'd put all of his friends on the payroll of the circus. "His money flowed to them freely and even his income from pictures wasn't sufficient to make up the slack."[3]

Her statements about Tom's finances are intriguing, especially in light of the fact that Olive managed to go broke after she and Tom divorced, despite the fact that the oil wells on her ranch were profitable. Further, Olive hounded Tom for money for decades after she went broke.

Tom did indeed feel a responsibility to keep his fellow cowboys employed—to pass his good fortune on to the men who, in his words, "…polished saddle leather and dragged our muddy loops…banded together with strong and everlasting ties of an enduring friendship."[4]

Tom told Olive that he felt like he could make as big a profit with his own circus that Sells-Floto had made with Tom as its headline attraction. Olive recalled that she felt "a premonition of disaster."[5]

As soon as Tom closed the deal for the purchase of the circus he was back in tight financial straits. He was personally responsible for the financial well-being of a giant operation. There were five mounted cages for wild animals, including "Babe, the whimsical elephant." There were 26 house trailers and a tent for the band. There were three big top tents, purchased by Sam Dill in mid-1934 with profits from Tom's appearances with the show. Circus animals had to be housed and fed. The performers and carnys had to be housed and fed. Keeping the equipment, including trucks and trailers, in working order was expensive. Tents and bleachers had to be maintained.

Olive recalled that Tom was broke by the time the circus took to the road for its first engagement.

Once again Tom's business acumen was lacking even if his enthusiasm wasn't. He renamed the operation the Tom Mix Circus and prepared for the 1935 season with great energy. At great cost, he had all of the vehicles and equipment repainted with his TM brand and the name "Tom Mix Circus." Tom was determined to make a success of his new circus, but he needed capital.

But Tom's luck held, again. As much as Tom needed money, a tiny, low-rent movie studio needed a movie star for its next picture. Nat Levine, a fifth-rate movie producer who owned a flea bag movie studio called Mascot Pictures, called Tom to see if Tom would star in his next serial called *The Miracle Rider*.[6]

Serials were like television shows of today. Before television, audiences used to go to the movies and see multiple films. The show would open with several serials, each with a chapter of 15 minutes in length. There would then be a matinee and then the feature film. Serials were often called 'cliffhangers' because the hero faced an insurmountable danger at the end of the chapter only to come back the next week and escape the dilemma. In short, audiences were left like their hero, hanging from a cliff until the next week. Most serials starred movie actors either on their way up or on their way down the career ladder. Indeed, an unknown John Wayne—the former prop man named Marion Morrison—starred in two serials for Mascot in 1932, *Shadow of the Eagle* and *Hurricane Express*. Wayne would go on to make dozens of low-budget westerns for Mascot and its successive incarnations, Lone Star, Monogram and Republic.

Tom knew that *The Miracle Rider* was not going to be a major Fox Studios production, but he needed cash. Nat Levine offered Tom $40,000 to star in the serial.[7]

Production would take about one month. Tom agreed to work for Mascot and do the serial because he needed the money to buy new trucks and equipment for his circus. Plus, Tom knew that the publicity from the movie would help ticket sales at the circus.[8]

He was already spending top dollar to hire the best circus talent on the market. First and foremost, Tom hired John Agee, the former equestrian director with the Ringling Brothers and Barnum Bailey Circus. Agee, a grizzled half-Indian with a crippled right hand, worked "magic" with horses, according to Gene Autry, who hired Agee after Tom's circus went bust.[9]

Tom also hired D.E. Turney as circus manager, and C.O. Robinson as band director. Robinson brought along a six-piece band.[10]

For circus performers, Tom hired Jack Knapp, the rodeo clown; and wild west cowboys Ed Hendershot and Herman Nolan.[11]

The Tom Mix Circus began the 1935 season in Compton, California, then traveled to Hollywood for a five-day stand. Tom then shut the show down to begin working on the new serial.

Production began on *The Miracle Rider* in April 1935. He plays Texas Ranger Tom Morgan, whose mission is to prevent the Ravenhead Indians from being run off their land by a sinister villain who is mining an explosive mineral. Tom rode Tony, Jr. and several doubles in the film.[12]

Nat Levine was thrilled with his new production. Tom looked the same on film as he had for the past 20 years. At 55, he was in top physical condition and still rode like the wind and handled his action sequences perfectly. Despite his superior health, he was suffering from some lingering effects of a series of bad horse falls during circus performances. Tom had to bring in stuntman Cliff

Lyons to handle a few of the tougher scenes, and the studio utilized Lyons to double for Tom during shooting in order to expedite the production.[13]

The film is not one of Tom's best, but as fate would have it, it has survived in mass release. Because the copyright expired long ago, many video and DVD distributors have released it and it is readily available from on-line video and DVD retailers.

Despite the creakiness of the production, Tom is in fine form. The film opens with a moving shot of Tom galloping Tony, Jr. at a dead run, sitting the horse with ease. In the opening chapter, Tom rides into town and dismounts with an elan that only a horseman of great skill can achieve.

Throughout the serial, Tom, though not a good actor, performs with a naturalness that is difficult to achieve on film. He has a comedic scene where he catches two children trying to steal a pie from a windowsill that plays like many of the comedic scenes from Tom's silent films. Indeed, his greatest weakness as an actor was his propensity to lapse into pantomime in a style that was popular in silent films but unnecessary in sound films. When the adventure begins, Tom chases thieves who have stolen money from the reservation, wrestles with bad guys on runaway trucks, flies experimental airplanes, and engages in all manner of shoot outs and fist fights.

Tom is said to have enjoyed working on the serial, due in no small part to the participation of the two directors, Armand Schaeffer and B. Reeves Eason. Schaeffer directed Tom in *Terror Trail* at Universal. Eason was close to Tom because his sister, Teddy, was Tom's longtime secretary.[14]

Indeed, Teddy was widely believed to be madly in love with Tom. Grief stricken, she committed suicide in 1940, shortly after Tom's death.

Tom was thrilled when audiences flocked to the theaters to see the serial, which the June 15, 1935 issue of the *Philadelphia Enquirer* called "excellent." "Tom Mix makes a big comeback," the newspaper gushed.[15]

The Miracle Rider grossed $1 million at the box office, Mascot's highest grossing film ever.

21

Despite the success of *The Miracle Rider*, Tom never made another film. He owned a circus and he had expenses to meet, and to make the circus profitable he had to get out on the road and perform.

And perform he did. The show resumed its tour in Hollywood and traveled to Monterey, California and then on to Salinas and Eureka. The biggest crowd in the history of Tom's circus came out in Eureka and Tom gave a terrific show. The tour continued up the Pacific Coast to Portland, Oregon and Tacoma and Bellingham, Washington before traveling on to Butte and Helena, Montana. From there, Tom's circus moved on to Laramie and Harding, Wyoming. The show then traveled through Colorado and Nebraska, arriving in the plains during the heat of summer. Crowds fell off slightly, but the show continued to draw record attendance.[1]

And, as often happens with such entertainment venues, there were tragedies and obstacles. Bad weather plagued the show at every turn. Olive said "rain, the bane of any circus, seemed to be following Tom's circus around like a hound dog."[2]

In Montana, a gang of thugs sabotaged the show when Tom wouldn't pay protection money.[3]

Then, to Tom's surprise, Ruth disappeared for several days to elope again, this time to rodeo cowboy Harry Knight. Knight was the champion bronc rider from Canada. The two got hitched in Reno, Nevada on June 6, 1935. When the news hit the press, Tom was stunned. Ruth had said nothing to him about her intentions.[4]

Crooked cops shook the show down for "fines" when it played Kentucky, causing Tom to pull stakes and hit the road in the middle of the night to avoid paying.

Heavy summer rains and flooding hurt attendance in Kansas and Missouri. The old adage "the show must go on" was the mantra as Tom and his circus did their best, often performing in cold, knee-deep mud or in dry, blistering heat.[5]

Tom put on a brave face, telling the entire circus contingent each day that "tomorrow it will be better. It has to be." Indeed, bandleader C.O. Robinson remembered that Tom ran his circus with "reckless courage."[6]

Robinson said Tom could not abide yes-men, and left the decision-making to his key employees, never undermining those upon whom he had bestowed positions of authority.

After one incident involving the circus band, Tom told Robinson, "You don't need to explain anything to me. I hired you to run my band and as long as you give me the kind of music I want I will never ask you to hire a certain man, fire a man, or not to fire a man. That is your job and you run it. When you can't do that to my satisfaction I'll get someone who can."[7]

Tom's push to make his circus successful took all of his concentration and physical effort. He worked tirelessly, no doubt finding vitality in the cheers of his fans and the loyalty of his performers. For Tom, the early days of his new circus were a time of great risk and the rush of emotions that came along with such a big gamble.

While Tom was immersed in his circus, his old pal Will Rogers was using his celebrity and financial wealth to take trips around the world. Rogers and his pilot Wiley Post were flying from the Yukon to the Far East on August 16, 1935 when their plane crashed onto a frozen lake near Point Barrow, Alaska.[8]

Tom was devastated by the news and raced back to Los Angeles for the funeral. He was so overcome with grief that he barely spoke to anyone during the wake or after the service.[9] Surely Tom saw the harbinger of his own death one day. He had been stubbornly clinging to the lifestyle of his youth, roaming the country to perform for the people. No doubt Rogers was similarly traveling to keep himself engaged and vital. Tom never wrote down his emotions at this time, but surely he must have been staggered by the sudden death of the man who was so instrumental in the days when Tom was learning to cowboy in Oklahoma. Little did Tom know that he would die a violent death just five years later.

To keep his circus afloat, Tom sold his fleet of expensive cars and his Beverly Hills home. He invested everything he had in one last gamble. One wonders if such a big risk was because of some single-minded drive to succeed or because of a fear of failure, of having to give up being the Tom Mix the world knew and loved. Olive said, "He was literally a poor man despite the millions he had made as the highest paid star on the screen.".[10]

Near the end of the season, on October 4, 1935, Tom was again injured when his horse fell during a performance in Alva, Oklahoma and Tom's leg was broken.[11]

The season was nearly over, so Ruth finished out the tour as headliner. The show finished up in Barstow, California and set up winter quarters in nearby Compton.

In 1935 the Tom Mix Circus traveled 13,275 miles and gave 216 performances. Despite record crowds at many locations, the returns were not enormous. The Great Depression was still gripping the nation and Tom had competition from other wild west shows and circuses.[12]

Faced with having to purchase new tents and grandstands, and adding some additional acts—including two elephant acts—to increase the show's potential, Tom made ends meet by cutting the travel budget slightly and by staying longer in some cities and shortening the touring schedule.

After the painful horse fall that broke his leg, Tom changed mounts in 1936. Having retired Tony in 1929 and then Tony, Jr. in 1935, Tom began riding Warrior, a tall, white horse with a striking presence.[13]

The year 1936 was similar to 1935. Good attendance at some locations was offset by bad weather and bad luck. The tour opened on March 11 in Compton, California and then moved on to Oregon and then Idaho, where a wind storm damaged tents and a grandstand. Good luck prevailed through Wyoming, Colorado, Kansas, Iowa and South Dakota.

On May 20, 1936, in Neenah, Wisconsin, a freak tornado blew up and nearly flattened the tent during a performance. Tom and three other circus employees were injured rescuing some of the circus animals. Despite his injuries, Tom headed an all-night search party for the small daughter of a spectator who had disappeared during the panic as spectators fled for cover. The child was found near dawn wandering in a nearby field.[14]

Tom's five-day stand in Chicago drew 103,000 people, roughly 20,000 per performance. Fresh from this triumph, the circus headed east into Ohio and Pennsylvania, and then on to Connecticut, Rhode Island, Massachusetts and New Jersey.[15]

As August gave way to September, Tom and his circus headed south to Maryland, Virginia, North Carolina, South Carolina and Georgia. Dodging a polio epidemic in Macon, Georgia, Tom turned the show around and picked up shows in Tennessee and ended the season in Anniston, Alabama on November 5, 1936, where the show pitched camp at a 47-acre lot owned by the U.S. Pipe Company.[16]

The circus made a profit that year, thanks to the large crowds when the weather was good.

Olive said Tom was in good form in 1936, and the improved financial condition brightened his demeanor. She saw no trace of the financial worries on Tom's face when she attended a performance of the circus in Austin, Texas. "I was worried that Tom's financial troubles might affect his performances, but my fear was groundless. He was more brilliant than ever. His flash, fire and unexcelled physical aura dazzled the thousands of persons who came to him wherever the circus played."[17]

At the close of the 1936 season, the Tom Mix Circus had traveled 12,236 miles to 25 states that year and gave 217 performances.

During the winter break in Alabama, Tom and the circus performers repaired equipment and rehearsed new acts. Winter in Alabama is mild, but wet. Winter showers pounded the region and on February 6, 1937, a strong thunderstorm blew across Alabama. Lightning struck the circus' cook tent, setting it afire, and damaged several trucks. Fifty miles away, flood waters caused the Coosa River to overflow its banks, flooding Gadsden, Alabama. The Red Cross rushed in and issued a call for help. Tom heard of the flood and packed up circus tents, 1,500 folding chairs and a light plant with a generator to aid the Red Cross' efforts. Etowah County residents were dumbstruck as the famous movie hero Tom Mix rode into town astride a gleaming truck and came to their rescue.[18]

On March 31, 1937, the Tom Mix Circus opened its season in Anniston.[19]

The show then headed for Birmingham, then back to Gadsden, where crowds turned out to cheer Tom Mix, the movie hero who was a real life hero when the city was in need. Tom then headed to Huntsville for a successful performance. The show then headed to Arkansas, Tennessee, Illinois, Missouri and Indiana. Rain prevented the show from performing in Mansfield, Ohio, but the weather cleared for shows in Akron and Youngstown, Ohio. The Pennsylvania and New York shows were highly successful, but returns dipped in Massachusetts thanks to a freak cold spell and heavy rains. The show did good business in Connecticut and New Hampshire.[20]

Tom played a stand in Concord, New Hampshire for the state prison inmates.

Weather continued to be a constant problem, and competition from other circuses had intensified as the national economy continued to struggle. Handbills for competitors often covered over Tom's advertisements. Circuses often raced each other to the next town, trying to lock up the audience dollars before the other circus arrived.[21]

Tom faced a new enemy as the show traversed Connecticut and Massachusetts when labor union activists from the Congress of Industrial Organizations attempted to unionize Tom's circus employees, without success.

The show moved on to New York and good attendance.

In Pennsylvania, a car pulled out in front of a circus truck and trailer. The truck driver slammed on the brakes, jack-knifing the trailer, which broke loose and careened down a mountainside. Thankfully, there were no serious injuries.

Three other vehicle accidents occurred in Pennsylvania, injuring horses, four zebras and a llama.[22]

The crowds began to thin out by mid-season, mostly due to bad weather and the weak national economy.

In 1937, Tom reduced the size of the circus, its travel schedule and the number of stands, giving more performances per city in hopes of further increasing profits. The circus traveled only 10,521 miles and gave 195 performances, including a stand at the Canadian National Exposition in Toronto, Canada.[23]

As the show made its way along the summer tour, Tom received word that his mother's health was failing. On July 25, 1937, Elizabeth Mix died at age 79.[24]

Once again, at a critical time of Tom's life, there is no recording of Tom's reaction to his mother's death. He was no doubt saddened by her passing.

Tom looked forward to a profitable 1938 season, but national events overtook him. America had begun to climb out of the Great Depression by 1937, but the economy slowed drastically the following year. By 1938, Tom's circus was beset with poor attendance, poor weather conditions and increasing disloyalty by his circus performers.

There was competition even from Tim McCoy, the cowboy star whose pedigree included cowboying in Wyoming and a stint as a cavalry officer and as adjutant general of Wyoming territory. McCoy had semi-retired from the movies, preferring, as Tom did, the sawdust trail to Hollywood. McCoy's show opened on April 14, 1938 in Chicago, Illinois and did good business at first, but began to falter and closed a mere 21 days later. The failure of McCoy's show was not lost on Tom. McCoy had invested $300,00 of his own money and was now flat broke. Tom, like McCoy, had his entire net worth invested in his show.[25]

The circus arrived in cities where, in previous years, audiences had flocked to the show. This time the crowds didn't come. Tom slashed his ticket prices by more than half, from 50 cents down to 20 cents. Attendance picked up some, but at the cost of profitability. Suddenly Tom was having to avoid creditors and stiff some vendors to keep the show going.

By this time Tom employed only 50 performers and 11 band members.[26]

Circus performers and staff members began leaving. Some took equipment with them when they went. Tom was particularly devastated when old friend Pat Chrisman, the wrangler who had sold Tom his wonder horse, Tony, and who had stayed on as a horse trainer for Tom for more than 20 years, stole one of Tom's beloved pistols and sold it for $100 to a Tom Mix fan. When word of Chrisman's betrayal circulated around the circus, performers expected fireworks.

Instead, Tom called Chrisman into his motor home and the two men talked quietly. The weight of Chrisman's Judas act seemed to have shattered Tom. "Gypsy" Joe Bowers was present for the exchange. He related later that Tom seemed on the verge of tears. His voice sounded as if he had a lump in his throat. "If you'd only asked me, I would have given you anything, Pat, you know that," Bowers recalled Tom saying. "But after all these years together you sneak in and just take it. You better pack your things and clear out."[27]

After that incident, Tom seemed to have lost his vigor. Black despair overwhelmed him. Olive recalled that Tom was in a state of "inner turmoil," and he turned to Ruth for comfort and support.

"Perhaps he couldn't have done it that year if Ruth had not been with him," Olive recalled.[28]

Seeds of doubt began to take hold in Tom's mind. When the show arrived in Auburn, California for a performance, Tom became overwhelmed. Ruth found him in his trailer just before the show was to begin, overcome with "nerves...blanched and shaking," Olive said.[29]

Despite the many injuries he had received during his lengthy career as a cowboy, wild west show performer and movie star, Tom always maintained himself in top physical condition. The word most often used to describe him was "robust."

Now, something had changed. Tom's once dazzling smile seemed forced and his eyes lacked their former luminescence. Tom's smile hid unspoken pain. A photo of Tom and Ruth, taken around this time in 1938, shows Tom's deteriorated condition. He is a shell of his former self.

Olive Mix recalled that Tom's behavior had become erratic, and there were increasing reports of incidents of Tom losing his temper while on the road. Olive called Tom's outbursts "emotionalism that resulted from Tom's losing contact, at times, with the man he really was."[30]

After a performance in a small New England town—which town is not recorded—Tom showed up at Ruth's trailer. He looked gaunt, pale and upset. Ruth remembered that for the first time in her life, her father looked "old." He was visibly distraught.[31]

Tom asked Ruth to go for a drive with him and she immediately agreed. She noticed her father's voice was weak and quavering. Tom apologized to Ruth for the lateness of the hour. "I've got to talk to you tonight," Tom said shakily. They drove down to the banks of a nearby river to talk. Tom told Ruth that he'd seen the handwriting on the wall. He was broke and his circus was going to fail. Ruth noticed that her father's dark eyes were restless and hollow. She could see that his face was ashen.[32]

"It seems a little fantastic that I've reached this stage of life only to end up a failure," Tom said darkly. "A personal failure. I've failed my family. And in doing that I've failed myself."

Ruth demurred, trying to lift her father's spirits. He waved her off. "When you were a baby, Ruth, I kept thinking that one day we'd be living in our own little world, as a family should. But I kept putting that day off until it was too late."[33]

Tom told Ruth that he was going to accept an offer to tour Europe on the vaudeville circuit. He didn't want to bail on the circus tour, but he knew that he had to in order to keep from being completely bankrupt. "Ruth, I guess there's one thing about life that keeps us tough and urges us on, and that's doing things we don't want to do."[34]

Without telling anyone associated with the show, Tom signed a contract to travel to England for a vaudeville tour. He knew he had to make some big bucks—and quick—to survive. He told Ruth the English tour "was the best thing to do. We can get our debts cleared off—and then we can start fresh again."[35]

Tom then told Ruth he wanted to be alone for a minute and take a walk. As he walked away, Ruth began to cry. Tom was gone for more than an hour. Ruth heard Tom's car starting up the hill and raced up the hill to catch her father, who, in his grief, forgot Ruth was there. She walked back to the circus in tears, but when she arrived at Tom's trailer found him in a deep sleep.

Olive said the next morning, Ruth, bleary eyed from a fitful night of worrying about her father's condition, went to Tom's trailer to check on him and found he was gone. He'd left a note for her: "I'm off for Europe, Ruth," the note said. "I tried to tell you last night that I'd have to do this alone—but I just couldn't do it. You see, the creditors insist that a Mix stay with the circus while I'm in Europe. I know you're going to bring it through for us. After our talk last night…now I'm sure there is a future."[36]

Olive said Ruth never saw her father alive again.[37]

Olive and Ruth Mix's version of Tom's flight to Europe differs from other accounts.

"Gypsy Joe" Bowers said Tom and Ruth discussed how the show would finish the season, and Ruth vowed to keep going as long as she could do so. She would take over as headliner and Tom would simply leave, without fanfare, for England. Tom and Bowers then slipped off into the night when the show reached Kansas

City, Missouri. He and Bowers simply loaded up Tom's horse and they vanished.[38]

Another account is that Tom left the circus in mid-May 1938 and traveled to Chicago. This account says that Tom went to Europe from Chicago, which cannot be confirmed.[39]

Whichever way it happened, the Tom Mix Circus continued on with Ruth as star. Ticket sales plummeted as most people wanted to see Ruth only if she was with Tom. By herself, Ruth was not a big enough draw to lure patrons to the circus.

Tom sailed for England with Warrior, his new 17.5 hand white circus horse, and a small entourage in tow. Tom told the press the horse's name was "Tony II," and the press picked up the headlines that Tom Mix and Tony were coming to the Emerald Isles. Mabel went with Tom to England for part of the tour, but she remained in the background.

Away from the grimness of the circus, Tom began to relax and eat, and during the voyage across the Atlantic Ocean he put on weight. By the time he arrived in England, he looked like his former self. The color had returned to his cheeks and he was no longer gaunt and desperate-looking.

Tom's arrival in Southhampton, England on May 20, 1938 was reminiscent of his triumphant 1925 English tour. He stepped off the ship on a misty morning, dressed in his trademark black Tom Mix Stetson and a trench coat. Customs inspectors were surprised to find that Tom had eight pistols and five rifles in his possession, as England banned possession of firearms and Tom had failed to obtain an import license to bring the guns into the country for his performances. Tom was cleared by customs, but not until one reporter quipped that Tom's arrival was "the largest armed force that has tried to land on British soil since…the Stuarts 200 years ago."[40]

Everywhere he went, Tom was deluged with cheering fans. His opened at the Palladium Theater in London and, according to Bowers, was a "sensation." Tom's show was small. He appeared with Tony II, did some trick shooting and trick roping, and then talked with audiences about his career. The show was kept small on purpose. The idea was to earn some quick cash in the low-cost world of vaudeville. Tom and his horse would perform, keeping the overhead low along the way.

Tom toured the theater circuit owned by impresario George Black, including the Birmingham Hippodrome. Everywhere he went, Tom left a trail of admirers in his wake. He stopped for a short while in the tony town of Harrogate, in the Midlands of England.[41]

A haven for the ultra-wealthy, Tom cut a dashing figure in his cowboy attire wherever he went. He rode Warrior through the streets of London, just as he'd ridden Tony in 1925, and the crowds choked the street to watch him gallop by. Photos of Tom's triumphant ride through Hyde Park and the streets of Westminster show Tom, dressed in his finest ivory suit with decorative piping and a brilliant white Stetson, riding atop Warrior, his beautiful white coat shimmering. Tom looks every bit the movie hero. In one photo, Tom rides Warrior down a street choked with spectators. He is seen passing a pub called the Marlborough Head, and traffic has come to a standstill.

As news of Tom's success spread across Europe, the famed Circus Belli of Denmark contacted Tom about performing in Denmark. Tom also received offers to perform in the Soviet Union, provided he spend his entire earnings in that country.

Back home, the Tom Mix Circus died a quick and painful death in Pecos, Texas on September 10, 1938.[42]

Olive was with Ruth that last night and both were in tears. Ruth told her mother, "I'm glad Daddy wasn't here to see it die."[43]

Ruth wrote a lengthy letter to Tom to inform him of the demise of the circus. Tom wrote back that he was doing well in Europe and hoped that the money he was making could be used to restart the circus upon his return.[44] One wonders if Tom thought of Zack Miller and the 101 Ranch show, which had collapsed in 1936. Tom's circus had suffered the same fate just two years later. Perhaps Tom had a new sympathy for Zack, despite their hatred of each other.

The failure of the Tom Mix Circus was not isolated. The old-fashioned truck circuses were too costly to run and a victim of the hard economic times. Circuses such as Ringling Brothers and Barnum and Bailey had switched to rail, traveling by train to reduce costs.

Despite Tom's success in England, in the wee quiet hours he continued to brood and often drank too much. His famous optimism, a trait which made him so popular with audiences, was reserved for public appearances. At times, Tom's comments to the press seemed to betray his true emotions. During an interview for the English press before Tom's Christmas show in Brighton, Tom offered an odd comment. After wishing the local children a happy holiday season, Tom said he always took a keen interest in children, and added, rather darkly, "I hope their parents [and] guardians take an interest in them too, and bring them up to be better citizens than we are. We've made our mistakes."[45]

Tom's success in England was the stuff of legend. While news of Hitler's military buildup in Germany put all of Europe on edge—especially Great Britain—Tom drew record crowds wherever he went.

Circus Belli offered Tom $3,250 a day—cash to be paid daily—to headline the show. He would perform nightly, including a Sunday matinee and three weekday matinees, for a total of nine shows per week from April 29 to July 31, 1939. The circus retained the option to continue Tom's contract through October. Tom insisted that the circus cover his transportation and livestock costs and the contract was signed on March 17, 1939.[46]

Tom arrived in Horsens, Denmark on April 18, 1939 with Mabel, "Gypsy Joe" Bowers, Jack Knapp and Bud and Rosa Carlell and Warrior, Tom's horse. More than 10,000 people turned out and mobbed Tom at his arrival.

The Circus Belli was overwhelmed by the response to Tom's arrival. The show had to buy a bigger tent just to cover the larger crowds. Each show was sold out. Tom performed to 3,000 cheering fans each performance.

When he was before the cheering crowds, Tom was affable and charismatic. He would ride into the ring, resplendent in his white circus outfit, a gleaming white Tom Mix Stetson on his head. He would perform his time-honored trick roping and trick shooting acts to thunderous applause.[47]

When Tom was alone, before the performances or after, or when he had retired for the evening, he was a different person. To those behind the scenes, Tom was dark and moody. He brooded a lot and was often short-tempered. He was particularly jealous of Mabel, often lashing out at reporters and others who came into contact with his wife. Some discounted Tom's actions as mere protectiveness, but others saw that Tom was an aging man with a young wife who feared losing his young bride to a younger man.[48]

Tom continued to drink heavily, sometimes alarmingly. Circus staff began riding herd on him, even locking him in his hotel room at night to ensure that he didn't disappear. Tom became as hostile to the Circus Belli staff constraining him as he was to the Fox Studio brass ten years before.[49]

Surely, he missed the wide open spaces of America's western landscape. He was in a foreign country among people whose language he did not speak, and he was being reined in like a dressage horse, forced to perform a series of tightly controlled movements. Tom was no dressage horse. He was a wild bronco, kicking at the fences of life.

Tom argued with Circus Belli management about his drinking. He was told to stop drinking before a performance, and his movements were restricted by stage managers prior to each show. Tom retaliated by sneaking bottles of whiskey backstage and into his hotel rooms. When the circus was set to stage a command performance for Denmark's king, Tom was found drunk and passed out in his quarters. He was quickly sobered up and made his performance on time. Tom went through his show a little woozy, but he managed to perform his act without a glaring screw up.[50]

Despite his growing irascibility and heavy drinking, Circus Belli extended Tom's contract past the July date. Tom continued to draw record crowds and, when not drinking, he was his old self. When he was a little shaky from drink during a couple of performances, rumors began to spread that Tom had died and that an imposter had taken his place with the show. The rumor spread quickly and Tom had to appear before the press to give interviews, proving that he was indeed alive.

Tom was so popular that German Chancellor and Nazi party leader Adolph Hitler issued an invitation for Tom to come to Germany. Tom allegedly sent back a terse reply stating, "I'll tour Germany and see my fans, but only over your dead body."

While Tom's contract was supposed to continue until October 1, Tom and Mabel left Denmark abruptly on September 2, 1939 when Hitler attacked Poland and war broke out in Europe.[51]

22

Tom returned to the United States in early September 1939. War had broken out in Europe and Tom, Mabel, "Gypsy Joe" Bowers, Jack Knapp and Bud and Rosa Carlell fled to the states. Tom stayed on the road, traveling with his vaudeville act, making just enough money to hang on. He was a proud man, and he did his best to put his best face forward. He continued to dress in the finest custom-made western finery. When he could no longer afford custom tailored costumes, he sat up late into the night embroidering his own costumes.

Daughter Thomasina remembered seeing her father sitting over a sewing machine with his reading glasses perched on the end of his nose, monogramming his own costumes.[1]

Here the story of Tom's life becomes frayed.

Some historians note that Tom returned broke. Such is not the case. Tom had roughly $100,000 in assets, including his small ranch at 13753 Osborne in Pacoima, a Los Angeles suburb, where he kept Tony, Tony Jr., and what was left of his personal property, including his 1937 Cord Roadster.[2]

Tom felt that his success in Europe proved he was still a crowd-pleaser, so he went to Hollywood to stage a movie comeback.

One story is that in April of 1940, Tom was in Hollywood. He got dressed in his gaudiest suit and returned to Fox Studios, now called 20th Century Fox, where director John Ford, who had worked with Tom on several hit films at Fox Studios, was directing Henry Fonda in *The Grapes of Wrath*. Ford is said to have welcomed Tom warmly when he visited the set. Tom walked with Ford to Ford's office, where Tom proposed a film venture starring Tom and directed by Ford. Ford is said to have rebuffed Tom, but gently.[3]

Ford basically told Tom that he was "washed up" in Hollywood, that the movies had outgrown his gaudy style of westerns. It is certain that Tom could not believe his ears, as most of the duded-up B-western heroes at Republic, PRC, Columbia, and the other studios were basically emulating his formula. Tom then went to visit Lefty Hough, who had managed many of Tom's productions back in the silent movie days. The two men shared a warm and nostalgic reunion.[4]

As if to prove to Hollywood that he was not old hat, Tom challenged his old friend and fellow 101 Ranch alumnus—and cinema rival—Buck Jones to a chariot race. Jones, still working steadily in matinee westerns and enormously popular with fans, took the bait and the two men agreed to race at the 15th Annual Newhall-Saugus Rodeo on Sunday, April 28, 1940.[5]

The rodeo was an enormously popular event, and many of Hollywood's biggest stars were there to perform or organize the event, including Gary Cooper, Clark Gable, Errol Flynn, William S. Hart, Gene Autry, Roy Rogers, "Hopalong Cassidy" actor William Boyd, Tex Ritter, Gordon "Wild Bill" Elliott, Edgar Bergen, Jerry Cologna, Marian Marsh, Noah Berry Jr, Wallace Beery, Rex Bell, Jack Benny, Leo Carrillo, Jackie Cooper, Andy Devine and Guinn "Big Boy" Williams.

The grandstand was packed with fans as the race began and Tom, throwing caution to the winds, drove like a wild cowboy possessed. The crowd went wild, cheering in a frenzy as Tom drove with complete abandon, defeating Jones handily.[6]

Later that week Tom continued his rounds of Hollywood. He went to see muscular cowboy star George O'Brien. O'Brien had started his career as a crew member on Tom's Fox Studio's films.[7]

When Tom worked with John Ford on several films, Ford took a liking to O'Brien. Both Ford and O'Brien were Irish and Ford had a strong loyalty to the Irish in Hollywood.

In 1925, when Ford was casting his epic western "The Iron Horse," Tom tried to get Ford to cast him in the lead. Ford chose O'Brien. The film, the first big-budget western Ford directed, was a smash. Ironically enough, Tom appears in a scene where Irish laborers complain about their pay. Tom is basically an extra, standing in the crowd, his face unshaven. It is unknown if Tom went to lend his support to Ford or O'Brien, or basically just ended up on the set when the scene was shot.

When Tom arrived at RKO Studios, the former FBO Studios where he had made his last silent movies, O'Brien welcomed him warmly. Tom talked to O'Brien about the two men making a movie together, and O'Brien liked the idea. Unfortunately, RKO cancelled O'Brien's contract before a deal could be struck.[8]

Olive insisted in her autobiography that Tom returned from Denmark with enough cash to pay off his creditors and was excited about touring South America that next winter—which is summer in the southern hemisphere.[9]

There is some evidence also that Tom was considering retiring to the wilds of Argentina to raise horses.[10]

Tom wandered the desert southwest, trying to drum up some financial support for a new circus venture, and he talked to Ruth about rejoining him on the sawdust trail.[11]

Ruth Mix's story gets as murky here as Tom's. In Olive's autobiography, she notes that Ruth had overseen the demise of the Tom Mix Circus and in September 1938 married rodeo promoter John Guthrie. Guthrie also performed as a trick shot artist on occasion. The marriage ended quickly and soon afterward she married Willacy County Sheriff Howard Cragg of Raymondville, Texas.[12]

Cragg made national headlines in November 1936, when he investigated the deaths of Luther Blanton and his son, John, two residents of San Perlita, Texas, who disappeared while hunting on the famous King Ranch. Some local residents of the town of El Sauz claimed that the two were murdered by King Ranch fence riders, and that the Kleberg family covered up the incident.[13]

Olive said Ruth and Cragg were building a new house on their ranch. She had no telephone, but she and Tom had exchanged letters about Ruth going on the tour with Tom in South America. Olive recalled that Tom was excited about performing with Ruth again, though Ruth had some misgivings about the venture.[14]

Cragg is not mentioned in any other document other than Olive's autobiography as having been married to Ruth. Indeed, Ruth later married a man named William Hickman Hill and eventually moved to Corpus Christi, Texas, where she lived until her death.

Olive said Tom told Ruth in a letter that he was driving to Hollywood to discuss a new picture deal and that he was stopping in Chicago on the way to negotiate the South American tour.[15]

In early October Tom stopped at the King Ranch in Texas where he was photographed by Jimmy Dodd sitting in a lawn chair in front of his 1937 Cord roadster. It is a candid shot of Tom, hatless, looking relaxed, albeit tired.[16]

On October 10, 1940, Tom arrived in El Paso, Texas, where he checked into the Ranchhotel, a dude ranch north of the city. He spent the day visiting two friends, Gene Sterling, a 17-year-old actor who had appeared as a small child in some of Tom's Fox films, and Slim Harris, a horse trainer.[17]

The next morning, Friday, October 11, 1940, Tom gave Sterling a ride to Las Cruces, New Mexico, a mere 22 miles from El Paso. Sterling remembered that Tom, always a speed demon behind the wheel, floored the supercharged sports car, hitting a top speed of 150 miles per hour on the short drive to Las Cruces. Tom invited Sterling to join him on the trip to Tucson, but Sterling begged off. Sterling helped Tom load a silver suitcase onto the driver's side back seat behind Tom. That suitcase would later be instrumental in his death.

Later that morning, Tom arrived in Lordsburg, New Mexico, a short distance from Las Cruces, where he appeared as Grand Marshal of the city's famous Fair Day Parade. Tom rode a borrowed horse named Smokey, who looked a lot like Tony, from F.B. Daniels, an agent for the Southern Pacific Railroad. Daniels was proud to lend his spirited horse to the famous movie cowboy.[18]

After the parade, Tom continued on to Tucson, where he spent the rest of the day visiting with Walt Coburn, a noted western writer, and Sheriff Ed Nichols, of Pima County, Arizona. Coburn said the events of the day were "destined to remain branded in my memory for all time."[19]

"That warm sunny day...my wife had gone to town and had left a message on the telephone pad in the den. The message was from Sheriff Ed Echols saying that he was bringing Tom Mix out that afternoon for a drink. I had just finished eating when the front doorbell rang, and when I got out on the screen porch there stood Sheriff Ed Echols and Tom Mix, and the sheriff's car was parked on the gravel driveway in front of the long hitchrack."[20]

Coburn recalled nearly 30 years later that Tom had spent considerable time ringing a circa 1780 mission bell hanging from Coburn's front porch, listening to its dulcet tone. "If you ever take a notion to sell that old bell, I'd like to have it. Where the hell did you get it?" Tom asked. Coburn said Tom was also interested in a genuine oxbow Coburn had hanging from a wall and Coburn's hideaway bar.[21]

Coburn said they rolled cigarettes from imported English Three Castles tobacco, "not with Bull Durham," and enjoyed drinks on the porch.[22]

The three men, "with cigarettes lit and warmed by good whiskey," began reminiscing about their lives. They talked about the Alaska Yukon Pacific Exposition in 1909 and when Ed Echols won the steer roping at the 1912 Calgary Stampede. They recalled the golden days of working for the 101 Ranch and Tom recalled working a spring roundup in Montana "along about 1904-1905" for the Circle Diamond Ranch. Tom said that he and a cowboy named Henry Grammar hired on with the Circle Diamond, working for a foreman named Johnny Survant and that Survant shot a sheep shearer in a saloon fight.

It is interesting that Coburn recalled this story as it is the only time Tom claimed to have ridden roundup in Montana in 1904 or 1905. Coburn details Tom's story at length, but there is no evidence to show that Tom was in Montana at the time.[23]

In 1904 Tom was tending bar in Guthrie, Oklahoma and breaking horses on the side. In 1905 Tom was working for the 101 Ranch, appearing in New York City in April with the show and in June 1905 at the famed Buffalo Chase at the

101. It is likely that either Tom was telling a tall tale or that Coburn was embellishing.

Tom joked that Echols had settled down since becoming sheriff. "There was a time, Ed, when you sowed a goodly crop of wild oats yourself. When you were wild and reckless and didn't give a damn." Echols responded that being a sheriff had "sawed my horns off."[24]

Echols recalled how he'd joined the 101 Ranch show in 1907 and met Tom then. The two men then reminisced about Will Rogers, a lifelong friend of both men until his death in 1935.[25]

The men whiled away the afternoon, talking philosophically about life. Coburn recalled that Tom was bitter about his failed marriages. "When a man's been married half a dozen times any sentiment about wedding anniversaries is cold as the ashes of last year's campfire. Payin' all those alimonies sorta drowns out the romance," Tom said.[26]

It is interesting that Tom was married to Mabel at this time, though traveling without her. Coburn did not mention that Tom spoke warmly about Mabel as he mused about his failed marriages, causing one to speculate on the state of his marriage to Mabel at the time of his death.

Tom told Coburn and Echols that he'd made millions in his career and that he'd "had a hell of a good time spending a lot of money." Tom said he never claimed to be an actor, but "I was the best showman on earth, even better than Buffalo Bill Cody who never made a movie in his life."[27]

Actually Cody did make a silent film reenacting highlights of his life shortly before his death, but Tom may not have known it.

The men then went to the Santa Rita Hotel bar, talking with local cowboys and hotel owner Nick Hall. Tom and Coburn swapped stories about stuntman Yakima Canutt and about the 101 Ranch days, including stories about such luminaries as Hoot Gibson and Buck Jones. They enjoyed a dinner of mesquite grilled steaks and Mexican beer at Coburn's home. Tom gave Coburn a paperback copy of his autobiography, "Ropin' A Million," which Tom autographed for the famed writer.[28]

Tom then returned to his hotel. Restless, Tom went back to the hotel bar and joined Maurice Carl and the hotel band for drinks until the wee hours of the morning.[29]

Tom awoke early the next morning, Saturday, October 12, 1940, and spent a short while talking with Echols, who had stopped by to visit. Tom asked the hotel to call Coburn and tell him that Tom would not be able to make lunch that day.[30]

Tom then used a hotel phone and telephoned a filling station near the Cragg Ranch in Texas to leave a message for Ruth to call him at the hotel in Tucson. Ruth called Tom later that morning, and Tom told her that the South American deal was set and the tour was to begin in February 1941. Tom told Ruth he hoped to make a movie between October and the February start date.[31]

Ruth told her father that she wasn't sure, that in her mind she'd given up show business to be Mrs. Cragg. Tom asked Ruth to join him in California, where he was going to firm up the contract for his new movie. She agreed to come.[32]

Olive said that after Tom spoke to Ruth he jumped into his Cord convertible and sped off. There is some evidence to suggest that Tom checked out of his room and then spent more than a half an hour talking with Tucson motorcycle policeman Richard Lease and Nick Hall, the Santa Rita Hotel owner. Lease would be the first official to be notified of Tom's death.[33]

Tom told them he'd decided to head to Florence to visit with Harry Knight, the Canadian bronc riding champion who had been briefly married to Ruth. Tom wanted to visit with Knight, who was in the cattle ranching business with Twain and Bill Clemons, descendants of Samuel Clemons, who wrote under the nomme de plume of Mark Twain.[34]

After that he intended to drive to Prescott to visit Lester and Grace Ruffner. He had written the Ruffner's from Denmark on July 26, 1939, telling them that he would visit when he returned from Europe.[35]

As was his habit, Tom apparently floored the accelerator on his yellow Cord as he headed west out of Tucson on Highway 80. At about 2:15 p.m., just before Tom reached Florence, Arizona, he missed a detour and rolled his fancy car. He was killed instantly when the silver suitcase Gene Sterling had put on the back seat flew forward and slammed into the back of Tom's neck, breaking it.[36]

John Adams of Oracle, Arizona and A. Armeta of Gasa Grande, Arizona and the rest of the road crew working on the highway rushed to Tom's car and found the star dead. There was not a scratch on him.[37]

Echols rushed to the accident site along with an ambulance and Dick Lease in tow. Nick Hall, the hotel manager, called Walt Coburn and Ruth to tell them the news.

Coburn was devastated. "I poured a big shot of Bushmill's Irish whiskey and took my drink out on the porch where we had sat the day before. The shock of Tom's sudden death left me sort of numb and bewildered, and I wanted to be alone for awhile."

"My wife had already left for town so I was alone with my grief. The October afternoon was warm and a few scattered clouds were in the sky, but the sun had lost its warmth as I took my drink outside to the long hitchrack. My thoughts were of yesterday when Tom Mix was alive. So very much alive." Coburn finished his drink, went out to his stable, saddled his horse, Tex, and rode into the desert to grieve.[38]

"I kept talking to Tex, low toned, as I untangled a witch's knot in the long black mane, telling him how my old friend Tom Mix had died a tragic death that day. I figured Tom was crowding 60 and was past the prime of his life. His career as a star of Western movies was over and done with. Far worse things could have happened to Tom Mix than sudden death. Old age and being broke would have been his ultimate future, and the prideful man could not possibly have taken in his stride old age and its infirmities and uselessness."[39]

Coroner E.O. Divine declined to call an inquest and determined that Tom was killed instantly in the wreck, that he had been traveling at about 80 miles per hour when he crashed through the barricade and overturned the Cord on the Arizona sand.[40]

At the time of his death Tom was wearing a light, cream-colored casual suit, his TM diamond and platinum belt buckle, a white Stetson (though he had stopped wearing the enormous "Tom Mix"-style Stetsons in favor of the lower-crowned, smaller-brimmed cowboy hats of the day), and he had in his pockets $6,000 in cash and $1,500 in travelers' checks.[41]

He also had in his pants pocket a note written on the Tucson hotel stationary that Ruth would call him at 8:30 a.m. from Raymondville, Texas.[42]

Mabel Mix was notified of Tom's death and asked her friend Mary Stone to fly with her to Arizona to retrieve Tom's body. They boarded Hollywood stunt pilot Paul Mantz' sleek red airplane and flew east.[43]

The plane returned to Hollywood's Union Air Terminal to a city in mourning. Most of Tom's contemporaries, older movie stars themselves, were aging gently. It had seemed that Tom had found eternal youth and energy, and now he was dead. Mary Pickford, who was "America's Sweetheart" at the height of her silent movie stardom, said she felt as if Tom had died as he would have wanted to. "I think he would have wanted it to come as quickly as it did," Pickford said. Cowboy star William S. Hart, who had retired from movies in 1925 and was experiencing a resurgence in popularity with the release of his prelude to the hit movie *Stagecoach*, was devastated by Tom's death. "It's just too awful. My recollections of Tom are still very vivid. He was wonderful."[44]

Tom's body was taken to Pierce Brothers' Mortuary. A funeral service was held at the Little Church of Flowers and the elite of Hollywood turned out. Tom was laid out in a large brass coffin, dressed in his favorite white western suit. Studio bosses Carl Laemmle of Universal, William Fox of Fox Studios, Jack Warner of Warner Brothers, Louis B. Mayer of MGM, Samuel Goldwyn of Goldwyn Studios and producer Hal Roach were present. Hollywood stars turned out in profusion, especially those who had started back in the silent movie days. Among them were Buster Keaton, Charlie Chaplin, Clark Gable, Harry Carey, Gary Cooper and Mickey Rooney. Cowboy stars were in abundance, including Buck Jones and Hoot Gibson, who knew Tom from the 101 Ranch days, and Gene Autry. George O'Brien was also in attendance. The most notable cowboy star in attendance was the retired William S. Hart, who Tom had replaced as the Number One cowboy at the box office. Hart appeared devastated by Tom's death, perhaps seeing in Tom's death a foretelling of his own demise. Pima County Sheriff Ed Echols attended the funeral and was visibly grief-stricken.[45]

Cowboy actor Monte Blue, a close friend of Tom's whose wife was Mabel's maid of honor at her and Tom's wedding, read the Masonic ritual.[46]

There are divergent accounts as to whether or not Rudy Vallee, the 1920s crooner, sang "Empty Saddles" at the funeral. Some accounts say that he did, other say he did not. In 1983, Valle said emphatically that he did not sing at Tom's funeral. Valle posited that the confusion probably came from the fact that he sang "The Last Round Up" at William S. Hart's funeral in 1946.

The funeral procession continued to Forest Lawn Memorial Park, in Glendale, California, the site of many celebrity graves. Tom's pallbearers were Monte Blue, John Ford, cameraman Dan Clark, director B. Reeves Eason, Eugene Biscailuz, Ivon D. Parker (Tom's lawyer and friend), Herman Nowlin and Monte Stone.[47]

After Tom's death, efforts to get his coffin draped with an American flag ran into trouble. The U.S. Government still listed Tom as a deserter. Tom's alleged ties to the Texas Rangers were proven to be false. Efforts to get the U.S. Marshal's office to decorate Tom's coffin were met with a denial. Despite years of public relations, the truth was that Tom was not entitled to a flag-draped coffin.

Director John Ford, who was connected at the highest levels with the U.S. military's propaganda efforts in Hollywood, intervened and got Tom's status as a deserter changed and Tom was buried with military honors.[48]

When Tom's 15-page will, which he signed on January 31, 1938, was probated it turned out his worth was about $115,000, but he had debts equaling about half that amount. Tom left his entire estate to Mabel and Thomasina. Tom explicitly disinherited all of his former wives and, oddly enough, Ruth, who is listed as Ruth Mix Knight. Tom left Tony, his beloved horse, to Ivon Parker, his lawyer. Parker was also named executor, and Tom also bequeathed numerous items of his personal property to Parker, who years later donated these items to the Tom Mix Museum in Dewey, Oklahoma.[49]

Tom also appointed his longtime secretary, Teresa Eason, aka Teddy, to be guardian of Thomasina's estate. Teddy Eason, sister of director B. Reeves Eason, was secretly in love with Tom for years. A homely woman who was hard of hearing, her soft, passive demeanor and sweet smile hid a longing for Tom of which she never spoke. Shortly after Tom's death, a grief-stricken Teddy took her own life.[50]

Less than a month after Tom's death, on November 24, 1940, Victoria sued Tom's estate for $50,000, the entire value of Tom's assets after the estate's debt were paid. Victoria claimed Tom borrowed the money from her in 1928 and 1929, when Tom was at the height of his earnings.[51]

Two years to the day after Tom's death, his wonder horse Tony fell ill and on October 12, 1942, was euthanized.[52]

In the years to come Mabel would return to the sawdust trail, billing herself as "Mrs. Tom Mix."[53]

Ruth's history is as muddied as her father's. No other historian mentions Howard Cragg. Ruth went on to tour with various circuses, including the Shrine Circus, before marrying again to William Hill. The couple lived in Corpus Christi, Texas, where they raised a family. Ruth became a saleswoman at Lichtenstein's department store and then as a secretary at Reynolds Metal. Hill died in 1976 and Ruth passed away on September 21, 1977.[54]

Olive Stokes Mix remarried and lived for 32 years after Tom's death, passing away in Los Angeles on November 1, 1972.

Victoria Ford Mix DeOlzabel died in Beverly Hills, California on July 24, 1964.

An ironic footnote: Lucille Mulhall, the famous cowgirl who once turned Tom's head and then became his friend for decades, died in an automobile accident less than one mile from the famed Mulhall Ranch in Oklahoma on December 21, 1940. She was 55.[55]

Sid Jordan, who served with Tom as a lawman in Oklahoma and went on to become his closest friend and devise some of Tom's greatest stunts, worked sporadically in movies until the early 1940s. He died in Hemet, California on September 30, 1970.

CONCLUSION

Tom Mix was the biggest movie star of his day, maybe even of all time. During a period when movie tickets cost a nickel Tom amassed a fortune of $6 million, losing much of it to the stock market crash of 1929 and to his single-minded determination to keep his circus alive.

He was born the son of a lumberman with a talent for horses and, learning at his father's side, Tom became the consummate equestrian. He deserted from the Army out of boredom and wandered west, where he fulfilled his dream of becoming a frontier lawman and skilled cowboy.

He became a movie star more out of the luck of being in the right place in the right time, but also because he had a personal charisma and devil-may-care attitude that translated well to the silent movie audiences of his day. He was the prototype for all the squeaky-clean western heroes who would follow, from Gene Autry and Roy Rogers to the myriad of other B-Western stars who rode the celluloid west.

The pressures of being one of the biggest stars in the world—and the expensive lifestyle that went along with such status—were enormous, made more so by the crush of the Great Depression and the lack of money worldwide. Still, Tom managed to earn more per week as a circus performer than many of Hollywood's top stars of that day. Tom Mix was paid $17,500 per week when he was king of the western cinema. In contrast, Autry and Rogers only earned $75 per week in the height of their fame at Republic Studios.

Free with his money, always ready to bail out a friend or pick up the check for a night on the town, Tom was the archetypal cowboy. He worked all week being a cowboy, then blew his payday on Saturday night revelry, as cowboys have done throughout American history.

Through it all, one thing remains clear. Tom Mix was happiest during the salad days of his early wild west show career at the 101 Ranch and his days as a star at Selig Polyscope. When he became a big star at Fox Studios, Tom was as constrained as a wild pony caught in a corral, always looking for a way to leap the high fence and gallop off into the horizon, free and unencumbered. In 1926, at the height of his fame, Tom reminisced about the days when he was a freewheeling cowboy. "In the old days, with the blue sky above me, a good horse under me, the vast acreage of the 101 Ranch rolling green about me and a bacon-filled atmosphere from the chuck wagon calling me, I was the richest of men. How rich, the recent years have told me," Tom told *101 Ranch Magazine*. "My fondest recollections are those of my early days on the 101 ranch...working under the 101 brand."[1]

Tom had only about $115,000 in assets and $60,000 in debts when he died. Olive stated in her autobiography that Tom did not own a home at the time of his death, but records indicate he owned a small home and some land located at 13753 Osborne in Pacoima, California, a lower-middle-class suburb of Los Angeles. He drove an exotic Cord sports car, which he raced around the country like a cowboy galloping across the great western plains. At the end of his life, Tom was—again—what he once was and always wanted to be, a footloose cowboy wandering the west in search of new adventures.

Walt Coburn perhaps said it best when he paid tribute to Tom in an article he wrote in 1968. "Tom had roped his million and squandered the money like a cowpuncher in town. [His death] was a spectacular end to the greatest Western cowboy star that was even known on the silver screen. If Tom Mix had deliberately planned the manner of his passing, it could never have been more fitting. Tom Mix had seen his last sunset in the welcome companionship of his old and true friend, Ed Echols. A crimson sunset in a spectacular sky, with a panoramic view of the desert and mountain ranges and Old Mexico. He had heard the sound of the quail and mourning doves blending into the hushed twilight of that last sundown.

"All men are born to die. But is given to few men that though they are long dead, they shall never die...He lived his own legend in real life and on the silver screen, and that legend is destined to live on forevermore."[2]

EPILOGUE

Tom Mix's' life story is the story of America. A child of poverty with a unique charm and a gift who rose to the heights of world fame. It is also the story of modern man, brought down by hard economic times and a rapidly changing culture.

Today, the name Tom Mix is still recognizable in the modern culture, even in cases where people don't remember exactly who Tom was.

Unfortunately, much of what is "known" about Tom Mix is incorrect. Thanks to Tom's adoption of the resumes of Will Rogers and Buck Jones, to name a few, his history is muddied by PR versions of his life. Even worse, books have been written which accept much of that false history as fact. Amazingly one book even contained a lengthy—and completely fictitious—memoir of a woman who claimed that she was Tom's daughter. The book even contains pictures of Tom and Victoria Mix and misidentifies Victoria as another fictitious woman to whom Tom was allegedly married. Additionally, the book asserts that this bogus daughter used to play with John Wayne, who was allegedly a frequent house guest at Tom's mansion. As Wayne carried a vehement grudge against Tom from 1926 until Tom's death, it is highly improbable that he spent any time at Tom's home.

Thankfully, much of the official record of Tom's life still exists, though many have chosen to ignore the facts and print the legend.

Preserving Tom's celluloid legacy are silent and early sound film collectors who maintain libraries of Tom's surviving films. Many of them, most notably Grapevine Films in Arizona, sell Tom's films on the internet.

Also, the Tom Mix Museum in Dewey, Oklahoma, preserves Tom's life in a nice, albeit small, museum. Many of Tom's personal effects are on display, including Tom's saddle, bridle and breastplate, which adorn a fiberglass Tony. It is an interesting place. The most intriguing item in the museum is the silver suitcase which broke Tom's neck, complete with the dent where it collided with Tom's head, killing him.

Tom's legacy is remembered also in a roadside monument along Highway 80 just outside of Florence, Arizona. It was dedicated by the Pima County Historical Society on December 5, 1947. Sheriff Ed Echols and Gene Autry, then the biggest cowboy star in the movies, attended the dedication. Autry sang "Empty Saddles" for the crowd in attendance. Sadly, this monument has been vandalized and disfigured on several occasions by thoughtless thugs who clearly have no idea of who Tom was. Recently, on May 6, 2005, thieves stole the inch-thick steel statue of the horse from atop the monument. As this book goes to press, the whereabouts of the statue are unknown.

As a youth, Tom Mix dreamed of leaving Pennsylvania and becoming a cowboy. Photo circa 1893.

Tom and third wife, Olive, shortly after their wedding, 1909. Notice how Tom stands with his back to her as if he is the sole subject of the photo.

William S. Hart, the first major cowboy star, emphasized realism. In 1920, Tom replaced Hart as the king of the cowboys by focusing on tongue-in-cheek humor and breathtaking stunts.

Tom at the height of his stardom at Selig Polyscope, before he left the ailing studio and became the top movie star at Fox Studios.

Literally glowing on the screen, Tom insisted that his cinematographers back light all of his scenes to make him radiate with on-screen charisma. By 1925, Tom was making more money than nearly every star in Hollywood and he was famous throughout the entire developed world.

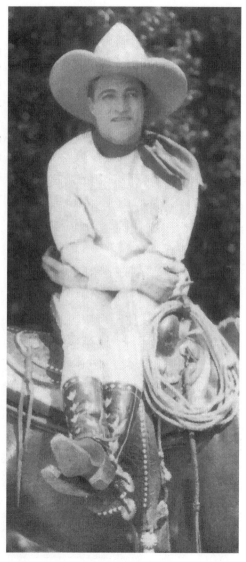

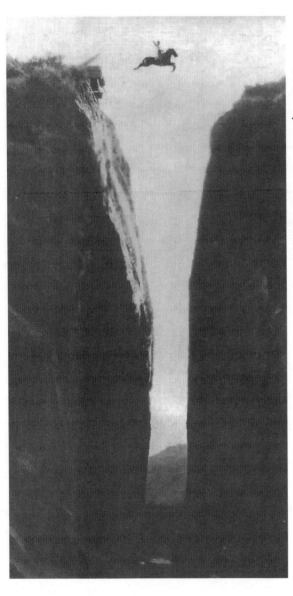

The famous jump over Newhall Pass in *Three Jumps Ahead* (1923). Revisionists claim the jump was a camera trick or that a stuntman did the jump. Note the ramp on the left side of the pass. If the jump were a camera trick, no ramp would have been needed. Those on the set that day say Tom did the jump, but he used a stunt double for his wonder horse, Tony.

Tom kept himself in peak physical condition so that he could do all of his own stunts. He realized that his sobriquet "the idol of every American boy" brought with it great responsibility. He publicly extolled clean living and healthy habits and never drank or smoked on film. He took great pains to keep his often wild and wooly private life away from the press and the public.

Fired by Fox Studios at the peak of his fame, Tom switched to struggling FBO Studios (later RKO) and then left the movies to headline with the Sells Floto Circus. His Tom Mix Circus began with great fanfare, but the depression took its toll on the circus' finances. Tom and daughter, Ruth, toured together and remained close until Tom's death.

Tom and Victoria Mix, right, posed for the press with President and Mrs. Coolidge during a visit to the White House in 1925. Tom was a lifelong Republican.

By the time Tom began touring with the circus, his marriage to fourth wife, Victoria, was over. He often spent time in the company of various circus showgirls. He later married a circus aerialist.

Still in peak condition at age 52, Tom returned to the movies to raise money for his circus ventures. Here, Tom scales a rope to the top of a castle tower in *My Pal the King* (1932)

Tom and Paul Hurst during a break in filming of *My Pal the King* (1932) The film contains the only surviving motion picture film of the Tom Mix Circus, which was incorporated into the plot of the film.

By 1938, Tom's circus was broke. Tom was broke too. He had sunk all of his money into the venture. Emaciated, exhausted and suffering from episodes of deep depression, Tom disappeared one night and fled to Europe where he was promised a fortune to perform in England and Denmark. The European tour would restore Tom's finances and his health.

At right, Tom as he appeared in *Rider of Death Valley* (1932), perhaps his finest film.

Fleeing financial ruin back in the United States, Tom arrived in London in 1938 and took the city by storm. His success in England resulted in an offer to headline with Circus Belli in Denmark for a salary of $20,000 per week. When Tom returned home in 1939, he had paid off all of his debts. A year later, Tom died in a car accident in Arizona on his way to another movie comeback.

Tom Mix, bottom left, as he saw himself. At the height of his fame, Tom realized that the best time of his life had been spent as a free-wheeling young cowboy on the 101 Ranch in northern Oklahoma. "In the old days, with the blue sky above me, a good horse under me, the vast acreage of the old 101 Ranch rolling green about me and a bacon-filled atmosphere from the chuck wagon calling me, I was the richest of men. How rich, the recent years alone have told me," he said somberly.

Filmography

Films made for Selig Polyscope Company: (All films are silent.)

Ranch Life in the Great Southwest (1909) P: William Selig; D: Frank Boggs; W: William Selig. Cast: Tom Mix, Pat Long, Johnny Mullins, Harry Grammar, Olive Stokes Mix. One reel. Released August 9, 1909. May have been released on August 9, 1910.

On the Little Big Horn, or Custer's Last Stand (1909) P: William Selig; D: Frank Boggs; W: Lannier Bartlett. Cast: Hobart Bosworth, Betty Harte, Frank Maish, Tom Mix. One reel. Released November 27, 1909. Disputed title.

In the Days of Daring (1909) P: William Selig; D: Tom Mix. Cast: Tom Mix. Disputed title.

Taming Wild Animals (1910) P: William Selig; D: Frank Boggs. Cast: Tom Mix, Kathlyn Williams, Tom Santschi.

Up San Juan Hill (1910) P: William Selig; D: Frank Boggs; W: Edward McWade. Cast: Tom Mix, Betty Harte, Tom Santschi. Disputed title.

Pride of the Range (1910) P: William Selig; D: Frank Boggs. Cast: Tom Mix, Tom Santschi, Betty Harte; Hoot Gibson, Milt Brown, Al Green. Disputed title.

The Pony Express (1910) Cast: Tom Mix. Disputed title.

The Millionaire Cowboy (1910) P: William Selig; D: Frank Boggs; W: Lanier Bartlett. Cast Tom Mix.

Briton and Boer (1910) P, D, W: William Selig. Cast: Tom Mix. Disputed title.

An Indian Wife's Devotion (1910) P, D, W: William Selig. Cast: Tom Mix.

The Trimming of Paradise Gulch (1910) P: William Selig, D: Frank Boggs; W: Lanier Bartlett. Cast: Tom Mix. Director is also listed as Otis Turner. One reel. Released June 2, 1910.

The Range Riders (1910) P: William Selig; D: Lynn Reynolds. Cast: Tom Mix, Myrtle Steadman, William V. Mong, Olive Stokes. One reel. Released June 9, 1910. May have been released on June 9, 1909.

In Old California, When the Gringos Came (1911) P: William Selig; D: Frank Boggs; W: Lanier Bartlett. Cast: Tom Mix, Kathlyn Williams, Tom Santschi.

In the Days of Gold (1911) P: Hobart Bosworth and F.E. Montgomery; D: Frank Boggs; W: Hobart Bosworth and F.E. Montgomery. Cast: Hobart Bosworth, Betty Harte, Roy Watson, Frank Richardson, Tom Santschi, Tom Mix.

The Schoolmaster of Mariposa (1911) P: William Selig; D: Frank Boggs; W: Lanier Bartlett. Cast: Hobart Bosworth, Betty Harte, Tom Mix.

Rescued by Her Lions (1911) P: William Selig; D: Frank Boggs; W: Edward McWade. Cast: Kathlyn Williams, Tom Santschi, Charles Clary, Tom Mix. Disputed title.

The Totem Mark (1911) P: William Selig; D: Frank Boggs; W: Edward McWade. Cast: Kathlyn Williams, Tom Santschi, Charles Clary, Tom Mix, Joseph Girard.

Kit Carson's Wooing (1911) P: William Selig; D: Frank Boggs; W: Lanier Bartlett. Cast: Hobart Bosworth, Betty Harte, Tom Mix, Tom Santschi.

Lost in the Arctic (1911) P: William Selig; D: Frank Boggs; W: Edward McWade. Cast: Kathlyn Williams, Tom Santschi, Charles Clary and Tom Mix.

Lost in the Jungle (1911) P: William Selig; D: Frank Boggs; W: Edward McWade. Cast: Kathlyn Williams, Tom Santschi, Charles Clary and Tom Mix.

The Cowboy and the Shrew (1911) Cast: Tom Mix, Herbert Rawlinson. One reel. Released April 10, 1911.

Wheels of Justice (1911)P: William Selig; D: Frank Boggs; W: Edward McWade. Cast: Kathlyn Williams, Tom Santschi, Charles Clary, Tom Mix, Joseph Girard. One reel. Released May 11, 1911.

Back to the Primitive (1911) 1911)P: William Selig; D: Frank Boggs; W: Edward McWade. Cast: Kathlyn Williams, Charles Clary, Tom Mix, Joseph Girard. One reel. Released May 11, 1911.

The Rose of Old San Augustine (1911) P: William Selig, D: Otis Turner. Cast: Kathlyn Williams, W.H. Stowell, Charles Clary, Tom Mix, Frank Weed, Vera Hamilton, True Broadman, Harrison Gray. One reel. Released June 1, 1911.

Captain Kate (1911) P: William Selig; D: Frank Boggs; W: Edward McWade. Cast: Kathlyn Williams, Tom Santschi, Charles Clary, Tom Mix, Frank Weed, Frank Smith, Tom Anderson. One reel. Released July 13, 1911.

Saved by the Pony Express (1911) P: William Selig; D,W:. Cast: Tom Mix. One reel. Released July 29, 1911.

Dad's Girls (1911) P: William Selig; D, W: Otis Turner. Cast: Kathlyn Williams, Frank Weed, Olive Stokes, Tom Mix, Stan Twist, Charles Clary, William Stowell, Louis Pierce. One reel. Released September 12, 1911.

Told in Colorado (1911) P: William Selig; D, W: Joseph A. Golden. Cast: William Duncan, T.J. Carrigan, Myrtle Steadman, Tom Mix, Olive Stokes, Otis B. Thayer. One reel. Released October 10, 1911.

Why the Sheriff Is a Bachelor (1911) D,W: Joseph A. Golden. Cast: Tom Mix, Myrtle Steadman, T.J. Carrigan, O.B. Thayer, William Duncan, George Hooker, Olive Stokes, George Allen. One reel. Released October 24, 1911.

Western Hearts (1911) D,W: Joseph A. Golden. Cast: Tom Mix, T.J. Carrigan, Otis B. Thayer, Myrtle Steadman, William Duncan, Ralph Kennedy, Dick Trenthwick. One reel. Released November 7, 1911.

The Tell-Tale Knife (1911) P, D: William Duncan. Cast: Tom Mix, William Duncan, Rex de Rosselli, Myrtle Steadman, Charles Tipton, Leon Watson. One reel. Released November 25, 1911.

A Romance of the Rio Grande (1911) P,D: Colin Campbell; W: Lanier Bartlett. Cast: Tom Mix, Betty Harte, William Duncan, Myrtle Steadman, George Hooker. One reel. Released December 12, 1911.

The Bully of Bingo Gulch (1911) D,W: Otis B. Thayer. Cast: William Duncan, Tom Mix, Charles Farra, Myrtle Steadman and Rex de Rosselli. One reel. Released December 26, 1911.

Outlaw Reward (1912). Cast: Tom Mix. Disputed title.

The Cowboy's Best Girl (1912) D: O.B. Thayer; W: Everitt McNeil. Cast: Myrtle Steadman, Rex de Rosselli, William Duncan, Tom Mix, Olive Mix, Robert Perry, Francis Carroll, Charles Canterbury, Florence Dye. One reel. Released January 16, 1912.

The Diamond S Ranch (1912) P: William Selig; D: Otis B. Thayer. Cast: Tom Mix, Frank Marsh, Olive Stokes Mix. One reel. Released February 29, 1912.

A Reconstructed Rebel (1912) P: William Selig; D: Colin Campbell; W:Lanier Bartlett. Cast: Tom Mix, Hobart Bosworth, Betty Harte, Tom Santschi. One reel. Released May, 1912.

How It Happened (1913) P, D, W: William Duncan. Tom Mix, Hobart Bosworth, Betty Harte, Tom Santschi. One reel. Released January 31, 1913.

Cowboy Millionaire (1913) P: William Selig; D: Tom Mix. Cast: Tom Mix. One reel. Released January 31, 1913.

The Range Law (1913) P: William Selig; D, W: William Duncan. Cast: William Duncan, Myrtle Steadman, Tom Mix and Lester Cuneo. One reel. Released February 14, 1913.

Juggling With Fate (1913) P: William Selig; D: Tom Mix; W: Edward McWade. Cast: Tom Mix, Myrtle Steadman, Lester Cuneo, Rex de Rosselli. One reel. Released March 3, 1913.

The Sheriff of Yavapai County (1913) P, D, W: William Duncan. Cast: William Duncan, Myrtle Steadman, Tom Mix, Lester Cuneo, Rex de Rosselli. One reel. Released March 21, 1913.

Pauline Cushman, the Federal Spy (1913) P: William Selig; W: Charles O. Nelson. Cast: Charles Clary, T.J. Commerford, Winnifred Greenwood, Lafayette McKee, Harry Lonsdale, Grant Forman, Walter Roberts, Tom Mix. One reel. Released March 27, 1913.

The Life-Timer (1913) P,D,W: William Duncan. Cast: William Duncan, Myrtle Steadman, Tom Mix, Florence Dye, Lester Cuneo. One reel. Released March 27, 1913.

The Shotgun Man and the Stage Driver (1913) P,D,W: William Duncan. Cast: William Duncan, Tom Mix, Myrtle Steadman, Florence Dye. One reel. Released April 3, 1913.

A Prisoner of Cabansas (1913) P,D: Colin Campbell; W: R.L. Terwilliger. Cast: Tom Mix, Tom Santschi, Bessie Eyton. One reel. Released April 3, 1913.

That Mail Order Suit (1913) D: William Duncan; W: Edgar Hungerford. Cast: Lester Cuneo, Tom Mix and Myrtle Steadman. One reel. Released April 18, 1913.

His Father's Deputy (1913) P,D,W: William Duncan. Cast: William Duncan, Tom Mix, Lester Cuneo, Rex de Rosselli, Marshal Stedman. One reel. Released May 17, 1913.

The Noisy Six (1913) P,D: Colin Campbell; W: O.A. Nelson. Cast: Tom Mix, Betty Harte, Bessie Eyton. One reel. Released May 21, 1913.

Religion and Gun Practice (1913) P, D: William Duncan; W: A.W. Corey. Cast: William Duncan, Myrtle Steadman, Tom Mix, Rex de Rosselli, Lester Cuneo. One reel. Released May 26, 1913.

The Wordless Message (1913) P, D: Colin Campbell; W: Hettie Gray Baker. Cast: Tom Mix, Tom Santschi. One reel. Released May 29, 1913.

Taming of a Tenderfoot (1913) D: William Duncan; W: Cornelius Shea. Cast: Lester Cuneo, Tom Mix, Myrtle Steadman, Florence Dye. One reel. Released June 7, 1913.

The Law and the Outlaw (1913) P, D: William Duncan; W: Tom Mix and U.E. Hungerford. Cast: William Duncan, Tom Mix, Myrtle Stedman, Lester Cuneo, J. Edgar Hungerford. Two reels. Released June 7, 1913.

Made a Coward (1913) P, D: William Duncan; W: A.W. Collins. Cast: William Duncan, Tom Mix, Lester Cuneo, Rex de Rosselli, Myrtle Stedman, Florence Dye. One reel. Released June 11, 1913.

Songs of Truce (1913) P, D: Colin Campbell; W: Hettie Gray Baker. Cast: Tom Mix, Tom Santschi, Kathlyn Williams. One reel. Released June 28, 1913.

The Marshal's Capture (1913) P,D: William Duncan; W: Elizabeth Frazer. Cast: William Duncan, Tom Mix, Lester Cuneo, Myrtle Stedman. One reel. Released June 28, 1913.

Sallie's Sure Shot (1913) P, D: William Duncan; W: Cornelius Shea. Cast: William Duncan, Tom Mix, Lester Cuneo, Myrtle Steadman. One reel. Released July 4, 1913.

Bud Doble Comes Back (1913) P, D: Colin Campbell; W: Frank Clark. Cast: Tom Mix, Tom Santschi. One reel. Released July 11, 1913.

The Only Chance (1913) D: William Duncan; W: C. Chester Wesley. Cast: William Duncan, Lester Cuneo, Tom Mix, Rex de Rosselli. One reel. Released July 14, 1913.

The Taming of Texas Pete (1913) P, D: William Duncan; W: Joseph F. Poland. Cast: William Duncan, Tom Mix, Betty Kastner, Myrtle Stedman. One reel. Released July 24, 1913.

The Stolen Moccasins (1913) P, D: William Duncan; W: Cornelius Shea. Cast: William Duncan, Myrtle Stedman, Tom Mix, Cornelius Shea. One reel. Released July 26, 1913.

An Apache's Gratitude (1913) P, D, W: William Duncan. Cast: William Duncan, Myrtle Stedman, Tom Mix, Jim Robson, Rex de Rosselli. One reel. Released August 1, 1913.

The Good Indian: A Saving Service Rewarded (1913) P: William Selig; D: William Duncan; W: Ethel C. Unland. One reel. Released August 22, 1913.

How Betty Made Good (1913) D: William Duncan; W: Ethel C. Unland. Cast: Lester Cuneo, Myrtle Stedman, Tom Mix, Rex de Rosselli, Howard Farrell, Sid Jordan, Vic Frith. One reel. Released August 27, 1913.

Howlin' Jones (1913) D: William Duncan; W: O.H. Nelson. Cast: William Duncan, Rex de Rosselli, Tom Mix, Sid Jordan, Vic Frith, Florence Dye, Myrtle Stedman, George Panky. One reel. Released September 4, 1913.

Tobias Wants Out (1913) P: Oscar Eagle; W: Arthur P. Hankins. Cast: Tom Mix. One reel. Released September 11, 1913.

The Rejected Lover's Luck (1913) D: William Duncan; W: Cornelius Shea. Cast: Lester Cuneo, Rex de Rosselli, Tom Mix, Myrtle Stedman, Vic Frith. One reel. Released September 19, 1913.

The Cattle Thief's Escape (1913) D: William Duncan; W: R.E. Hicks. Cast: William Duncan, Rex de Rosselli, Tom Mix, Myrtle Stedman, Lester Cuneo. One reel. Released October 1, 1913.

Saved from the Vigilantes (1913) D: William Duncan; W: Malcolm Douglass. Cast: William Duncan, Myrtle Stedman, Tom Mix, Hugh Mosher, Olive Stokes Mix, Rex de Rosselli. One reel. Released October 9, 1913.

The Silver Grindstone (1913) D: William Duncan; W: Eugene P. Lyle. Cast: William Duncan, Myrtle Stedman, Florence Dye, Tom Mix, Lester Cuneo, Rex de Rosselli. One reel. Released October 14, 1913.

Dishwash Dick's Counterfeit (1913) D: William Duncan and B. Williams. Cast: Rex de Rosselli, Myrtle Stedman, Tom Mix, Lester Cuneo. One reel. Released October 21, 1913.

A Muddle in Horse Thieves (1913) P: William Selig; D: Tom Mix; W: Elizabeth Frazer. Cast: Tom Mix. One reel. Released October 25, 1913.

The Sheriff and the Rustler (1913) P,D: William Duncan; W: Tom Mix. Cast: Lester Cuneo, Tom Mix, George Panky, Rex de Rosselli, Neil Broaded, Vic Frith, B.L. Jones. Two reels. Released November 1913.

The Schoolmarm's Shooting Match (1913) D: William Duncan; W: Cornelius Shea. Cast: William Duncan, Myrtle Stedman, Lester Cuneo, Rex de Rosselli, Tom Mix, Hugh Mosier, William Jones. One reel. Released November 7, 1913.

The Child of the Prairies (1913) P: William Duncan; W: Tom Mix. Cast: Tom Mix, Lester Cuneo, Florence Dye, Myrtle Stedman, Vic Frith, Hugh Mosier, Sid Jordan. One reel. Released November 13, 1913.

The Escape of Jim Dolan (1913) P: William Selig; D: Colin Campbell; W: Tom Mix. Tom Mix, Betty Harte, Tom Santschi, Lester Cuneo, Nip Van, Myrtle Stedman, Rex de Rosselli, Vic Frith, Sid Jordan, Hugh Mosier. One reel. Released November 13, 1913.

Local Color (1913) P: William Selig; W, D: Tom Mix. Cast: Tom Mix. One reel. Released November 21, 1913. Disputed title, believed confused with 1916 film of same title.

Cupid in the Cow Camp (1913) Cast: Tom Mix, Myrtle Stedman, Lester Cuneo, Vic Frith, Sid Jordan, Rex de Rosselli, Art Cook, Marshall Stedman. One reel. Released November 26, 1913.

Physical Culture on the Quarter Circle V Bar (1913) D: William Duncan; W: Edwin Ray Coffin. Cast: William Duncan, Rex de Rosselli, Tom Mix, Lester Cuneo, Myrtle Stedman, Florence Dye, Hugh Mosier. One reel. Released December 11, 1913.

Buster's Little Game (1913) P, D: William Duncan; W: C.W. Vansant. Cast: William Duncan, Lester Cuneo, Myrtle Stedman, Florence Dye, Rex de Rosselli, Tom Mix. One reel. Released December 17, 1913.

Mother Love vs. Gold (1913) P, D: William Duncan; W: John M. Kiskadden. Cast: Willian Duncan, Myrtle Stedman, Lester Cuneo, Tom Mix, Florence Dye, Rex de Rosselli. One reel. Released December 23, 1913.

The Sheriff's Girl (1914) P: William Selig. Cast: Tom Mix. Disputed title.

Buffalo Hunting (1914) P: William Selig; D: F.J. Grandon; W: Gilson Willets. Cast: Tom Mix. Disputed title. Possibly produced by 101 Ranch's film studio and released in 1912.

Single Shot Parker (1914) P: William Selig. Cast: Tom Mix. Disputed title. Most likely a reissue title of *The Heart of Texas Ryan* (1916).

By Unseen Hand (1914) P, D: William Duncan; W: Hardee Kirkland. Cast: William Duncan, Lester Cuneo, Rex de Rosselli, Tom Mix, Myrtle Stedman, Marshall Stedman. One reel. Released January 7, 1914.

A Friend in Need (1914) P,D,W: William Duncan. Cast: William Duncan, Florence Dye, Eleanor Blevins, Lester Cuneo, Tom Mix, Charles Wheelock. One reel. Released January 22, 1914.

The Little Sister (1914) P: William Duncan; D: William Selig; W: Merla Marion Metcalfe. Cast: Tom Mix, William Duncan, Grace Tregarthen, Lester Cuneo, Charles Wheelock. One reel. Released February 5, 1914.

Shotgun Jones (1914) P, D: Colin Campbell; W: Bertrand W. Sinclair, Bertha M. Bower. Cast: Tom Mix. Two reels. Released April 14, 1914.

Me an' Bill (1914) P: William Selig; D, W: Colin Campbell. Cast: Tom Mix. Two reels. Released June 6, 1914.

When the Cook Fell Ill (1914) P, D: Colin Campbell; W: B.M. Bower. Cast: Tom Mix, Wheeler Oakman, Frank Clark, Frank Feehan. One reel. Released June 9, 1914.

The Leopard's Foundling (1914) P: Kathlyn Williams; D: Colin Campbell; W: Mabel Heckes Justice. Cast: Kathlyn Williams, Tom Mix. One reel. Released June 11, 1914.

In Defiance of the Law (1914) P, D: Colin Campbell; W: James Oliver Curwood. Cast: Tom Mix, Wheeler Oakman, Bessie Eyton, Joe King, Frank Clark, Baby Lillian Wade, Lillian Hayward. Three reels. Released June 13, 1914.

The Wilderness Trail (1914) P, D: Colin Campbell; W: James Oliver Curwood. Cast: Wheeler Oakman, Joe King, Tom Mix, Kathlyn Williams, Bessie Eyton, Lillian Hayward, Frank Clark. One reel. Released June 26, 1914.

Wiggs Takes the Rest Cure (1914) P, D: F. J. Grandon, W: W.E. Wing. Cast: Tom Mix. One reel. Released June 26, 1914.

Lure of the Ladies (1914) P, D: Oscar Eagle; W: Will M. Hough. Cast: Tom Mix. One reel. Released July 7, 1914.

Etienne of the Glad Heart (1914) P, D: Colin Campbell; W: Mabel Heckes. Cast: Tom Mix, Wheeler Oakman, Bessie Eyton, Frank Clark, Lillian Hayward. Two reels. Released July 15, 1914.

His Fight (1914) P, D: Colin Campbell; W: James Oliver Curwood. Cast: Tom Mix, Tom Santschi, Kathlyn Williams. One reel. Released July 20, 1914.

The Reveler (1914) P, D: Colin Campbell; W: B.M. Bower. Cast: Tom Mix. One reel. Released July 31, 1914.

When the West Was Young (1914) P, D: Colin Campbell; W: Cyrus Townsend Brady. Cast: Bessie Eyton, Wheeler Oakman, Jack McDonald, Gertrude Ryan, Frank Clark, Tom Mix, Harry Lonsdale. Two reels. Released August 1914.

The White Mouse (1914) P, D: Colin Campbell; W: James Oliver Curwood. Cast: Tom Mix, Wheeler Oakman, Bessie Eyton, Joe King. Two reels. Released August 4, 1914.

Chip of the Flying U (1914) D: Colin Campbell; W: B.M. Bower. Cast; Tom Mix, Kathlyn Williams, Frank Clark, Wheeler Oakman, Bessie Eyton, Fred Huntley. Three reels. Released August 17, 1914.

To Be Called For (1914) P, D: F.J. Grandon; W: Wallace C. Clifton. Cast: Tom Mix. One reel. Released August 19, 1914.

The Fifth Man (1914) P, D: F. J. Grandon; W: James Olliver Curwood. Cast: Tom Mix, Tom Santschi, Frank Walsh, Charles Clary, Bessie Eyton, Lafe McKee, Roy Watson. Three reels. Released August 22, 1914.

Jim (1914) P, D: F.J. Grandon; W: Wallace C. Clifton. Cast: Tom Mix. One reel. Released September 2, 1914.

The Lonesome Trail (1914) P,D: Colin Campbell; W: B.M. Bower. Cast: Tom Mix, Kathlyn Williams. One reel. Released September 2, 1914.

The Livid Flame (1914) P,D: F.J. Grandon; W: Walter E. Wing. Cast: Tom Mix. Two reels. Released September 3, 1914.

Four Minutes Late (1914) P, D: F.J. Grandon; W: James Oliver Curwood. Cast: Tom Mix. One reel. Released September 9, 1914.

The Real Thing In Cowboys (1914) P, D: Tom Mix. W: Hettie Gray Baker. Cast: Tom Mix, Goldie Colwell, Miss Townsend. One reel. Released September 10, 1914.

Hearts and Masks (1914) P, D: Colin Campbell; W: Harold McGrath. Cast: Tom Mix, Kathlyn Williams. Three reels. Released September 15, 1914.

The Way of the Bad Man (1914) P, D, W: Tom Mix. Cast: Tom Mix, Leo Maloney, Goldie Colwell, Roy Watson. One reel. Released September 16, 1914.

The Moving Picture Cowboy (1914) P: Lester Cuneo; D, W: Tom Mix. Cast: Tom Mix, Ellinor Blevins, Lester Cuneo, Sid Jordan, W.L. Lewis, Charles Wheelock, Bobby Murdock. Two reels. Released September 16, 1914.

The Mexican (1914) P, D: Tom Mix. W: Lynn Reynolds. Cast: Tom Mix, Lillian Wade, Leo Maloney, Goldie Colwell. One reel. Released September 24, 1914.

The Going of the White Swan (1914) P, D: Colin Campbell; W: Gilbert Parker. Cast: Bessie Eyton, Wheeler Oakman, Tom Mix, Frank Clark, Roy Clark, Joe King. Two reels. Released September 28, 1914.

Jimmy Hayes and Muriel (1914) P, D: Tom Mix; W: Sidney Porter. Cast: Tom Mix, Goldie Colwell, Leo Maloney, Roy Watson. One reel. Released September 28, 1914.

Why The Sheriff Is A Bachelor (1914) P, D, W: Tom Mix. Cast: Tom Mix, Leo Maloney, Goldie Colwell, Roy Watson. One reel. Released October 10, 1914.

Garrison's Finish (1914) P, D: F.J. Grandon, W: B.M. Ferguson. Cast: Tom Mix. Three reels. October 10, 1914.

The Losing Fight (1914) P, D, W: Colin Campbell. Cast: Tom Mix. One reel. Released October 15, 1914.

The Ranger's Romance (1914) P, D, W: Tom Mix. Cast: Tom Mix, Goldie Colwell, Roy Watson, Inez Walker. One reel. Released October 15, 1914.

The Tell-Tale Knife (2nd version) (1914) P, D, W: Tom Mix. Cast: Tom Mix, Goldie Colwell, Harry Loverin, Leo Maloney, Hoot Gibson. One reel. Released October 15, 1914.

Out of Petticoat Lane (1914) P, D, W: F.J. Grandon. Cast: Tom Mix. Two reels. Released October 24, 1914.

The Sheriff's Reward (1914) P, D, W: Tom Mix. Cast: Tom Mix, Goldie Colwell, Leo Maloney, Roy Watson. One reel. Released October 24, 1914.

The Scapegoat (1914) P, D, W: Tom Mix. Cast: Tom Mix, Goldie Colwell, Leo Maloney. One reel. Released October 24, 1914.

If I Were Young Again (1914) P, D: F. J. Grandon; W: Gilson Willets. Cast: Tom Mix. Two reels. Released October 24, 1914.

Young Girl and Mine (1914) D: F. J. Grandon; W: Gilson Willets. Cast: Kathlyn Williams, Tom Mix. One reel. Released October 31, 1914.

The Tell-Tale Knife (3rd version) (1914) P, D, W: Tom Mix. Cast: Tom Mix, Goldie Colwell, Roy Watson, Inez Walker. One reel. Released November 7, 1914.

Saved by a Watch (1914) P, D, W: Tom Mix. Cast: Tom Mix, Goldie Colwell, Leo Maloney, Inez Walker. One reel. Released November 11, 1914.

The Rival Stage Lines (1914) P, D: Tom Mix; W: Allen A. Martin. Cast: Tom Mix, Goldie Colwell, Leo Maloney, Sid Jordan, Inez Walker, Lynn F. Reynolds. One reel. Released November 12, 1914.

In the Days of the Thundering Herd (1914) P: William Selig; D: Colin Campbell; W: Gilson Willets. Cast: Tom Mix, Bessie Eyton, Red Wing, Wheeler Oakman, John Bowers, Major Gordon "Pawnee Bill" Lillie. Five reels. Released November 12, 1914.

The Soul Mate (1914) P, D: F. J. Grandon; W: Mark Reardon. Cast: Tom Mix, Kathlyn Williams. One reel. Released November 14, 1914.

Lure of the Windigo (1914) P: William Selig; D: F. J. Grandon; W: Mabel Heckes Justice. Cast: Tom Mix. Two reels. Released November 28, 1914.

The Man from the East (1914) P: William Selig; D, W: Tom Mix. Cast: Tom Mix, Goldie Colwell, Leo Maloney, Pat Chrisman, Inez Walker, Hoot Gibson, R.H. Kelly, C.W. Bachman, Ed Jones, Susie Morella. One reel. Released November 28, 1914.

Wade Brent Pays (1914) D: F. J. Grandon; W: Marie Wing, F. J. Grandon. Cast: Tom Mix, Tom Santschi. One reel. Released December 8, 1914.

Cactus Jake, Heart Breaker (1914) D: Tom Mix; W: Edwin Ray Coffin. Cast: Tom Mix, Goldie Colwell, Leo Maloney, Josephine Miller. One reel. Released December 10, 1914.

Flower of Faith (1914) P, D: F. J. Grandon; W: Will M. Hough. Cast: Kathlyn Williams, Tom Mix. Two reels. Released December 10, 1914.

A Militant School Ma'am (1914) P: William Selig; D: Tom Mix; W: Ray Coffin. Cast: Tom Mix, Goldie Colwell, Leo Maloney. One reel. Released December 28, 1914.

Weary Goes Wooing (1915) Cast: Tom Mix. Disputed title.

Cactus Jim (1915) Cast: Tom Mix, Goldie Colwell, Lynn Reynolds. Disputed title.

Western Justice (1915) Cast: Tom Mix. (Contains rodeo footage of Tom only). Re-release title or disputed title.

Harold's Bad Man—A Story of Luck and Love (1915) P, D: Tom Mix; W: Edwin Ray Coffin. Cast: Tom Mix, Goldie Colwell, Leo Maloney, Pat Chrisman, Sid Jordan, Ed Jones. One reel. Released January 1, 1915.

Cactus Jim's Shop Girl (1915) P: William Selig; D: Tom Mix; W: Ray Coffin. Cast: Tom Mix, Goldie Colwell, Lynn Reynolds, Sid Jordan. One reel. Released January 9, 1915.

Heart's Desire (1915) P: William Selig; D: F. J. Grandon; W: Wallace C. Clifton. Cast: Tom Mix. One reel. Released January 13, 1915.

The Grizzly Gulch Chariot Race (1915) P: William Selig; D: Tom Mix; W: O.A. Nelson. Cast: Tom Mix, Inez Walker, Sid Jordan, Dick Crawford, Roy Watson. One reel. Released January 13, 1915.

Forked Trails (1915) P: William Selig; D: Tom Mix; W: William McLeod Raine. Cast: Tom Mix, Goldie Colwell, Sid Jordan, Pat Chrisman. One reel. Released January 16, 1915.

Roping A Bride (1915) P, D: Tom Mix. W: E. Lynn Summers. Cast: Tom Mix, Goldie Colwell, Sid Jordan, C.W. Bachman, Roy Watson, Inez Walker. One reel. Released January 26, 1915.

Bill Hayward, Producer (1915) P: William Selig; D: Tom Mix; W: Cecille B. Peterson. Cast: Tom Mix, Mabel van Buren, Sid Jordan, Goldie Colwell, Roy Watson, George Fawcett, Pat Chrisman, Dick Hunter, Dick Crawford, Ed Jones. One reel. Released February 1, 1915.

Hearts of the Jungle (1915) P: William Selig; D: F.J. Grandon; W: Wallace C. Clifton. Cast: Tom Mix. One reel. Released February 11, 1915.

Slim Higgins (1915) P, D, W: Tom Mix. Cast: Tom Mix, Goldie Colwell, Roy Watson, Pat Chrisman. One reel. Released February 11, 1915.

A Child of the Prairie (1915) (2nd version) P: William Selig; D, W: Tom Mix. Cast: Tom Mix, Louella Maxim, Baby Norma Maxam, Ed J. Brady, Fay Robinson, Rose Robinson. Two reels. Released February 24, 1915.

The Man From Texas (1915) P, D, W: Tom Mix. Cast: Tom Mix, Leo Maloney, Sid Jordan, Hoot Gibson, Goldie Colwell, Louella Maxam, Ed Brady. Two reels. Released February 24, 1915.

The Stagecoach Driver and the Girl (1915) P, D, W: Tom Mix. Cast: Tom Mix, Goldie Coldwell, Louella Maxim, Sid Jordan, Ed Brady, Ed Jones. One reel. Released February 26, 1915.

Jack's Pals (1915) P, D: P.J. Grandon; W: C.B. Murphy. Cast: Tom Mix. One reel. Released March 3, 1915.

The Puny Soul of Peter Rand (1915) D: F.J. Grandon; W: Walter E. Wing. Cast: Tom Mix, Tom Santschi. One reel. Released March 6, 1915.

Sagebrush Tom (1915) P, D, W: Tom Mix. Cast: Tom Mix, Myrtle Stedman, Goldie Colwell, Ed J. Brady. One reel. Released March 8, 1915.

The Outlaw's Bride (1915) P: William Selig; D: Tom Mix; W: Cornelius Shea. Cast: Tom Mix, Eugenie Ford, Ed J. Brady, Pat Chrisman. One reel. Released March 13, 1915.

Ma's Girls (1915) P, D, W: Tom Mix. Cast: Tom Mix, Eugenie Forde, Goldie Colwell, Ed J. Brady, Louella Maxam. One reel. Released March 20, 1915.

The Legal Light (1915) P: William Selig; D: Tom Mix; W: Edwin Ray Coffin. Cast: Tom Mix, Eugenie Forde, Ed J. Brady. One reel. Released March 20, 1915.

Getting A Start In Life (1915) P, D: Tom Mix; W: James Oliver Curwood. Cast: Tom Mix, Louella Maxam, Sid Jordan. One reel. Released March 29, 1915.

Mrs. Murphy's Cooks (1915) P, D, W: Tom Mix. Cast: Tom Mix, Louella Maxam, Anna Dodge. One reel. Released April 3, 1915.

The Face At The Window (1915) P, D: F.J. Grandon; W: Wallace C. Clifton. Cast: Tom Mix. One reel. Released April 10, 1915.

The Conversation of Smiling Tom (1915) P, D: Tom Mix; W: Emma Bell. Cast: Tom Mix, Sid Jordan, Louella Maxam, Eugenie Forde, William Brunton. One reel. Released April 10, 1915.

An Arizona Wooing (1915) P, D: Tom Mix; W: William McLeod Raine. Cast: Tom Mix, Bessie Eyton, Sid Jordan, Pat Chrisman, Louella Maxam, Billy Brunton. One reel. Released April 26, 1915.

A Matrimonial Boomerang (1915) P: William Selig; D: Tom Mix; W: Edith Blumer. Cast: Tom Mix, Louella Maxam, Pat Chrisman, Howard Farrell. One reel. Released April 30, 1915.

Saved By Her Horse (1915) P, D: Tom Mix; W: Cornelius Shea. Cast: Tom Mix, Louella Maxam, Sid Jordan, Pat Chrisman. One reel. Released May 26, 1915.

Pals in Blue (1915) P: William Selig; D, W: Tom Mix. Cast: Tom Mix, Ada Gleason, Sid Jordan, Howard Farrell, Pat Chrisman, Edward Bradley, Bob Anderson, Al Merrill, Eugenie Ford. Three reels. Released May 26, 1915.

The Heart of the Sheriff (1915) P, D, W: Tom Mix. Cast: Tom Mix, Sid Jordan, Louella Maxam. One reel. Released June 8, 1915.

The Girl of Gold Gulch (1915) P, D: Tom Mix; W: Cornelius Shea. Cast: Tom Mix, Victoria Forde, Joe Ryan, Ed Jones. One reel. Released June 10, 1915.

The Parson Who Fled West (1915) P, D: Burton L. King; W: Malcolm Douglas. Cast: Tom Mix. One reel. Released July 3, 1915.

The Foreman of the Bar Z Ranch (1915) P, D: Tom Mix. W: Wallace C. Clifton. Cast: Tom Mix, Louella Maxam, Pat Chrisman. One reel. Released July 15, 1915.

The Child, the Dog and the Villain (1915) P, D: Tom Mix; W: Campbell McCullock. Cast: Tom Mix, Louella Maxam, Sid Jordan, Pat Chrisman, Leo Maloney, Pearl Hoxie. One reel. Released July 17, 1915.

The Taking of Mustang Pete (1915) P, D: Tom Mix; W: Emma Bell. Cast: Tom Mix, Louella Maxam, Pat Chrisman, Leo Maloney, Henry Pagett. One reel. Released July 24, 1915.

The Gold Dust and the Squaw (1915) P, D: Tom Mix; W: Cornelius Shea. Cast: Tom Mix, Betty O'Neal, Sid Jordan, Leo Maloney, Pat Chrisman, Bob Anderson. One reel. Released July 31, 1915.

The Lucky Deal (1915) P, D, W: Tom Mix. Cast: Tom Mix, Betty O'Neal, Sid Jordan, Leo Maloney, Pat Chrisman. One reel. Released August 7, 1915.

Never Again (1915) P, D, W: Tom Mix. Cast: Tom Mix, Victoria Forde, Sid Jordan, Leo Maloney. One reel. Released August 8, 1915.

How Weary Went Wooing (1915) P, D: Tom Mix; W: B.M. Bower. Cast: Tom Mix, Victoria Forde, Sid Jordan, Leo Maloney. One reel. Released September 4, 1915.

Never Again (1915) (2nd version) P, D, W: Tom Mix. Cast: Tom Mix, Victoria Forde, Sid Jordan, Leo Maloney. One reel. Released September 11, 1915.

The Range Girl and the Cowboy (1915) P, D, W: Tom Mix. Cast: Tom Mix, Victoria Forde, Leo Maloney, Sid Jordan. One reel. Released September 11, 1915.

The Auction Sale of Run Down Ranch (1915) P, D: Tom Mix; W: Cornelius Shea. Cast: Tom Mix, Victoria Forde, Pat Chrisman, Leo Maloney, Joe Simkins. One reel. Released September 11, 1915.

Her Slight Mistake (1915) P, D: Tom Mix, W: E. Winthrop Sargent. Cast: Tom Mix, Howard Farrell, Leo Maloney, Pat Chrisman, Ethelyn (Babe) Chrisman. One reel. Released September 18, 1915.

The Girl and the Mail Bag (1915) P, D: Tom Mix; W: Cornelius Shea. Cast: Tom Mix, Victoria Forde, Leo Maloney, Sid Jordan. One reel. Released September 25, 1915.

The Stagecoach Guard (1915) P, D, W: Tom Mix. Cast: Tom Mix, Victoria Forde, Sid Jordan. One reel. Released October 9, 1915.

The Brave Deserve the Fair (1915) P: William Selig; D, W: Tom Mix. Cast: Tom Mix, Leo Maloney, Victoria Forde, Sid Jordan. Two reels. Released October 9, 1915.

The Race for a Gold Mine (1915) P, D: Tom Mix; W: Cornelius Shea. Cast: Tom Mix, Victoria Forde, Sid Jordan, Pat Chrisman. One reel. Released October 16, 1915.

The Foreman's Choice (1915) P, D: Tom Mix; W: Cornelius Shea. Cast: Tom Mix, Victoria Forde, Pat Chrisman, Sid Jordan, Howard Farrell. One reel. Released October 20, 1915.

Athletic Ambitions (1915) P, D, W: Tom Mix. Cast: Tom Mix, Victoria Forde, Pat Chrisman, Sid Jordan, Howard Farrell. One reel. Released October 23, 1915.

The Tenderfoot's Triumph (1915) P, D: Tom Mix; W: Cornelius Shea. Cast: Tom Mix, Hazel Daley, Joe Simkins, Sid Jordan, Pat Chrisman. One reel. Released October 29, 1915.

The Chef At Circle G (1915) P: William Selig; D: Tom Mix; W: Edwin Ray Coffin. Cast: Tom Mix, Hazel Page, Pat Chrisman, Sid Jordan. One reel. Released October 30, 1915.

The Impersonation of Tom (1915) P, D: Tom Mix; W: Cornelius Shea. Cast: Tom Mix, Hazel Daley, Sid Jordan, Pat Chrisman. One reel. Released November 6, 1915.

With the Aid of the Law (1915) P, D: Tom Mix; W: Marshal E. Gamon. Cast: Tom Mix. One reel. Released November 11, 1915.

Bad Man Bobbs (1915) P, D: Tom Mix; W: Edwin Ray Coffin. Cast: Tom Mix, Ethelyn (Babe) Chrisman, Sid Jordan, Pat Chrisman. One reel. Released November 11, 1915.

On the Eagle's Trail (1915) P, D: Tom Mix; W: Cornelius Shea. Cast: Tom Mix, Victoria Forde, Joe Simkins, Sid Jordan. One reel. Released November 27, 1915.

The Wagon Trail (1916) Cast: Tom Mix. Disputed title.

The Long Trail (1916) P: William Selig; D: Frank Boggs; W: Tom Mix. Cast: Tom Mix, Frank Walsh. Disputed title.

The Desert Calls Its Own (1916) Cast: Tom Mix, Victoria Forde, Ethelyn (Babe) Chrisman, Sid Jordan, Pat Chrisman. One reel. Released January 1, 1916.

A Mix-Up in the Movies (1916) P, D, W: Tom Mix. Cast: Tom Mix, Pat Chrisman, Babe Chrisman, Joe Simkins, Sid Jordan. One reel. Released January 22, 1916.

Making Good (1916) P, D, W: Tom Mix. Cast: Tom Mix, Victoria Forde, Pat Chrisman, Joe Ryan. One reel. Released January 23, 1916.

The Passing of Pete (1916) P, D, W: Tom Mix. Cast: Tom Mix, Victoria Forde, Ethelyn (Babe) Chrisman, Sid Jordan, Betty Keller. One reel. Released February 11, 1916.

A $5,000 Elopement (1916) P, D: Tom Mix; W: Cornelius Shea. Cast: Tom Mix, Victoria Forde, Sid Jordan, Joe Ryan, Chet Ryan. One reel. Released March 3, 1916.

Trilby's Love Disaster (1916) P, D, W: Tom Mix. Cast; Tom Mix, Victoria Forde, Ethelyn (Babe) Chrisman, Joe Ryan, Betty Keller. One reel. Released March 4, 1916.

Along the Border (1916) P, D, W: Tom Mix. Cast: Tom Mix, Victoria Forde, Sid Jordan, Joe Ryan, Joe Simkins. One reel. Released March 18, 1916.

Too Many Chefs (1916) P, D, W: Tom Mix. Cast: Tom Mix, Victoria Forde, Joe Ryan. One reel. Released April 1, 1916.

The Man Within (1916) P: William Selig; D: Tom Mix; W: E. Lynn Summers. Cast; Tom Mix, Victoria Forde, Sid Jordan, Pat Chrisman, Joe Ryan. Three reels. Released April 15, 1916.

The Sheriff's Duty (1916) P, D, W: Tom Mix. Cast: Tom Mix, Betty Keller, Pat Chrisman, Sid Jordan, Joe Ryan. One reel. Released April 22, 1916.

Crooked Trails (1916) P, D, W: Tom Mix. Cast: Tom Mix, Victoria Forde, Pat Chrisman, Sid Jordan, Joe Ryan. One reel. Released May 13, 1916.

Going West to Make Good (1916) P, D, W: Tom Mix. Cast: Tom Mix, Victoria Forde, Joe Ryan. One reel. Released May 13, 1916.

The Cowpuncher's Peril (1916) P, D, W: Tom Mix. Tom Mix, Victoria Forde, Pat Chrisman, Joe Ryan. One reel. Released May 26, 1916.

Taking A Chance (1916) P, D, W: Tom Mix. Cast: Tom Mix, Victoria Forde, Pat Chrisman, Joe Ryan. One reel. Released June 3, 1916.

Some Duel (1916) P, D, W: Tom Mix. Cast: Tom Mix, Victoria Forde, Joe Ryan, Sid Jordan, Pat Chrisman. One reel. Released June 17, 1916.

Legal Advice (1916) P, D, W: Tom Mix. Cast: Tom Mix, Sid Jordan, Victoria Forde, Pat Chrisman, Joe Ryan, George Panky. One reel. Released June 24, 1916.

Shooting Up the Movies (1916) P, D, W: Tom Mix. Cast: Tom Mix, Victoria Forde, Sid Jordan, Howard Farrell, Hazel Daly, Joe Ryan. Two reels. Released July 1, 1916.

Local Color (aka Local Color on the A-1 Ranch) (1916) P, D, W: Tom Mix. Cast: Tom Mix, Victoria Forde, Sid Jordan, Joe Simkins, Joe Ryan. One reel. Released July 7, 1916.

An Angelic Attitude (1916) P, D: Tom Mix; W: Edwin Ray Coffin. Cast: Tom Mix, Victoria Forde, Joe Ryan, Sid Jordan. One reel. Released July 15, 1916.

A Western Masquerade (1916) P, D, W: Tom Mix. Cast: Tom Mix, Victoria Forde, Joe Ryan, Sid Jordan. One reel. Released July 22, 1916.

A Bear of a Story (1916) P, D, W: Tom Mix. Cast: Tom Mix, Victoria Forde, Sid Jordan, Betty Keller. One reel. Released July 29, 1916.

Roping A Sweetheart (1916) P, D, W: Tom Mix. Cast: Tom Mix, Victoria Forde, Sid Jordan, Pat Chrisman. One reel. Released August 5, 1916.

Tom's Strategy (1916) P, D, W: Tom Mix. Cast: Tom Mix, Victoria Forde, Betty Keller, Howard Farrell. One reel. Released August 12, 1916.

The Taming of Grouchy Bill (1916) P, D, W: Tom Mix. Cast: Tom Mix, Victoria Forde, Sid Jordan, Joe Ryan. One reel. Released August 19, 1916.

The Pony-Express Rider (1916) P, D, W: Tom Mix. Cast: Tom Mix, Pat Chrisman, Sid Jordan, Victoria Forde, Joe Ryan. Two reels. Released August 26, 1916.

A Corner in Water (1916) P, D, W: Tom Mix. Cast: Tom Mix, Victoria Forde, Pat Chrisman, Joe Ryan, Chet Ryan. One reel. Released September 2, 1916.

The Raiders (1916) P, D, W: Tom Mix. Cast: Tom Mix, Victoria Forde, Pat Chrisman, Sid Jordan. One reel. Released September 9, 1916.

The Canby Hill Outlaws (1916) P, D, W: Tom Mix. Cast: Tom Mix, Victoria Forde, Pat Chrisman, Sid Jordan. One reel. Released September 10, 1916.

A Mistake in Rustlers (1916) P, D, W: Tom Mix. Cast: Tom Mix, Victoria Forde, Leo Maloney, Sid Jordan, Pat Chrisman. One reel. Released September 23, 1916.

An Eventful Evening (1916) P, D: Tom Mix; W: Victoria Forde. Cast: Tom Mix, Victoria Forde, Betty Keller, Pat Chrisman. One reel. Released September 30, 1916.

The Way of the Red Man (1916) W, D: Tom Mix. Cast: Tom Mix. One reel. Released October 3, 1916. Disputed title.

A Close Call (1916) P, D, W: Tom Mix. Cast: Tom Mix, Victoria Forde, Pat Chrisman, Joe Ryan, Sid Jordan. One reel. Released October 7, 1916.

Tom's Sacrifice (1916) P, W: Victoria Forde. Cast: Tom Mix, Victoria Forde, Joe Ryan, Howard Farrell, Joe Simkins, Sid Jordan. One reel. Released October 14, 1916.

When Cupid Slipped (1916) P, W: Victoria Forde. D: Tom Mix. Cast: Tom Mix, Pat Chrisman, Victoria Forde, Sid Jordan. One reel. Released October 21, 1916.

The Sheriff's Blunder (1916) P, D, W: Tom Mix. Cast: Tom Mix, Sid Jordan, Victoria Forde. Two reels. Released November 4, 1916.

Mistakes Will Happen (1916) P, D, W: Tom Mix. Cast: Tom Mix, Victoria Forde, Pat Chrisman, Sid Jordan. One reel. Released November 11, 1916.

The Golden Thought (1916) P, D: Tom Mix; W: J.A. Lacy. Cast: Tom Mix, Victoria Forde, Sid Jordan, Earl Deming, Alice Burke, Barney Furey, Lily Clark, Pat Chrisman. Two reels. Released December 9, 1916.

Twisted Trails (1916) P, D: Tom Mix; W: Edwin Ray Coffin. Cast: Tom Mix, Bessie Eyton, Eugenie Besserer, Al W. Filson, William Machin, Pat Chrisman, Sid Jordan. Three reels. Released December 11, 1916.

Starring in Western Stuff (1916) P, D, W: Tom Mix. Cast: Tom Mix, Victoria Forde, Sid Jordan, Pat Chrisman, Ethelyn (Babe) Chrisman, Pete Bender. One reel. Released December 23, 1916.

The Saddle Girth (1917) P, D, W: Tom Mix. Cast: Tom Mix, Louella Maxam, Sid Jordan. One reel. Released January 23, 1917.

The Luck That Jealousy Brought (1917) P, D: Tom Mix; W: Cornelius Shea. Cast: Tom Mix, Louella Maxam, Sid Jordan, Pat Chrisman. One reel. Released January 24, 1917.

Films made for Fox Studios: (All films are silent.)

Hearts and Saddles (1917) P: William Fox; D: Tom Mix and Robert Eddy; W: Tom Mix. Cast: Tom Mix, Victoria Forde, Sid Jordan, Pat Chrisman, Victor Portez, George Panky. Two reels. Released March 11 or March 19, 1917.

A Roman Cowboy (1917) P: William Fox; D, W: Tom Mix. Cast: Tom Mix, Sid Jordan, Victoria Forde, Vic Frith. Two reels. Released May 6 or May 13, 1917.

Six-Cylinder Love (1917) P: William Fox; D, W: Tom Mix. Cast: Tom Mix, Victoria Forde, Sid Jordan. Two reels. Released June 10 or June 11, 1917.

A Soft Tenderfoot (1917) P: William Fox; D, W: Tom Mix. Cast: Tom Mix, Victoria Forde, Pat Chrisman, Sid Jordan, Billy Mason. Two reels. Released July 5 or July 23, 1917.

Durand of the Badlands (1917) P: William Fox; D: Richard Stanton; W: Maibelle H. Justice. Cast: Dustin Farnum, Tom Mix, Winifred Kingston, Frankie Lee, Babe Chrisman, Lee Morris, Amy Jerome, Tony. Five reels. Released August 12, 1917.

Tom and Jerry Mix (1917) P, D, W: Tom Mix. Cast: Tom Mix, Victoria Forde, Sid Jordan, Pat Chrisman, Floyd Anderson (aka Floyd Taliaferro Alderson aka Wally Wales). Two reels. Released September 2 or September 3, 1917.

Cupid's Round-up (1918) P: William Fox; D: Edward LeSaint; W: Charles Kenyon. Cast: Tom Mix, Wanda Petit, Roy Watson, E.B. Tilton, Edwin Booth, Verne Mersereau, Al Padgett, Eugenie Forde. Five reels. Released January 13, 1918.

Six-Shooter Andy (1918) P: William Fox; D: Sidney Franklin and Chester Franklin; W: Bernard McConville. Cast: Tom Mix, Pat Chrisman, Enid Markey, Sam DeGrasse, Bert Woodruff, Bob Fleming, Jack Planck, Ben Kammer, George

Stone, Lewis Sargent, Buddy Messinger, Raymond Lee, Virginia Lee Corbin, Violet Radcliff, Beulah Burns, Thelma Burns, Charles Stevens, Vivian Planck, Dick Hunter. Five reels. Released February 24, 1918.

Western Blood (1918) P: William Fox; D, W: Lynn Reynolds, story by Tom Mix. Cast: Tom Mix, Victoria Forde, Barney Furey, Pat Chrisman, Frank Clark, Buck Jones. Five reels. Released April 14, 1918.

Aces High (1918) P: William Fox; D, W: Lynn Reynolds. Cast: Tom Mix, Lawrence Payton, Virginia Lee Corbin, Pat Chrisman, Kathleen O'Connor, Lloyd Pearl, Lewis Sargent, Colin Chase, Jay Horley, Georgie Johnson. Five reels. Released June 9, 1918.

Who Is Your Father? (1918) P: William Fox and Henry Lehrmann; D, W: Tom Mix. Cast: Tom Mix. Two reels. Released June 30 or July 7, 1918.

Mr. Logan, U.S.A. (1918) P: William Fox; D, W: Lynn Reynolds. Cast: Tom Mix, Kathleen O'Connor, Smoke Turner, Dick Le Reno, Val Paul, Maude Emory, Charles LeMoyne, Jack Dill. Five reels. Released September 8, 1918.

Fame and Fortune (1918) P: William Fox; D: Lynn Reynolds; W: Bennett Cole, story by Charles A. Seltzer. Cast: Tom Mix, Kathleen O'Connor, Virginia Lee Corbin, Jay Morley, Pat Chrisman, Lawrence Peyton, Colin Chase, Virginia Brown Faire, Lewis Sargent, George Nicholls, Charles McHugh, Annette DeFoe, Val Paul, Jack Dill, E.N. Wallock, Clarence Burton. Five reels. Released October 20 or November 8, 1918.

Treat 'Em Rough (1919) P: William Fox; D, W: Lynn Reynolds, story by Charles A. Seltzer. Cast: Tom Mix, Jane Novak, Smoke Turner, Jack Curtis, Charles LeMoyne, Val Paul. Five reels. Released January 5, 1919.

Hell Roaring Reform (1919) P: William Fox; D: Edward LeSaint; W: Charles Kenyon, sotry by Anthony Roach. Cast: TomMix, Kathleen O'Connor, Smoke Turner, George Berrell, Jack Curtis, Cupid Morgan. Five reels. Released February 16, 1919.

Fighting for Gold (1919) P: William Fox; D: Edward LeSaint; W: Charles Kenyon, story by W. McLeod Raine. Cast: Tom Mix, Lucille Young, Teddy

Sampson, Sid Jordan, George Nichols, Jack Nelson, Harry Lonsdale, Robert Dunbar, Frank Clark, Hattie Buskirk. Five reels. Released March 30, 1919.

The Coming of the Law (1919) P: William Fox, D: A. Rosen; W: Denison Clift, story by Charles A. Seltzer. Cast: Tom Mix, Jane Novak, Brownie Vernon, George Nichols, Jack Curtis, Sid Jordan, Smoke Turner, Charles LeMoyne, Pat Chrisman, Lewis Sargent, Jack Dill, Harry Dunkinson, Banty Caldwell, Earl Simpson, Dick Hunter, Buck Jones, Pedro Leone, Vic Frith. Five reels. Released May 11, 1919.

The Wilderness Trail (1919) P: William Fox; D: Edward LeSaint; W: Charles Kenyon, story by Frank Williams. Cast: Tom Mix, Colleen Moore, Sid Jordan, Frank M. Clark, Lulu Warrenton, Pat Chrisman, Jack Nelson. Five reels. Released July 6, 1919.

Rough Riding Romance (1919) P: William Fox; D: Arthur Rossen; W: Charles Kenyon. Cast; Tom Mix, Sid Jordan, Juanita Hansen, Pat Chrisman, Jack Nelson, Spottiswood Aitken, Frankie Lee. Five reels. Released August 24, 1919.

The Speed Maniac (1919) P: William Fox; D; Edward LeSaint; W: Denison Clift, story by H. H. van Loan. Cast: Tom Mix, Eva Novak, Buck Jones, Charles K. French, Ernest Shields, Jack Curtis, Helen Wright. Five reels. Released October 19,1919.

The Feud (1920) P: William Fox; D: Edward LeSaint; W: Charles Kenyon, story by Charles Kenyon. Cast: Tom Mix, Eva Novak, Claire McDowell, J. Arthur Mackey, John Cosar, Molly McConnell, Lloyd Bacon, Sid Jordan, Lucretia Harris, Guy Eakins, Jean Calhoun, Joseph Bennett, Frank Thorne, Nelson McDowell. Five reels. Released December 7, 1919 or January 25, 1920.

The Cyclone (1920) P: William Fox; D: Cliff Smith; W: J. Anthony Roach. Cast: Tom Mix, Colleen Moore, William Ellingford, Buck Jones, Henry Herbert. Five reels. Released January 24 or January 25, 1920.

The Dare-Devil (1920) P: William Fox; D, W: Jacques Jaccard, story by Tom Mix. Cast: Tom Mix, Eva Novak, Lucille Young, Pat Chrisman, Charles K. French, Lee Shumway, Sid Jordan, Harry Dunkinson, Lafe McKee, George Hernandez. Five reels. Released March 7 or March 20, 1920.

Desert Love (1920) P: William Fox; D, W: Jacques Jaccard, story by Tom Mix. Cast: Tom Mix, Eva Novak, Francelia Billington, Lester Cuneo, Charles K. French, Jack Curtis. Five reels. Released April 11 or April 24, 1920.

The Terror (1920) P: William Fox; D, W: Jacques Jaccard, story by Tom Mix. Cast: Tom Mix, Lester Cuneo, Francelia Billington, Lucille Young, Joseph Bennett, Charles K. French, Wilbur Higby. Five reels. Released May 16 or May 19, 1920.

Three Gold Coins (1920) P: William Fox; D: Clifford Smith; W: Alvin Weitz, story by H.H. van Loan. Cast: Tom Mix, Sid Jordan, Pat Chrisman, Margaret Loomis, Bert Hadley, Frank Whitson, Bonnie Hill, Walt Robbins, Sylvia Jocelyn, Dick Rush, Margaret Collington, Frank Weed. Five reels. Released July 4, 1920.

The Untamed (1920) P: William Fox; D, W: Emmett J. Flynn, story by Max Brand. Cast: Tom Mix, Pauline Starke, Sid Jordan, George Siegman, Philo McCullough, James Barrows, Charles K. French, Pat Chrisman, Gloria Hope, Frank Clark, Major J.A. McGuire, Joe Connelly, Buster, the horse. Six reels. Released August 29 or September 5, 1920.

The Texan (1920) P: William Fox; D: Lynn Reynolds; W: Lynn Reynolds and Jules Furthmann, story by J.B. Hendrix. Cast: Tom Mix, Sid Jordan, Gloria Hope, Robert Walker, Charles J. French, Ben Corbett, Pat Chrisman. Five reels. Released October 31, 1920.

Prairie Trails (1920) P: William Fox; D: George Marshall; W: Frank H. Clark, story by J.B. Hendrix. Cast: Tom Mix, Kathleen O'Connor, Robert Walker, Charles K. French, Sid Jordan, Gloria Hope, William Elmer, Harry Dunkinson. Five reels. Released December 20, 1920.

The Road Demon (1921) P: William Fox; D, W: Lynn Reynolds. Cast: Tom Mix, Sid Jordan, Claire Andersen, Charles K. French, Lloyd Bacon, George Hernandez, Charles Arling, Harold Goodwin, Billy Elmer, Lee Phelps, Frank Tokawaja. Five reels. Released February 20, 1921.

Hands Off (1921) P: William Fox; D: George Marshall; W: Frank H. Clark, story by William MacLeod Raines. Cast: Tom Mix, Pauline Curley, Charles K. French, Lloyd Bacon, Frank Clark, Sid Jordan, William McCormick, Virginia Warwick, J. Webster Dill, Marvin Loback. Five reels. Released April 3, 1921.

A Ridin' Romeo (1921) P: William Fox; D, W: George Marshall, story by Tom Mix. Cast: Tom Mix, Sid Jordan, Pat Chrisman, Rhea Mitchell, Harry Dunkinson, Eugenie Ford. Five reels. Released May 22, 1921.

Big Town Round-up (1921) P: William Fox; D, W: Lynn Reynolds, story by William MacLeod Raines. Cast: Tom Mix, Ora Carew, Gilbert Holmes, Harry Dunkinson, Laura LaPlante, William Buckley, William Elmer, William Crinley. Five reels. Released July 3, 1921.

After Your Own Heart (1921) P: William Fox; D: George Marshall; W: John Montague and Tom Mix, story by W.W. Cook. Cast: Tom Mix, Ora Carew, George Hernandez, William Buckley, Sid Jordan, Betty Jewel, Charles K. French, Duke Lee, James Mason, J. Gordon Russell, Bill Ward, E.C. Robinson. Five reels. Released August 7, 1921.

The Night Horseman (1921) P: William Fox; D, W: Lynn Reynolds. Cast: Tom Mix, Mary Hopkins, Harry Lonsdale, Joseph Bennett, Sid Jordan, Cap Anderson, Bert Sprotte, Lon Poff, Charles K. French. Five reels. Released September 18, 1921.

The Rough Diamond (1921) P: William Fox; D, W: Edward Sedgewick, story by Tom Mix. Cast: Tom Mix, Sid Jordan, Eva Novak, Hector Sarno, Edwyn Brady. Five reels. Released October 30, 1921.

Trailin' (1921) P: William Fox; D, W: Lynn Reynolds, story by Max Brand. Cast: Tom Mix, Sid Jordan, Eva Novak, Bert Sprotte, James Gordon, Duke Lee, William Duvall, Harry Dunkinson, Al Fremont, J. Farrell McDonald, Bert Hadley, Caroll Halloway. Five reels. Released December 11, 1921.

Sky High (1922) P: William Fox; D, W: Lynn Reynolds. Cast: Tom Mix, Sid Jordan, Eva Novak, J. Farrell McDonald, William Buckley, Pat Chrisman, Adele Warner, Wynn Mace. Five reels. Released January 15, 1922.

Chasing the Moon (1922) P: William Fox; D, W: Edward Sedgewick, story by Tom Mix and Edward Sedgewick. Cast: Tom Mix, Eva Novak, William Buckley, Sid Jordan, Elsie Danbric, Wynn Mace. Five reels. Released February 26, 1922.

Up and Going (1922) P: William Fox; D, W: Lynn Reynolds, story by Tom Mix. Cast: Tom Mix, Eva Novak, Sid Jordan, Patsy Ruth Miller, Bert Sprotte, Joe Harris Al Fremont, Earl Simpson, William Conklin, Tom O'Brien, Pat Chrisman, Paul Weigel. Five reels. Released April 2, 1922.

The Fighting Streak (1922) P: William Fox; D, W: Arthur Rosson, story by G. Owen Baxter. Cast: Tom Mix, Patsy Ruth Miller, Gerald Pring, Al Fremont, Bert Sprotte, Robert Fleming, Sid Jordan. Five reels. Released May 14, 1922.

For Big Stakes (1922) P: William Fox; D, W: Lynn Reynolds. Cast: Tom Mix, Patsy Ruth Miller, Sid Jordan, Bert Sprotte, Joe Harris, Al Fremont, Earl Simpson. Five reels. Released June 18, 1922.

Just Tony (1922) P: William Fox; D, W: Lynn Reynolds, story by Max Brand. Cast: Tom Mix, Claire Adams, J.P. Lockney, Duke Lee, Frank Campeau, Walt Robbins. Five reels. Released August 20, 1922.

Do and Dare (1922) P: William Fox; D, W: Edward Sedgwick, story by Marion Brooks. Cast: Tom Mix, Claire Adams, Dulcie Cooper, Claude Peyton, Jack Robbins, Hector Sarno, Wilbur Higby, Bob Klein, Gretchen Hartman. Five reels. Released October 1, 1922.

Tom Mix in Arabia (1922) P: William Fox; D, W: Lynn Reynolds. Cast: Tom Mix, Claire Adams, Norman Shelby, George Hernandez, Edward Peil, Ralph Yearsley, Eugene Corey, Hector Sarno, Barbara Bedford. Five reels. Released November 5, 1922.

Catch My Smoke (1922) P: William Fox; D: William Beaudine; W: Jack Strumwasser, story by J.B. Adams. Cast: Tom Mix, Lillian Rich, Claude Peyton, Gordon Griffith, Harry Griffith, Robert Milash, Pat Chrisman, Cap Anderson, Ruby LaFayette. Five reels. Released December 3 or December 31, 1922.

Romance Land (1923) P: William Fox; D: Edward Sedgwick; W: Joseph F. Poland, story by Kenneth Perkins. Cast: Tom Mix, Pat Chrisman, Barbara Bedford, Frank Brownlee, George Webb, Wynn Mace. Five reels. Released February 3 or February 11, 1923.

Three Jumps Ahead (1923) P: William Fox; D, W: John Ford. Cast: Tom Mix, Alma Bennett, Edward Peil, Joe Girard, Virginia True Boardman, Margaret Joslin, Harry Todd, Franke Ford, Earl Simpson. Five reels. Released March 25, 1923.

Stepping Fast (1923) P: William Fox; D: Joseph J. Franz; W: Bernard McConville, story by Bernard McConville. Cast: Tom Mix, Claire Adams, Donald McDonald, Hector Sarno, George Siegman, Edward Peil, Tom Squire, Edward Jobson, Ethel Wales, Minna Redman, Earl Simpson. Five reels. Released May 13, 1923.

Soft Boiled (1923) P: William Fox; D, W: J.G. Blystone, story by Edward Moran. Cast: Tom Mix, Billie Dove, Joseph Girard, Tom Wilson, Lee Shumway, Frank Beal, Jack Curtis, Charles H. Mailes, Harry Dunkinson, Wilson Hummel. Eight reels. Released August 18 or August 26, 1923.

North of Hudson Bay (1923) P: William Fox; D: John Ford; W: Jules Furthmann. Cast: Tom Mix, Kathleen Key, Jennie Lee, Frank Campeau, Eugene Pallette, Will Walling, Frank Leigh, Fred Kohler. Five reels. Released September 10 or November 8, 1923.

The Lone Star Ranger (1923) P: William Fox; D, W: William Hillyer. Cast: Tom Mix, Billie Dove, Lee Shumway, Stanton Heck, Edward Peil, Frank Clark, Minna Redman, Francis Carpenter, William Conklin, Tom Lingham. Six reels. Released September 9 or October 15, 1923.

Mile-A-Minute Rodeo (1923) P: William Fox; D: Lambert Hillyer; W: Robert N. Lee, story by Max Brand. Six reels. Released October 28 or November 18, 1923.

Eyes of the Forest (1923) P: William Fox; D: Lambert Hillyer; W: LeRoy Stone, story by Shannon Fife. Cast: Tom Mix, Pauline Starke, Sid Jordan, Buster Gardner, J.P. Lockney, Tom Lingham, Edwin Wallock. Five reels. Released December 28 or December 30, 1923.

Ladies to Board (1924) P: William Fox; D: J.G. Blystone; W: Donald W. Lee, story by Dudley Pelley. Cast: Tom Mix, Gertrude Olmstead, Philo McCullough, Pee Wee Holmes, Gertrude Claire, Dolores Rousse. Six reels. Released February 3, 1924.

The Trouble Shooter (1924) P: William Fox; D: Jack Conway; W: Frederic Hatton, Fanny Hutton. Cast: Tom Mix, Frank Currier, Kathleen Key, J. Gunnis Davis, Mike Donlin, Dolores Rousse, Al Fremont, Charles McHugh, Earl Fox, Howard Truesdel. Six reels. Released May 4 or May 26, 1924.

The Heart Buster (1924) P: William Fox; D: Jack Conway; W: John Stone, story by George Scarborough. Cast: Tom Mix, Esther Ralston, Cyril Chadwick, William Courtwright, Frank Currier, Tom Wilson. Five reels. Released June 30 or July 6, 1924.

The Last of the Duanes (1924) P: William Fox; D: Lynn Reynolds; W: Edward Montayne, story by Zane Grey. Cast: Tom Mix, Marion Nixon, Brinsley Shaw, Frank Nelson, Lucy Beaumont, Harry Lonsdale. Seven reels. Released June 30 or August 24, 1924.

Oh, You Tony! (1924) P: William Fox; D: J.G. Blystone; W: Donald W. Lee. Cast: Tom Mix, Claire Adams, Dick La Reno, Earl Fox, Dolores Rousse, Charles K. French, Pat Chrisman, Miles McCarthy, Matilda Brundage, May Wallace. Seven reels. Released September 5 or September 21, 1924.

Teeth (1924) P: William Fox; D: John Blystone; W: Donald W. Lee, story by Clinton Stagge. Cast: Tom Mix, Lucy Fox, Edward Peil, George Bancroft, Lucien Littlefield, Duke, the dog. Seven reels. Released November 2 or November 3, 1924.

The Deadwood Coach (1924) P: William Fox; D, W: Lynn Reynolds, story by Clarence E. Mulford. Cast: Tom Mix, Doris May, George Bancroft, DeWitt Jennings, Bustern Gardner, Lucien Littlefield, Norman Wills, Nora Cecil, Clyde Kinney, Frank Coffyn, Sid Jordan. Seven reels. Released December 6 or December 7, 1924.

Dick Turpin (1925) P: William Fox; D: J.G. Blystone; W: Charles Kenyon, story by Charles Kenyon and Charles Darnton. Cast: Tom Mix, Kathleen Meyers, Philo McCullough, James Marcus, Lucille Hutton, Alan Hale, Bull Montana, Fay Holderness, Jack Herrick, Fred Kohler. Seven reels. Released February 1, 1925.

Riders of the Purple Sage (1925) P: William Fox; D: Lynn Reynolds; W: Edfrid Bingham, story by Zane Grey. Cast: Tom Mix, Beatrice Burnham, Arthur Morrison, Seesel Ann Johnson, Warner Oland, Fred Kohler, Joe Rickson, Charles LeMoyne, Marion Dixson, Dawn O'Day, Charles Newton, Mabel Ballin, Harold Goodwin, Wilfred Lucas. Six reels. Released March 8 or March 15, 1925.

The Rainbow Trail (1925) P: William Fox; D, W: Lynn Reynolds, story by Zane Grey. Cast: Tom Mix, Anne Cornwall, George Bancroft, Lucien Littlefield, Mark Hamilton, Thomas Delmar, Vivian Oakland, Steve Clemento, Fred de Silva, Doc Roberts, Carol Holloway, Diana Miller, Fred Dillon. Six reels. Released April 19 or May 24, 1925.

The Lucky Horseshoe (1925) P: William Fox; D: J.G. Blystone; W: John Stone, story by Robert Lord. Cast: Tom Mix, Billie Dove, Malcolm Waite, J. Farrell McDonald, Clarrisa Selwynne, Ann Pennington, J. Gunnis Davis. Five reels. Released August 23 or August 29, 1925.

The Everlasting Whisper (1925) P: William Fox; D: J.G. Blystone; W: Wyndham Gittens, story by J. Gregory. Cast: Tom Mix, Alice Calhoun, Robert Cain, George Berrell, Walter James, Virginia Madison, Karl Dane. Six reels. Released October 4 or October 11, 1925.

The Best Bad Man (1925) P: William Fox; D: J.G. Blystone; W: Lillie Hayward, story by Max Brand. Cast: Tom Mix, Clara Bow, Buster Gardner, Cyril Chadwick, Tom Kennedy, Frank Beal, Judy King, Tom Wilson, Paul Panzer. Five reels. Released November 15 or December 12, 1925.

The Yankee Señor (1925) P: William Fox; D: Emmett Flynn; W: Eve Unsell, story by Katherine F. Gerould. Cast: Tom Mix, Olive Borden, Tom Kennedy, Francis McDonald, Joseph Franz, Margaret Livingston, Alec B. Francis, Kathryn Hill, Martha Mattox, Raymond Wells, Eugene Pallette, Harry Seymore. Five reels. Released December 27, 1925 or January 10, 1926.

My Own Pal (1926) P: William Fox; D: J.G. Blystone; W: Lillie Hayward, story by Gerald Beaumont. Cast: Tom Mix, Olive Borden, Tom Santschi, Virginia Marshall, Bardson Bard, Hedda Nova, William Colvin, Virginia Warwick, Jay Hunt, Helen Lynch, Tom McGuire, Jacques Rollens. Five reels. Released February 14 or February 28, 1926.

Tony Runs Wild (1926) P: William Fox; D: Thomas Buckingham, W: Elfrid Bingham and Robert Lord, story by H. H. Knibbs. Cast: Tom Mix, Lawford Davidson, Jacqueline Logan, Duke Lee, Vivian Oakland, Edward Martindel, Raymond Wells, Lucien Littlefield, Jack Padjan, Marion Harlan, Richard Carter, Arthur Morrison, Tony, the wonder horse. Six reels. Released April 11 or April 18, 1926.

Hard Boiled (1926) P: William Fox; D: J.G. Blystone; W: Charles Darnton and John Stane, story by Shannon Fife. Cast: Tom Mix, Helen Chadwick, William Lawrence, Charles Conklin, Emily Fitzroy, Phyllis Haver, Dan Mason, Walter O'Donnell, Ethel Grey Terry, Edward Sturgis, Eddie Roland, Emmett Wagner. Six reels. Released June 6 or August 8, 1926.
No Man's Gold (1926) P: William Fox; D: Lewis Seiler; W: John Stone, story by J.A. Dunn. Cast: Tom Mix, Eva Novak, Frank Campeau, Forrest Taylor, Harry Grippe, Malcolm Waite, Mickey Moore, Tom Santschi. Six reels. Released August 8 or August 29, 1926.

The Great K&A Train Robbery (1926) P: William Fox; D: Lewis Seiler; W: John Stone, story by Paul J. Ford. Cast: Tom Mix, Dorothy Dwan, William Walling, Henry Grippe, Carl Miller, Edward Piel, Curtis McHenry. Five reels. Released October 17 or October 25, 1926.

The Canyon of Light (1926) P: William Fox; D: Benjamin Stoloff; W: John Stone, story by Kenneth Perkins. Cast: Tom Mix, Dorothy Dwan, Carl Miller, Ralph Sipperly, Barry Norton, Carmelita Geraghty, William Walling, Duke Lee. Six reels. Released December 5, 1926.

The Last Trail (1927) P: William Fox; D: Lewis Seiler; W: John Stone, story by Zane Grey. Cast: Tom Mix, Carmelita Geraghty, William Davidson, Frank Hagney, Lee Shumway, Robert Brower, Jerry the Giant, Oliver Eckhardt. Six reels. Released January 16 or January 23, 1927.

The Bronco Twister (1927) P: William Fox; D: Orville O. Dull; W: John Stone, story by Adela Rogers St. John. Cast: Tom Mix, Helene Costello, George Irving, Dorothy Kitchen, Paul Nicholson, Doris Lloyd, Malcolm Waite, Jack Pennick, Otto Fries. Six reels. Released March 13, 1927.

The Circus Ace (1927) P: William Fox; D: Ben Stoloff; W: Jack Jungmeyer, story by Harold Shumate. Cast: Tom Mix, Natalie Joyce, Jack Baston, Duke Lee, James Bradbury, Stanley Blystone, Dudley Smith, Buster Gardner, Clarence the kangaroo. Five reels. Released June 12 or June 26, 1927.

Tumbling River (1927) P: William Fox; D: Lewis Seiler; W: Jack Jungmeyer, story by J. E. Grimstead. Cast: Tom Mix, Dorothy Dwan, Edward Peil, William Conklin, Stella Essex, Elmo Billings, Wallace MacDonald, Buster Gardner, Harry Grippe, Buster, the horse. Five reels. Released August 14 or August 21, 1927.

Outlaws of Red River (1927) P: William Fox; D: Lewis Seiler; W: Harold Shumate, story by Gerald Beaumont. Cast: Tom Mix, Marjorie Daw, Arthur Clayton, William Conklin, Duke Lee, Johnny Downs, Francis McDonald, Virginia Marshall. Six reels. Released May 8 or August 17, 1927.

Silver Valley (1927) P: William Fox; D: Ben Stoloff; W: Harold Blipsitz, story by Harry S. Drago. Cast: Tom Mix, Tom Kennedy, Dorothy Dwan, Philo McCullough, Jocky Hoefli, Lon Poff, Harry Dunkinson, Clark Comstock. Five reels. Released October 2, 1927.

The Arizona Wildcat (1927) P: William Fox; D: R. William Neill; W: John Stone, story by Adela Rogers St. John. Cast: Tom Mix, Dorothy Sebastian, Ben Bard, Gordon Elliot, Monty Collins, Jr., Cissy Fitzgerald, Doris Dawson, Marcella Day. Five reels. Released November 20, 1927.

Daredevil's Reward (1928) P: William Fox; D: Eugene Ford; W: John Stone, story by John Stone. Cast: Tom Mix, Natalie Joyce, Lawford Davidson, Billy Bletcher, Harry Cording, William Welch. Five reels. Released January 15 or January 27, 1928.

Horseman of the Plains (1928) P: William Fox; D: Ben Stoloff; W: Fred Myton, story by Harry S. Drago. Cast: Tom Mix, Sally Blaine, Heime Conklin,

Charles Byer, Lew Harvey, Grace Marvin, William Ryno. Five reels. Released February 2 or March 11, 1928.

Hello Cheyenne (1928) P: William Fox; D: Eugene Ford; W: Fred K. Myton, story by Harry S. Drago. Cast: Tom Mix, Carol Lincoln, Jack Baston, Martin Faust, Joseph Girard, Al St. John, William Caress. Five reels. Released March 29 or May 13, 1928.

Painted Post (1928) P: William Fox; D: Eugene Ford; W: Buckleigh F. Oxford, story by Harry S. Drago. Cast: Tom Mix, Natalie Kingston, Philo McCullough, Al St. John, Fred Gamble. Five reels. Released June 1 or July 1, 1928.

Films made for Film Booking Office (FBO): (All films are silent.)

Son of the Golden West (1928) P: Joseph Kennedy; D: Eugene Forde; W: George Pyper. Cast: Tom Mix, Sharon Lyn, Lee Shumway, Tom Lingham, Fritzi Ridgeway, Duke Lee, Joie Ray, Wynn Mace, Mark Hamilton. Six reels. Released October 1, 1928.

King Cowboy (1928) P: Joseph Kennedy; D: Robert DeLacey; W: Frank Clark, story by S. E. V. Taylor. Cast: Tom Mix, Sally Blaine, Lew Meehan, Wynn Mace, Barney Furey, Robert Fleming, Frank Leigh. Seven reels. Released November 5 or November 26, 1928.

Outlawed (1929) P: Joseph Kennedy; D: Eugene Forde; W: George Pyper. Cast: Tom Mix, Sally Blaine, Ethan Laidlaw, Frank Clark, Barney Furey, Al Smith, Al Ferguson. Seven reels. Released January 1 or January 21, 1929.

The Drifter (1929) P: Joseph Kennedy; D: Robert DeLacey; W: George Pyper, story by Oliver Drake and Robert DeLacey. Cast: Tom Mix, Dorothy Dwan, Wynn Mace, Barney Furey, Al Smith, Frank Austin, Ernest Wilson, Joe Rickson. Six reels. Released February 25 or March 19, 1929.

The Big Diamond Robbery (1929) P: Joseph Kennedy; D: Eugene Forde; W: John Twist, story by Frank Clark. Cast: Tom Mix, Kathryn McGuire, Frank Beal, Ethan Laidlaw, Barney Furey, Martha Mattox, Ernest Hilliard. Seven reels. Released May 13, 1929.

Films made for Universal Studios: (All are sound films.)

The Cohens and Kellys In Hollywood (1932)P: Stanley Bergerman; D: John Francis Dillon; W: Howard J. Green. Cast: George Sidney, Charlie Murray, June Clyde, Norman Foster, Emma Dunn, Esther Howard, Edwin Maxwell, Dorothy Christie, Luis Alberni, Tom Mix, Sidney Fox, Lew Ayres, Boris Karloff, Genevieve Tobin. 75 mins. Released March 28, 1932.

Destry Rides Again (1932) P: Carl Laemmle, Jr.; D: Ben Stoloff; W: Richard Schayer and Isador Bernstein, story by Max Brand. Cast: Tom Mix, Claudia Dell, Earl Fox, Zasu Pitts, Stanley Fields, Francis Ford, Charles K. French, Edward J. LeSaint, Edward Piel, Sr., Frederick Howard, Robert Ruffner, John Ince, George Ernest, Ed Brady, Chris Martin. Six reels (56 minutes). Released April 4 or April 17, 1932.

The Rider of Death Valley (1932) P: Carl Laemmle, Jr.; D: Al Rogel; W: Jack Cunningham, story by Max Brand. Cast: Tom Mix, Lois Wilson, Fred Kohler, Sr., Mae Busch, Edmund Cobb, William Robertson, Edith Fellows, Forest Stanley, Pete Morrison, Iron Eyes Cody, Otis Harlan, Francis Ford. Seven reels (78 minutes). Released May 20 or May 26, 1932.

Texas Badman (1932) P: Carl Laemmle, Jr.; D: Edward Laemmle (retakes directed by Gene Lewis); W: Jack Cunningham. Cast: Tom Mix, Lucille Powers, Fred Kohler, Sr., Edward J. LeSaint, William Robertson, Franklyn Farnum, Dick Alexander, Bud Osborne, Joseph Girard, Lynton Brent, Buck Bucko, Tetsu Komai. Six reels (61 minutes). Released June 18 or June 30, 1932.

My Pal, the King (1932) P: Carl Laemmle, Jr., D: Kurt Neumann; W: Richard Schayer. Cast: Tom Mix, Mickey Rooney, Noel Francis, Paul Hurst, Stuart Holmes, Jim Thorpe, Finish Barton, Ferdinand Schumann-Heink, Jamnes Kirkwood, Wallis Clark, Christian Frank, Clarissa Selwynne. Seven reels (74 minutes). Released August 1 or August 4, 1932.

The Fourth Horseman (1932) P: Carl Laemmle, Jr.; D: Hamilton McFadden (retakes directed by Art Rosson); W: Jack Cunningham, story by Nina Putnam. Cast: Tom Mix, Margaret Lindsay, Fred Kohler, Sr., Raymond Hatton, Buddy Roosevelt, Edmund Cobb, Rosita Marstini, Richard Cramer, Duke Lee, Grace Cunard, Hank Mann, Fred Burns, Bud Osborne, Walter Brennan, Harry Allen,

Herman Nowlin, Paul Shawham, Frederick Howard, Helen Millard, Captain Anderson, Martha Mattox. Six reels (63 minutes). Released September 22 or September 29, 1932.

Hidden Gold (1932) P: Carl Laemmle, Jr.; D: Art Rosson; W: Jack Natteford and Jim Milhauser, story by Jack Natteford. Cast: Tom Mix, Raymond Hatton, Judith Barrie, Eddie Gribbon, Willis Clarke, Donald Kirke, Roy Moore. Six reels (61 minutes). Released October 19 or November 3, 1932.

Flaming Guns (1932) P: Carl Laemmle, Jr.; D: Art Rosson; W: Jack Cunningham, story by Peter B. Kyne. Cast: Tom Mix, Ruth Hall, William Farnum, Bud Osborne, Duke Lee, George Hackathorne, Pee Wee Holmes, Clarence Wilson, Slim Whitaker, Clyde Kinney, Fred Burns, Jimmy Shannon, William Steele, Walter Patterson, Robert Ruffner. Six reels (57 minutes). Released June 1932 or December 17, 1932.

Terror Trail (1933) P: Carl Laemmle, Jr.; D: Armand Schaefer; W: Jack Cunningham, story by Gran Taylor. Cast: Tom Mix, Naomi Judge, Raymond Hatton, Arthur Rankin, Francis McDonald, Lafe McKee, Bob Kortman, Hank Bell, John St. Polls, Frank Brownlee, Jay Wilsey, Henry Tenbrook, W. J. Holmes, Leonard Trainer, Jim Corley. Six reels (57 minutes). Released January 24 or February 2, 1933.

Rustler's Roundup (1933) P: Carl Laemmle, Jr.; D: Henry McRae; W: Frank Howard Clark, story by Ella O'Neill. Cast: Tom Mix, Noah Beery Jr., Diane Sinclair, William Desmond, Nelson McDowell, Douglas Dumbrille, Bud Osborne, Roy Stewart, Pee Wee Holmes, William Wagner, Frank Lackteen, Walter Brennan. Six reels (56 minutes). Released February 23 or September 1, 1933.

Films made for Mascot Studios: (Sound film)

The Miracle Rider (1935) P: Victor Zobel; D: Armand Schaefer and B. Reeves Eason; W: John Rathmell, story by Gerald Gerahty, Barney Sarecky and Wellyn Totman. Cast; Tom Mix, Joan Gale, Charles Middleton, Jason Robards, Edward Hearn, Ernie Adams, Edward Earle, Tom London, Niles Welsh, Edmund Cobb, Max Wagner, Charles King, George Chesebro, Stanley Price, George Burton,

Jack Rockwell, Bob Frazer, Bob Kortman. 33 reels (309 minutes). Released May 18, 1935.

Endnotes

Endnotes
Chapter One

1. Mix, Paul E. <u>Tom Mix: A Heavily Illustrated Biography with a Filmography</u>. Jefferson: McFarland, 1995, p. 8.
2. Ibid, p. 8.
3. Ibid, p. 8.
4. Ibid, p. 9.
5. Ibid, p. 8.
6. Ibid, p. 8.
7. Ibid, p. 10.
8. Ibid, p. 11.
9. Ibid, p. 11.
10. Ibid, p. 12.
11. Ibid, p. 13.
12. Kasson, Joy. <u>Buffalo Bill's Wild West: Celebrity, Memory and Popular History</u>. New York: Hill and Wang, 2000. p. 5.
13. Ibid, p. 5.
14. Mix, Paul E. <u>Tom Mix: A Heavily Illustrated Biography with a Filmography</u>. Jefferson: McFarland, 1995, p. 13.
15. McCoy, Tim and Ronald McCoy. <u>Tim McCoy Remembers the West</u>. Lincoln: University of Nebraska Press, 1977, p. 16.
16. Mix, Paul E. <u>Tom Mix: A Heavily Illustrated Biography with a Filmography</u>. Jefferson: McFarland, 1995, p. 13.
17. Ibid, p. 14.
18. Ibid, p. 14.
19. Ibid, p. 15-17.
20. Ibid, p. 16.
21. Ibid, p. 16.
22. Mix, Paul E. <u>Tom Mix: A Heavily Illustrated Biography with a Filmography</u>. Jefferson: McFarland, 1995, p. 16.

23. Birchard, Robert S. <u>King Cowboy: Tom Mix and the Movies</u>. Burbank: Riverwood Press, 1993. p. 4, 5.
24. Mix, Paul E. <u>Tom Mix: A Heavily Illustrated Biography with a Filmography.</u> Jefferson: McFarland, 1995, p. 14.
25. Ibid, p. 18.
26. Ibid, p. 18.
27. Ibid, p. 18.
28. Ibid, p. 23.
29. Ibid, p. 24.
30. Ibid, p. 24.
31. Ibid, p. 37.

Endnotes
Chapter Two

1. Mix, Paul E. <u>Tom Mix: A Heavily Illustrated Biography with a Filmography.</u> Jefferson: McFarland, 1995., p. 26.
2. Ibid, p. 28.
3. Ibid, p. 29.
4. Ibid, p. 29.
5. Ibid, p. 29.
6. Ibid, p. 31.
7. Ibid, p. 31.
8. Ibid, p. 32.
9. Ibid, p. 32.
10. Ibid, p. 37.
11. Ibid, p. 37.
12. Ibid, p. 37.
13. Wallis, Michael. <u>The Real Wild West: The 101 Ranch and the creation of the American West.</u> New York: St. Martin's Press, 1999. p. 116.
14. Mix, Paul E. <u>Tom Mix: A Heavily Illustrated Biography with a Filmography.</u> Jefferson: McFarland, 1995, p. 13.
15. Ibid, p. 37.
16. Ibid, p. 37.
17. Ibid, p. 44.
18. Ibid, p. 44.
19. Ibid, p. 47.
20. Ibid, p. 44.
21. Ibid, p. 37.

22. Ibid, p. 24.
23. Ibid, p. 31.
24. Ibid, p. 45.
25. Ibid, p. 44.
26. Ibid, p. 44.
27. Ibid, p. 45.
28. Ibid, p. 45
29. Carter, Joseph H. Never Met A Man I Didn't Like: The Life and Writings of Will Rogers. New York: Avon Books, 1991, p. 38.
30. Mix, Paul E. Tom Mix: A Heavily Illustrated Biography with a Filmography. Jefferson: McFarland, 1995, p. 45; Wallis, Michael. The Real Wild West: The 101 Ranch and the creation of the American West. New York: St. Martin's Press, 1999. p. 243.
31. Mix, Paul E. Tom Mix: A Heavily Illustrated Biography with a Filmography. Jefferson: McFarland, 1995, p. 45.
32. Wallis, Michael. The Real Wild West: The 101 Ranch and the creation of the American West. New York: St. Martin's Press, 1999, p. 351.
33. Carter, Joseph H. Never Met A Man I Didn't Like: The Life and Writings of Will Rogers. New York: Avon Books, 1991, p. 52.
34. Ibid, p. 70.
35. Mix, Olive Stokes and Eric Heath. The Fabulous Tom Mix. Englewood Cliffs: Prentice-Hall, 1957, p. 4.
36. Ibid, p. 4.
37. Ibid, p. 4.
38. Ibid, p. 4.
39. Ibid, p. 5.
40. Ibid, p. 5.
41. Ibid, p. 6.
42. Ibid, p. 7.
43. Mix, Paul E. Tom Mix: A Heavily Illustrated Biography with a Filmography. Jefferson: McFarland, 1995, p. 45.
44. Ibid, p. 45.
45. Ibid, p. 47.
46. Ibid, p. 47.
47. Ibid, p. 47.
48. Ibid, p. 47.
49. Mix, Paul E. Tom Mix: A Heavily Illustrated Biography with a Filmography. Jefferson: McFarland, 1995, p. 47.

50. Wallis, Michael. <u>The Real Wild West: The 101 Ranch and the creation of the American West.</u> New York: St. Martin's Press, 1999, p. 238.

Endnotes
Chapter Three

1. Mix, Paul E. <u>Tom Mix: A Heavily Illustrated Biography with a Filmography.</u> Jefferson: McFarland, 1995, p. 47.
2. Ibid, p. 47.
3. Ibid, p. 47.
4. Wallis, Michael. <u>The Real Wild West: The 101 Ranch and the creation of the American West.</u> New York: St. Martin's Press, 1999, p. 236.
5. Collings, Ellsworth and Alma Miller England. <u>The 101 Ranch</u>. Norman: University of Oklahoma Press, 1937, p. xxix.
6. Ibid, p. vii.
7. Ibid, p. vii.
8. Mix, Paul E. <u>Tom Mix: A Heavily Illustrated Biography with a Filmography.</u> Jefferson: McFarland, 1995, p. 47.
9. Ibid, p. 47.
10. Wallis, Michael. <u>The Real Wild West: The 101 Ranch and the creation of the American West.</u> New York: St. Martin's Press, 1999, p. 344.
11. Mix, Paul E. <u>The Life and Legend of Tom Mix.</u> Cranbury: A.S. Barnes and Co., Inc., 1972, p. 48.
12. Mix, Paul E. <u>Tom Mix: A Heavily Illustrated Biography with a Filmography.</u> Jefferson: McFarland, 1995,p. 45.
13. Mix, Paul E. <u>Tom Mix: A Heavily Illustrated Biography with a Filmography.</u> Jefferson: McFarland, 1995, p. 47.
14. Ibid, p. 47.
15. Ibid, p. 48.
16. Mix, Paul E. <u>Tom Mix: A Heavily Illustrated Biography with a Filmography.</u> Jefferson: McFarland, 1995, p. 48.
17. Wallis, Michael. <u>The Real Wild West: The 101 Ranch and the creation of the American West.</u> New York: St. Martin's Press, 1999, p. 239.
18. Nicholas, John H. <u>Tom Mix: Riding Up To Glory</u>. Oklahoma City: National Cowboy Hall of Fame, 1980, p. 11.
19. Carter, Joseph H. <u>Never Met A Man I Didn't Like: The Life and Writings of Will Rogers</u>. New York: Avon Books, 1991, p. 77.
20. Wallis, Michael. <u>The Real Wild West: The 101 Ranch and the creation of the American West.</u> New York: St. Martin's Press, 1999, p. 250.

End Notes
Chapter Four

1. Collings Ellsworth and Alma Miller England. <u>The 101 Ranch</u>. Norman: University of Oklahoma Press, 1937, p. ix.
2. Ibid, p. ix, x.
3. Ibid, p. 142.
4. Mix, Paul E. <u>Tom Mix: A Heavily Illustrated Biography with a Filmography.</u> Jefferson: McFarland, 1995, p. 48
5. Wallis, Michael. <u>The Real Wild West: The 101 Ranch and the creation of the American West.</u> New York: St. Martin's Press, 1999, p. 249.
6. Collings, Ellsworth and Alma Miller England. <u>The 101 Ranch</u>. Norman: University of Oklahoma Press, 1937, p. 142.
7. Wallis, Michael. <u>The Real Wild West: The 101 Ranch and the creation of the American West.</u> New York: St. Martin's Press, 1999, p. 250.
8. Ibid, p. 251; Collings, Ellsworth and Alma Miller England. <u>The 101 Ranch</u>. Norman: University of Oklahoma Press, 1937, p. 161.
9. Wallis, Michael. <u>The Real Wild West: The 101 Ranch and the creation of the American West.</u> New York: St. Martin's Press, 1999, p. 251.
10. Mix, Paul E. <u>Tom Mix: A Heavily Illustrated Biography with a Filmography.</u> Jefferson: McFarland, 1995, p. 48.
11. Wallis, Michael. <u>The Real Wild West: The 101 Ranch and the creation of the American West.</u> New York: St. Martin's Press, 1999, p. 227.
12. Ibid, p. 257, 278.
13. Ibid, p. 280.
14. Ibid, p. 280.
15. Ibid, p. 280.
16. Mix, Paul E. <u>Tom Mix: A Heavily Illustrated Biography with a Filmography.</u> Jefferson: McFarland, 1995, p. 48.
17. Ibid, p. 49.
18. Ibid, p. 49.
19. Ibid, p. 49.
20. Ibid, p. 49.
21. Ibid, p. 52.
22. Ibid, p. 50.
23. Ibid, p. 50.
24. Ibid, p. 50.

25. Virgines, George. "The Guns of Tom Mix." <u>Guns Magazine</u>. 2/1970, p. 45-47.
26. Mix, Paul E. <u>Tom Mix: A Heavily Illustrated Biography with a Filmography.</u> Jefferson: McFarland, 1995, p. 50.
27. Ibid, p. 50.
28. Ibid, p. 50.
29. Birchard, Robert S. <u>King Cowboy: Tom Mix and the Movies</u>. Burbank: Riverwood Press, 1993, p. 5.
30. The Sunday Oklahoman, 2/1/1981, p. 3,4
31. Mix, Paul E. <u>Tom Mix: A Heavily Illustrated Biography with a Filmography.</u> Jefferson: McFarland, 1995, p. 52.
32. Ibid, p. 53.
33. Ibid, p. 53.
34. Ibid, p. 54.
35. Mix, Olive Stokes and Eric Heath. <u>The Fabulous Tom Mix</u>. Englewood Cliffs: Prentice-Hall, 1957, p. 118.
36. Mix, Paul E. <u>The Life and Legend of Tom Mix.</u> Cranbury: A.S. Barnes and Co., Inc., 1972, p. 61.
37. Wallis, Michael. <u>The Real Wild West: The 101 Ranch and the creation of the American West.</u> New York: St. Martin's Press, 1999, p. 280.

End Notes
Chapter Five

1. Mix, Life, p. 70.
2. Mix, Paul E. <u>Tom Mix: A Heavily Illustrated Biography with a Filmography.</u> Jefferson: McFarland, 1995, p. 55.
3. Collings, Ellsworth and Alma Miller England. <u>The 101 Ranch</u>. Norman: University of Oklahoma Press, 1937, p. 103.
4. Ibid, p. 103.
5. Ibid, p. 103, 106.
6. Mix, Paul E. <u>The Life and Legend of Tom Mix.</u> Cranbury: A.S. Barnes and Co., Inc., 1972, p. 48.
7. Mix, Paul E. <u>Tom Mix: A Heavily Illustrated Biography with a Filmography.</u> Jefferson: McFarland, 1995, p. 55.
8. Mix, Olive Stokes and Eric Heath. <u>The Fabulous Tom Mix</u>. Englewood Cliffs: Prentice-Hall, 1957, p. 7.
9. Ibid, p. 10.
10. Ibid, p. 11.

11. Ibid, p. 11.
12. Ibid, p. 12.
13. Ibid, p. 14.
14. Ibid, p. 15.
15. Ibid, p. 15.
16. Ibid, p. 17.
17. Ibid, p. 17.
18. Ibid, p. 18.
19. Ibid, p. 18.
20. Ibid, p. 19.
21. Ibid, p. 21.
22. Ibid, p. 21.
23. Mix, Paul E. <u>The Life and Legend of Tom Mix.</u> Cranbury: A.S. Barnes and Co., Inc., 1972, p. 50.
24. Mix, Olive Stokes and Eric Heath. <u>The Fabulous Tom Mix</u>. Englewood Cliffs: Prentice-Hall, 1957, p. 6.
25. Trial transcript, Olive Stokes testimony, In the Chancery Court of Adams County, Mississippi, Zack T. Miller v. Tom Mix, et al. No. 5731, January 8, 1931, p. 21.
26. Mix, Olive Stokes and Eric Heath. <u>The Fabulous Tom Mix</u>. Englewood Cliffs: Prentice-Hall, 1957, p. 23.
27. Ibid, p. 23.
28. Ibid, p. 25.
29. Ibid, p. 31.
30. Ibid, p. 30.
31. Ibid, p. 34.
32. Ibid, p. 35.
33. Ibid, p. 36.
34. Ibid, p. 38.
35. Ibid, p. 39.

End Notes
Chapter Six

1. Mix, Olive Stokes and Eric Heath. <u>The Fabulous Tom Mix</u>. Englewood Cliffs: Prentice-Hall, 1957, p. 50.
2. Ibid, p. 48.
3. Ibid, p. 43.

4. Mix, Paul E. The Life and Legend of Tom Mix. Cranbury: A.S. Barnes and Co., Inc., 1972, p. 50.
5. Mix, Olive Stokes and Eric Heath. The Fabulous Tom Mix. Englewood Cliffs: Prentice-Hall, 1957, p. 49.
6. Ibid, p. 50.
7. Ibid, p. 50.
8. Ibid, p. 52.
9. Ibid, p. 51.
10. Ibid, p. 51.
11. Ibid, p. 52.
12. Ibid, p. 41.
13. Birchard, Robert S. King Cowboy: Tom Mix and the Movies. Burbank: Riverwood Press, 1993, p. 117.
14. Ibid, p. 31.
15. Mix, Olive Stokes and Eric Heath. The Fabulous Tom Mix. Englewood Cliffs: Prentice-Hall, 1957, p. 103.
16. Ibid, p. 52.
17. Ibid, p. 52.
18. Ibid, p. 53.
19. Ibid, p. 54.
20. Mix, Paul E. Tom Mix: A Heavily Illustrated Biography with a Filmography. Jefferson: McFarland, 1995, p. 55.
21. Mix, Olive Stokes and Eric Heath. The Fabulous Tom Mix. Englewood Cliffs: Prentice-Hall, 1957, p. 55.
22. Ibid, p. 55.
23. Ibid, p. 55.
24. Ibid, p. 56.
25. Ibid, p. 56.
26. Ibid, p. 56.
27. Ibid, p. 56.
28. Mix, Paul E. Tom Mix: A Heavily Illustrated Biography with a Filmography. Jefferson: McFarland, 1995, p. 55.
29. Mix, Olive Stokes and Eric Heath. The Fabulous Tom Mix. Englewood Cliffs: Prentice-Hall, 1957, p. 56.
30. Ibid, p. 57.
31. Ibid, p. 59.
32. Wallis, Michael. The Real Wild West: The 101 Ranch and the creation of the American West. New York: St. Martin's Press, 1999, p. 254.

33. Mix, Olive Stokes and Eric Heath. <u>The Fabulous Tom Mix</u>. Englewood Cliffs: Prentice-Hall, 1957, p. 59.
34. Mix, Paul E. <u>Tom Mix: A Heavily Illustrated Biography with a Filmography</u>. Jefferson: McFarland, 1995, p. 57.
35. Mix, Olive Stokes and Eric Heath. <u>The Fabulous Tom Mix</u>. Englewood Cliffs: Prentice-Hall, 1957, p. 60.
36. Ibid, p. 61.
37. Ibid, p. 62.
38. Ibid, p. 62.
39. Ibid, p. 63.
40. Ibid, p. 64.
41. Waldo, Anna Lee. <u>Prairie: The Legend of Charles Burton Irwin and the Y6 Ranch</u>. New York: Charter Books p. xii.
42. Ibid, p. xii.
43. Mix, Olive Stokes and Eric Heath. <u>The Fabulous Tom Mix</u>. Englewood Cliffs: Prentice-Hall, 1957, p. 65.
44. Ibid, p. 65.
45. Ibid, p. 65.
46. Ibid, p. 65.
47. Ibid, p. 66
48. Ibid, p. 66.
49. Ibid, p. 66.
50. Birchard, Robert S. <u>King Cowboy: Tom Mix and the Movies</u>. Burbank: Riverwood Press, 1993, p. 7.
51. Ibid, p. 8.
52. Mix, Olive Stokes and Eric Heath. <u>The Fabulous Tom Mix</u>. Englewood Cliffs: Prentice-Hall, 1957, p. 63.
53. Birchard, Robert S. <u>King Cowboy: Tom Mix and the Movies</u>. Burbank: Riverwood Press, 1993, p. 7.
54. Mix, Paul E. <u>Tom Mix: A Heavily Illustrated Biography with a Filmography</u>. Jefferson: McFarland, p. 66.
55. Horwitz, James. <u>They Went Thataway</u>. New York: E.P. Dutton, 1976, p. 67.
56. Mix, Paul E. <u>Tom Mix: A Heavily Illustrated Biography with a Filmography</u>. Jefferson: McFarland, 1995, p. 66.
57. Ibid, p. 65; Mix, Olive Stokes and Eric Heath. <u>The Fabulous Tom Mix</u>. Englewood Cliffs: Prentice-Hall, 1957, p. 69.
58. Mix, Paul E. <u>Tom Mix: A Heavily Illustrated Biography with a Filmography</u>. Jefferson: McFarland, 1995, p. 241.

59. Mix, Olive Stokes and Eric Heath. <u>The Fabulous Tom Mix</u>. Englewood Cliffs: Prentice-Hall, 1957, p. 68.
60. Norris, Merle. <u>The Tom Mix Book</u>. Waynesville: The World of Yesterday, 1989, p. 102.
61. Birchard, Robert S. <u>King Cowboy: Tom Mix and the Movies</u>. Burbank: Riverwood Press, 1993, p. 26.
62. Mix, Olive Stokes and Eric Heath. <u>The Fabulous Tom Mix</u>. Englewood Cliffs: Prentice-Hall, 1957, p. 76.
63. Birchard, Robert S. <u>King Cowboy: Tom Mix and the Movies</u>. Burbank: Riverwood Press, 1993, p. 8.
64. Ibid, p. 8, 9.
65. Mix, Paul E. <u>Tom Mix: A Heavily Illustrated Biography with a Filmography</u>. Jefferson: McFarland, 1995, p. 67.
66. Ibid, p. 67.
67. Birchard, Robert S. <u>King Cowboy: Tom Mix and the Movies</u>. Burbank: Riverwood Press, 1993, p. 9.
68. Ibid, p. 10.
69. Ibid, p. 10.
70. Ibid, p. 9.
71. Ibid, p. 10.
72. Wallis, Michael. <u>The Real Wild West: The 101 Ranch and the creation of the American West</u>. New York: St. Martin's Press, 1999, p. 353.
73. Birchard, Robert S. <u>King Cowboy: Tom Mix and the Movies</u>. Burbank: Riverwood Press, 1993, p. 10.
74. Wallis, Michael. <u>The Real Wild West: The 101 Ranch and the creation of the American West</u>. New York: St. Martin's Press, 1999, p. 354.
75. Birchard, Robert S. <u>King Cowboy: Tom Mix and the Movies</u>. Burbank: Riverwood Press, 1993, p. 10.
76. Ibid, p. 10.
77. Wallis, Michael. <u>The Real Wild West: The 101 Ranch and the creation of the American West</u>. New York: St. Martin's Press, 1999, p. 319.
78. Ibid, p. 319.
79. Ibid, p. 321.
80. Ibid, p. 323.
81. Ibid, p. 324.
82. Ibid, p. 325.
83. Mix, Olive Stokes and Eric Heath. <u>The Fabulous Tom Mix</u>. Englewood Cliffs: Prentice-Hall, 1957, p. 52.

84. Wallis, Michael. The Real Wild West: The 101 Ranch and the creation of the American West. New York: St. Martin's Press, 1999, p. 351.
85. Ibid, p. 352.
86. Birchard, Robert S. King Cowboy: Tom Mix and the Movies. Burbank: Riverwood Press, 1993, p. 10.
87. Mix, Olive Stokes and Eric Heath. The Fabulous Tom Mix. Englewood Cliffs: Prentice-Hall, 1957, p. 72.
88. Norris, Merle. The Tom Mix Book. Waynesville: The World of Yesterday, 1989, p. 102.
89. Mix, Paul E. Tom Mix: A Heavily Illustrated Biography with a Filmography. Jefferson: McFarland, 1995, p. 66.
90. Ibid, p. 67.
91. Ibid, p. 67.
92. Ibid, p. 67.
93. Ibid, p. 67.
94. Norris, Merle. The Tom Mix Book. Waynesville: The World of Yesterday, 1989, p. 61.
95. Mix, Olive Stokes and Eric Heath. The Fabulous Tom Mix. Englewood Cliffs: Prentice-Hall, 1957, p. 83.
96. Mix, Paul E. Tom Mix: A Heavily Illustrated Biography with a Filmography. Jefferson: McFarland, 1995, p. 69.
97. Emrich, David. Hollywood, Colorado. Lakewood: Post Modern Company, 1997. p. 39.
98. Mix, Paul E. Tom Mix: A Heavily Illustrated Biography with a Filmography. Jefferson: McFarland, 1995, p. 68.
99. Ibid, p. 70.
100. Ibid, p. 73, 74.
101. Ibid, p. 70.
102. Mix, Olive Stokes and Eric Heath. The Fabulous Tom Mix. Englewood Cliffs: Prentice-Hall, 1957, p. 91.
103. Mix, Paul E. Tom Mix: A Heavily Illustrated Biography with a Filmography. Jefferson: McFarland, 1995, p. 74.
104. Mix, Olive Stokes and Eric Heath. The Fabulous Tom Mix. Englewood Cliffs: Prentice-Hall, 1957, p. 92.
105. Norris, Merle. The Tom Mix Book. Waynesville: The World of Yesterday, 1989, p. 105.
106. Mix, Paul E. Tom Mix: A Heavily Illustrated Biography with a Filmography. Jefferson: McFarland, 1995, p. 70.

107. Ibid, p. 74.
108. Emrich, David. Hollywood, Colorado. Lakewood: Post Modern Company, 1997, p. 37.
109. Ibid, p. 37.
110. Mix, Paul E. Tom Mix: A Heavily Illustrated Biography with a Filmography. Jefferson: McFarland, 1995, p. 70.
111. Ibid, p. 70.
112. Ibid, p. 70.
113. Ibid, p. 70, 71.
114. Ibid, p. 70.
115. Mix, Olive Stokes and Eric Heath. The Fabulous Tom Mix. Englewood Cliffs: Prentice-Hall, 1957, p. 130.
116. Mix, Paul E. Tom Mix: A Heavily Illustrated Biography with a Filmography. Jefferson: McFarland, 1995, p. 74.
117. Emrich, David. Hollywood, Colorado. Lakewood: Post Modern Company, 1997, p. 37, 38.
118. Ibid, p. 38.

Endnotes
Chapter Seven

1. McClure, Arthur F. and Ken D. Jones. Heroes, Heavies and Sagebrush. South Brunswick: A.S. Barnes and Co., 1972, p. 48.
2. Everson, William K. The Hollywood Western. New York: Citadel Press, 1992, p. 69.
3. McClure, Arthur F. and Ken D. Jones. Heroes, Heavies and Sagebrush. South Brunswick: A.S. Barnes and Co., 1972, p. 65.
4. Horwitz, James. They Went Thataway. New York: E.P. Dutton, 1976, p. 83.
5. Horwitz, James. They Went Thataway. New York: E.P. Dutton, 1976, p. 90.
6. McClure, Arthur F. and Ken D. Jones. Heroes, Heavies and Sagebrush. South Brunswick: A.S. Barnes and Co., 1972, p. 56.
7. Birchard, Robert S. King Cowboy: Tom Mix and the Movies. Burbank: Riverwood Press, 1993, p. 275.
8. McClure, Arthur F. and Ken D. Jones. Heroes, Heavies and Sagebrush. South Brunswick: A.S. Barnes and Co., 1972, p. 48.
9. Mix, Paul E. Tom Mix: A Heavily Illustrated Biography with a Filmography. Jefferson: McFarland, p. 100.
10. McClure, McClure, Arthur F. and Ken D. Jones. Heroes, Heavies and Sagebrush. South Brunswick: A.S. Barnes and Co., 1972, p. 48.

11. Wallis, Michael. The Real Wild West: The 101 Ranch and the creation of the American West. New York: St. Martin's Press, 1999, p. 351.
12. Everson, William K. The Hollywood Western. New York: Citadel Press, 1992, p. 24.

End Notes
Chapter Eight

1. Mix, Olive Stokes and Eric Heath. The Fabulous Tom Mix. Englewood Cliffs: Prentice-Hall, 1957, p. 74.
2. Mix, Paul E. Tom Mix: A Heavily Illustrated Biography with a Filmography. Jefferson: McFarland, 1995, p. 76.
3. Ibid, p. 77; Mix, Olive Stokes and Eric Heath. The Fabulous Tom Mix. Englewood Cliffs: Prentice-Hall, 1957, p. 94.
4. Mix, Paul E. Tom Mix: A Heavily Illustrated Biography with a Filmography. Jefferson: McFarland, 1995, p. 77.
5. Ibid, p. 78.
6. Ibid, p. 78.
7. Ibid, p. 78.
8. Ibid, p. 79.
9. Ibid, p. 80.
10. Ibid, p. 81.
11. University of Oklahoma Library, Western History Collection, (WHC, MB, File Box 69)
12. Mix, Olive Stokes and Eric Heath. The Fabulous Tom Mix. Englewood Cliffs: Prentice-Hall, 1957, p. 97.
13. Ibid, p. 95.
14. Ibid, p. 96.
15. Ibid, p. 95.
16. Ibid, p. 98.
17. Ibid, p. 98.
18. Ibid, p. 100.
19. Mix, Paul E. Tom Mix: A Heavily Illustrated Biography with a Filmography. Jefferson: McFarland, 1995, p. 83.
20. Mix, Paul E. The Life and Legend of Tom Mix. Cranbury: A.S. Barnes and Co., Inc., 1972, p. 60.
21. Mix, Paul E. Tom Mix: A Heavily Illustrated Biography with a Filmography. Jefferson: McFarland, 1995, p. 52.
22. Ibid, p. 83.

23. Ibid, p. 83.
24. Ibid, p. 84.
25. Rosebrook, Jeb J. and Jeb S. Rosebrook. "Arizona's Celluloid Cowboys." <u>Arizona Highways</u>. July 1997. Vol. 73, Number 7. Phoenix: 1997, p. 20.
26. Ibid, p. 18.
27. Norris, Merle. <u>The Tom Mix Book</u>. Waynesville: The World of Yesterday, 1989, p. 78.
28. Mix, Paul E. <u>Tom Mix: A Heavily Illustrated Biography with a Filmography</u>. Jefferson: McFarland, 1995, p. 83.
29. Mix, Olive Stokes and Eric Heath. <u>The Fabulous Tom Mix</u>. Englewood Cliffs: Prentice-Hall, 1957, p. 117.

End Notes
Chapter Nine

1. Mix, Paul E. <u>Tom Mix: A Heavily Illustrated Biography with a Filmography</u>. Jefferson: McFarland, 1995, p. 86.
2. Ibid, p. 87
3. Ibid, p. 89
4. Ibid, p. 89
5. Ibid, p. 89

End Notes
Chapter Ten

1. Wyatt, Edgar H. <u>The Hoxie Boys: The Lives and Films of Jack and Al Hoxie</u>. Raleigh: Wyatt Classics, Inc., 1992, p. 92.
2. McLynn, Frank. <u>Villa and Zapata: A History of the Mexican Revolution</u>. New York: Carroll & Graf Publishers, 2000, p. 392.
3. Ibid, p. 393.
4. Ibid, p. 390-393

End Notes
Chapter Eleven

1. Birchard, Robert S. <u>King Cowboy: Tom Mix and the Movies</u>. Burbank: Riverwood Press, 1993, p. 111.
2. Birchard, Robert S. <u>King Cowboy: Tom Mix and the Movies</u>. Burbank: Riverwood Press, 1993, p. 19.

3. Mix, Olive Stokes and Eric Heath. The Fabulous Tom Mix. Englewood Cliffs: Prentice-Hall, 1957, p. 121.
4. Birchard, Robert S. King Cowboy: Tom Mix and the Movies. Burbank: Riverwood Press, 1993, p. 19.
5. Mix, Paul E. Tom Mix: A Heavily Illustrated Biography with a Filmography. Jefferson: McFarland, p. 93.
6. Birchard, Robert S. King Cowboy: Tom Mix and the Movies. Burbank: Riverwood Press, 1993, p. 17.
7. Ibid, p. 18.
8. Norris, Merle. The Tom Mix Book. Waynesville: The World of Yesterday, 1989, p. 43.
9. Birchard, Robert S. King Cowboy: Tom Mix and the Movies. Burbank: Riverwood Press, 1993, p. 128.
10. Mix, Olive Stokes and Eric Heath. The Fabulous Tom Mix. Englewood Cliffs: Prentice-Hall, 1957, p. 136.
11. Trial transcript, Olive Stokes testimony, In the Chancery Court of Adams County, Mississippi, Zack T. Miller v. Tom Mix, et al. No. 5731, January 8, 1931, p.19.
12. Mix, Paul E. Tom Mix: A Heavily Illustrated Biography with a Filmography. Jefferson: McFarland, 1995, p. 95.
13. Birchard, Robert S. King Cowboy: Tom Mix and the Movies. Burbank: Riverwood Press, 1993, p. 20.
14. Ibid, p. 121.
15. Ibid, p. 115.
16. Ibid, p. 115.
17. Mosley, Leonard. Zanuck: The Rise and Fall of Hollywood's Last Tycoon. New York: McGraw Hill, 1984, p. 38.
18. Birchard, Robert S. King Cowboy: Tom Mix and the Movies. Burbank: Riverwood Press, 1993, p. 116.
19. Ibid, p. 115.
20. Mix, Olive Stokes and Eric Heath. The Fabulous Tom Mix. Englewood Cliffs: Prentice-Hall, 1957, p. 122.
21. Birchard, Robert S. King Cowboy: Tom Mix and the Movies. Burbank: Riverwood Press, 1993, p. 124.
22. Mix, Olive Stokes and Eric Heath. The Fabulous Tom Mix. Englewood Cliffs: Prentice-Hall, 1957, p. 103.
23. Mix, Paul E. Tom Mix: A Heavily Illustrated Biography with a Filmography. Jefferson: McFarland, 1995, p. 117.

24. Mix, Olive Stokes and Eric Heath. <u>The Fabulous Tom Mix</u>. Englewood Cliffs: Prentice-Hall, 1957, p. 103.
25. Ibid, p. 103.
26. Mix, Olive Stokes and Eric Heath. <u>The Fabulous Tom Mix</u>. Englewood Cliffs: Prentice-Hall, 1957, p. 105.
27. Birchard, Robert S. <u>King Cowboy: Tom Mix and the Movies</u>. Burbank: Riverwood Press, 1993, p. 116.
28. Moore, Colleen. <u>Silent Star</u>. Garden City: Doubleday & Company, Inc., 1968, p. 49.
29. Ibid, p. 51.
30. Ibid, p. 52.
31. Ibid, p. 52.
32. Ibid, p. 51.
33. Ibid, p. 52.
34. Ibid, p. 51.
35. Ibid, p. 54.
36. Ibid, p. 56, 57.
37. Mix, Paul E. <u>Tom Mix: A Heavily Illustrated Biography with a Filmography</u>. Jefferson: McFarland, 1995, p. 269.
38. Birchard, Robert S. <u>King Cowboy: Tom Mix and the Movies</u>. Burbank: Riverwood Press, 1993, p. 154.
39. Moore, Colleen. <u>Silent Star</u>. Garden City: Doubleday & Company, Inc., 1968, p. 53, 54.
40. Ibid, p. 54.
41. Ibid, p. 57.
42. Ibid, p. 57.
43. Ibid, p. 58.
44. Ibid, p. 58.
45. Ibid, p. 55.
46. Ibid, p. 55.
47. Autry, Gene and Mickey Herskowitz. <u>Back In The Saddle Again</u>. Garden City: Doubleday & Co., 1978, p. 41.
48. Ibid, p. 41.
49. Birchard, Robert S. <u>King Cowboy: Tom Mix and the Movies</u>. Burbank: Riverwood Press, 1993, p. 166.
50. Kahn, Roger. <u>A Flame of Pure Fire: Jack Dempsey and the Roaring '20s</u>. New York: Harcourt Brace & Co., 1999, p. 355.

51. Nicholas, John H. <u>Tom Mix: Riding Up To Glory</u>. Oklahoma City: National Cowboy Hall of Fame, 1980, p. 19.
52. "Tom Mix's Daughter to Christen Daddy's Yacht," L.A. Examiner, 3/11/1923.
53. St. John, Adela Rogers. <u>The Honeycomb</u>. New York: Doubleday & Co., 1969, p. 164.
54. Ibid, p. 164.
55. Ibid, p. 165.
56. Autry, Gene and Mickey Herskowitz. <u>Back In The Saddle Again</u>. Garden City: Doubleday & Co., 1978, p. 43.
57. St. John, Adela Rogers. <u>The Honeycomb</u>. New York: Doubleday & Co., 1969. p. 165.
58. Ibid, p. 165.
59. Ibid, p. 166.
60. Ibid, p. 164.
61. Ibid, 360.
62. Moore, Colleen. <u>Silent Star</u>. Garden City: Doubleday & Company, Inc., 1968, p. 60.
63. St. John, Adela Rogers. <u>The Honeycomb</u>. New York: Doubleday & Co., 1969, p. 164.
64. Mix, Olive Stokes and Eric Heath. <u>The Fabulous Tom Mix</u>. Englewood Cliffs: Prentice-Hall, 1957, p. 138, 139.
65. Ibid, 139.
66. "Thomasina Mix Goblin Party Hostess," L.A. Examiner, 11/8/1925
67. Davis, Ronald. Duke: <u>The Life and Image of John Wayne</u>. Norman, University of Oklahoma Press, 1998, p. 228, 229.
68. Mix, Olive Stokes and Eric Heath. <u>The Fabulous Tom Mix</u>. Englewood Cliffs: Prentice-Hall, 1957, p. 121.
69. Birchard, Robert S. <u>King Cowboy: Tom Mix and the Movies</u>. Burbank: Riverwood Press, 1993, p. 24.
70. Ibid, p. 15.
71. Ibid, p. 184.
72. Mix, Olive Stokes and Eric Heath. <u>The Fabulous Tom Mix</u>. Englewood Cliffs: Prentice-Hall, 1957, p. 18.
73. Ibid, p. 152.
74. Mix, Paul E. <u>Tom Mix: A Heavily Illustrated Biography with a Filmography</u>. Jefferson: McFarland, 1995, p. 104.

75. Norris, Merle. The Tom Mix Book. Waynesville: The World of Yesterday, 1989, p. 13.
76. Letter from Louis A. Oaks to Tom Mix, 5/16/1923, Oklahoma Historical Society, Tom Mix Collection.
77. Birchard, Robert S. King Cowboy: Tom Mix and the Movies. Burbank: Riverwood Press, 1993, p. 122.
78. Ibid, p. 121
79. Ibid, p. 121.
80. Norris, Merle. The Tom Mix Book. Waynesville: The World of Yesterday, 1989 p. 75.
81. Mix, Paul E. The Life and Legend of Tom Mix. Cranbury: A.S. Barnes and Co., Inc., 1972, p. 62.
82. Mix, Paul E. Tom Mix: A Heavily Illustrated Biography with a Filmography. Jefferson: McFarland, 1995, p. 107, 108.
83. Mix, Olive Stokes and Eric Heath. The Fabulous Tom Mix. Englewood Cliffs: Prentice-Hall, 1957, p. 105, 106.

End Notes
Chapter Twelve

1. Birchard, Robert S. King Cowboy: Tom Mix and the Movies. Burbank: Riverwood Press, 1993, p. 188.
2. Ibid, p. 132.
3. Ibid, p. 132.
4. Mix, Paul E. Tom Mix: A Heavily Illustrated Biography with a Filmography. Jefferson: McFarland, 1995, p. 109, 110.
5. Ibid, p. 111, 112.
6. Cody, Iron Eyes and Collin Perry. Iron Eyes—My Life As A Hollywood Indian. New York: Everest House, 1982, p. 44.
7. Ibid, p. 45.
8. Nicholas, John H. Tom Mix: Riding Up To Glory. Oklahoma City: National Cowboy Hall of Fame, 1980, p. 41.
9. Birchard, Robert S. King Cowboy: Tom Mix and the Movies. Burbank: Riverwood Press, 1993, p. 128.
10. Norris, Merle. The Tom Mix Book. Waynesville: The World of Yesterday, 1989 p. 38.
11. Birchard, Robert S. King Cowboy: Tom Mix and the Movies. Burbank: Riverwood Press, 1993, p. 128.
12. Ibid, p. 128.

13. Ibid, p. 128.
14. Moore, Colleen. Silent Star. Garden City: Doubleday & Company, Inc., 1968, p. 53.

End Notes
Chapter Thirteen

1. Birchard, Robert S. King Cowboy: Tom Mix and the Movies. Burbank: Riverwood Press, 1993, p. 120.
2. Bell, Gene. "Who the Hell is Tom Mix?" www.classicImages.com. Lee Enterprises, 1999, page x.
3. Swindell, Larry. The Last Hero: A Biography of Gary Cooper. New York: Doubleday, 1980, p. 61.
4. McClure, Arthur F. and Ken D. Jones. Heroes, Heavies and Sagebrush. South Brunswick: A.S. Barnes and Co., 1972, p. 48.
5. Birchard, Robert S. King Cowboy: Tom Mix and the Movies. Burbank: Riverwood Press, 1993 p. 125.
6. Letter from Thomas Kellogg to Tom Mix, 3/12/1925, Oklahoma Historical Society, Tom Mix Collection, Box 1621.
7. Letter from George Holmes to Scotland Yard, 4/2/1925. Oklahoma Historical Society, Tom Mix Collection.
8. Mix, Paul E. Tom Mix: A Heavily Illustrated Biography with a Filmography. Jefferson: McFarland, 1995, p. 111.
9. Ibid, p. 111.
10. Ibid, p. 111.
11. Norris, Merle. The Tom Mix Book. Waynesville: The World of Yesterday, 1989, p. 59.
12. Mix, Paul E. The Life and Legend of Tom Mix. Cranbury: A.S. Barnes and Co., Inc., 1972, p. 107.
13. Nicholas, John H. Tom Mix: Riding Up To Glory. Oklahoma City: National Cowboy Hall of Fame, 1980, p. 44.
14. Letter from Dr. Arl Meyers to Tom Mix, 4/18/1925, Oklahoma Historical Society, Tom Mix Collection.
15. Mix, Paul E. Tom Mix: A Heavily Illustrated Biography with a Filmography. Jefferson: McFarland, 1995, p. 112.
16. Ibid, p. 112.
17. Ibid, p. 112.
18. Ibid, p. 112.
19. Ibid, p. 112.

20. Ibid, p. 112.
21. Nicholas, John H. Tom Mix: Riding Up To Glory. Oklahoma City: National Cowboy Hall of Fame, 1980, p. 44, 45.
22. Letter from W. Freeland Kendrick to Tom Mix, 7/7/1995, Oklahoma Historical Society, Tom Mix Collection.
23. Mix, Paul E. Tom Mix: A Heavily Illustrated Biography with a Filmography. Jefferson: McFarland, 1995, p. 114.

End Notes
Chapter Fourteen

1. Coburn, Walt. "Tom Mix's Last Sundown. Frontier Times. Vol. 42, No. 5, New Series No. 55. Austin: Western Publications, Inc., August, 1969, p. 9.
2. Birchard, Robert S. King Cowboy: Tom Mix and the Movies. Burbank: Riverwood Press, 1993, p. 119.
3. Eyles, Alan. John Wayne. Cranbury: A.S. Barnes and Co., Inc., 1976, p. 19.
4. Eyles, Alan. John Wayne. Cranbury: A.S. Barnes and Co., Inc., 1976, p. 20.
5. Roberts, Randy and James Olson. John Wayne: American. Lincoln: University of Nebraska Press, 1995, p. 61.
6. Ibid, p. 61.
7. Eyles, Alan. John Wayne. Cranbury: A.S. Barnes and Co., Inc., 1976, p. 22.
8. Birchard, Robert S. King Cowboy: Tom Mix and the Movies. Burbank: Riverwood Press, 1993, p. 124.
9. Ibid, p. 124.
10. Daily Variety, 5/26/1926.
11. Birchard, Robert S. King Cowboy: Tom Mix and the Movies. Burbank: Riverwood Press, 1993, p. 124.
12. Norris, Merle. The Tom Mix Book. Waynesville: The World of Yesterday, 1989, p. 193.
13. Ibid, p. 162, 163.
14. "Trip to Paris," Beverly Hills, Ca. Bulletin, 5/12/1927.
15. Mix, Olive Stokes and Eric Heath. The Fabulous Tom Mix. Englewood Cliffs: Prentice-Hall, 1957, p. 139.
16. Birchard, Robert S. King Cowboy: Tom Mix and the Movies. Burbank: Riverwood Press, 1993, p. 120.
17. Ibid, p. 119.
18. Mix, Olive Stokes and Eric Heath. The Fabulous Tom Mix. Englewood Cliffs: Prentice-Hall, 1957, p. 132.
19. Ibid, p. 133.

20. Ibid, p. 134.
21. Norris, Merle. <u>The Tom Mix Book</u>. Waynesville: The World of Yesterday, 1989 p. 38.
22. "Miss Mix Rides Like Her Veteran Daddy" Journal Miner, Prescott: Az. 11/4/1927.
23. Seattle Record, 11/4/1927.
24. Article, unknown author or publication, 10/4/1927, OHS/TMC, Box 1621.
25. Mix, Paul E. <u>Tom Mix: A Heavily Illustrated Biography with a Filmography.</u> Jefferson: McFarland, 1995, p. 115.
26. Streible, Dan. "Tom Mix meet Mr. Trotsky: Newsreels and Out-takes as Documentary." www. s.edu/park-row.html.
27. Mix, Olive Stokes and Eric Heath. <u>The Fabulous Tom Mix</u>. Englewood Cliffs: Prentice-Hall, 1957 p. 142.
28. Carter, Joseph H. <u>Never Met A Man I Didn't Like: The Life and Writings of Will Rogers</u>. New York: Avon Books, 1991, p. 78.
29. Autry, Gene and Mickey Herskowitz. <u>Back In The Saddle Again</u>. Garden City: Doubleday & Co., 1978, p. 43.
30. Carter, Joseph H. <u>Never Met A Man I Didn't Like: The Life and Writings of Will Rogers</u>. New York: Avon Books, 1991, p. 78.
31. Interview 5/15/1929, author unknown, publication unknown, Oklahoma Historical Society, Tom Mix Collection.

End Notes
Chapter Fifteen

1. Mix, Paul E. <u>Tom Mix: A Heavily Illustrated Biography with a Filmography.</u> Jefferson: McFarland, 1995, p. 115.
2. Birchard, Robert S. <u>King Cowboy: Tom Mix and the Movies</u>. Burbank: Riverwood Press, 1993, p. 216.
3. Mix, Paul E. <u>Tom Mix: A Heavily Illustrated Biography with a Filmography.</u> Jefferson: McFarland, 1995, p. 115
4. Birchard, Robert S. <u>King Cowboy: Tom Mix and the Movies</u>. Burbank: Riverwood Press, 1993, p. 221.
5. Ibid, p. 222.
6. Ibid, p. 223.
7. Ibid, p. 223.
8. Ibid, p. 221.
9. Ibid, p. 221.
10. Ibid, p. 223.

11. Ibid, p. 230.
12. Ibid, p. 223.
13. Ibid, p. 217.
14. Ibid, p. 226.
15. Gossard, Jr., Wayne H. "Three Ring Circus: The Tom Mix-Zack Miller Lawsuits 1929-1934." <u>The Chronicles of Oklahoma</u>. Norman: The Oklahoma Historical Society, Vol. LV111, Number 1. Spring, 1980, p. 7.
16. Ibid, p. 7.
17. Ibid, p. 7.
18. Ibid, p. 7,8.
19. Barra, Allen. <u>Inventing Wyatt Earp: His Life and Many Legends.</u> New York: Caroll & Graf Publishers, 1998, p. 341.
20. St. John, Adela Rogers. <u>The Honeycomb</u>. New York: Doubleday & Co., 1969, p. 165.
21. Ibid, p. 167.
22. Autry, Gene and Mickey Herskowitz. <u>Back In The Saddle Again</u>. Garden City: Doubleday & Co., 1978. p. 43.
23. Birchard, Robert S. <u>King Cowboy: Tom Mix and the Movies</u>. Burbank: Riverwood Press, 1993, p. 223.
24. Ibid, p. 223, 224.
25. Ibid, p. 226.
26. Roberts, Randy and James Olson. <u>John Wayne: American</u>. Lincoln: University of Nebraska Press, 1995, p. 83.
27. Roberts, Randy and James Olson. <u>John Wayne: American</u>. Lincoln: University of Nebraska Press, 1995, p. 61.

End Notes
Chapter Sixteen

1. Gossard, Jr., Wayne H. "Three Ring Circus: The Tom Mix-Zack Miller Lawsuits 1929-1934." <u>The Chronicles of Oklahoma</u>. Norman: The Oklahoma Historical Society, Vol. LV111, Number 1. Spring, 1980, p. 7.
2. Ibid, p. 8.
3. Ibid, p. 12.
4. Ibid, p. 8.
5. Ibid, p. 8.
6. Ibid, p. 8.
7. Ibid, p. 8.
8. Ibid, p. 8,9.

9. Collings, Ellsworth and Alma Miller England. The 101 Ranch. Norman: University of Oklahoma Press, 1937, p. 218.
10. Coburn, Walt. "Tom Mix's Last Sundown. Frontier Times. Vol. 42, No. 5, New Series No. 55. Austin: Western Publications, Inc., August, 1969, p. 10.

End Notes
Chapter Seventeen

1. Mix, Olive Stokes and Eric Heath. The Fabulous Tom Mix. Englewood Cliffs: Prentice-Hall, 1957, p. 139.
2. Ibid, p. 146.
3. Ibid, p. 148.
4. Mix, Paul E. Tom Mix: A Heavily Illustrated Biography with a Filmography. Jefferson: McFarland, 1995, p. 117.
5. Ibid, p. 114.
6. Mix, Olive Stokes and Eric Heath. The Fabulous Tom Mix. Englewood Cliffs: Prentice-Hall, 1957, p. 5.
7. Ibid, p. 147.
8. Mix, Paul E. Tom Mix: A Heavily Illustrated Biography with a Filmography. Jefferson: McFarland, 1995, p. 169.
9. Mix, Olive Stokes and Eric Heath. The Fabulous Tom Mix. Englewood Cliffs: Prentice-Hall, 1957, p. 147.
10. Ibid, p. 149.
11. Ibid, p. 149.
12. Ibid, p. 144, 145.
13. Ibid, p. 144.
14. Ibid, p. 145.
15. Ibid, p. 146.
16. Birchard, Robert S. King Cowboy: Tom Mix and the Movies. Burbank: Riverwood Press, 1993, p. 230
17. Mix, Paul E. Tom Mix: A Heavily Illustrated Biography with a Filmography. Jefferson: McFarland, 1995, p. 124, 125.
18. Birchard, Robert S. King Cowboy: Tom Mix and the Movies. Burbank: Riverwood Press, 1993, p. 229, 230.
19. "Lassoes Trouble" Brooklyn Eagle, 5/9/1929.
20. "Mix says 'Just Honest Working Man.'" Los Angeles Examiner, 5/9/1929.
21. Santa Barbara (Ca.) Press, 5/11/1929.
22. Birchard, Robert S. King Cowboy: Tom Mix and the Movies. Burbank: Riverwood Press, 1993, p. 230.

23. Mix, Paul E. Tom Mix: A Heavily Illustrated Biography with a Filmography. Jefferson: McFarland, 1995, p. 174.
24. Ibid, p. 174, 175.
25. Birchard, Robert S. King Cowboy: Tom Mix and the Movies. Burbank: Riverwood Press, 1993, p. 232.
26. Mix, Paul E. Tom Mix: A Heavily Illustrated Biography with a Filmography. Jefferson: McFarland, 1995, p. 175; Birchard, p. 232.
27. St. John, Adela Rogers. The Honeycomb. New York: Doubleday & Co., 1969, p. 164.
28. Ibid, p. 164.
29. Moore, Colleen. Silent Star. Garden City: Doubleday & Company, Inc., 1968, p. 53.
30. Ibid, p. 51.
31. "Tom Mix quits movies as wife brings suit," New York American, 12/13/1930.
32. Trial transcript, Zack Miller testimony, In the Chancery Court of Adams County, Mississippi, Zack T. Miller v. Tom Mix, et al. No. 5731, January 8, 1931, p. 4, University of Oklahoma Library, Western History Collection.
33. Trial transcript, Zack Miller testimony, In the Chancery Court of Adams County, Mississippi, Zack T. Miller v. Tom Mix, et al. No. 5731, January 8, 1931, p. 6, University of Oklahoma Library Western History Collection.
34. Trial transcript, Olive Stokes testimony, In the Chancery Court of Adams County, Mississippi, Zack T. Miller v. Tom Mix, et al. No. 5731, January 8, 1931, p. 2, University of Oklahoma Library, Western History Collection.
35. Trial transcript, Olive Stokes testimony, In the Chancery Court of Adams County, Mississippi, Zack T. Miller v. Tom Mix, et al. No. 5731, January 8, 1931, p. 18, University of Oklahoma Library, Western History Collection.
36. Trial transcript, Olive Stokes testimony, In the Chancery Court of Adams County, Mississippi, Zack T. Miller v. Tom Mix, et al. No. 5731, January 8, 1931, p. 19, University of Oklahoma Library, Western History Collection.
37. Trial transcript, Olive Stokes testimony, In the Chancery Court of Adams County, Mississippi, Zack T. Miller v. Tom Mix, et al. No. 5731, January 8, 1931, p. 20,21, University of Oklahoma Library, Western History Collection.
38. Trial transcript, Tom Mix testimony, In the Chancery Court of Adams County, Mississippi, Zack T. Miller v. Tom Mix, et al. No. 5731, January 8, 1931, p. 8, University of Oklahoma Library, Western History Collection.

39. Trial transcript, Tom Mix testimony, In the Chancery Court of Adams County, Mississippi, Zack T. Miller v. Tom Mix, et al. No. 5731, January 8, 1931, p. 20, University of Oklahoma Library, Western History Collection.
40. Trial transcript, Tom Mix testimony, In the Chancery Court of Adams County, Mississippi, Zack T. Miller v. Tom Mix, et al. No. 5731, January 8, 1931, p. 5, University of Oklahoma Library, Western History Collection.
41. Trial transcript, Tom Mix testimony, In the Chancery Court of Adams County, Mississippi, Zack T. Miller v. Tom Mix, et al. No. 5731, January 8, 1931, p. 6, University of Oklahoma Library, Western History Collection.
42. Trial transcript, Tom Mix testimony, In the Chancery Court of Adams County, Mississippi, Zack T. Miller v. Tom Mix, et al. No. 5731, January 8, 1931, p. 20, University of Oklahoma Library, Western History Collection.
43. Gossard, Jr., Wayne H. "Three Ring Circus: The Tom Mix-Zack Miller Lawsuits 1929-1934." The Chronicles of Oklahoma. Norman: The Oklahoma Historical Society, Vol. LV111, Number 1. Spring, 1980, p. 12.
44. Gossard, Jr., Wayne H. "Three Ring Circus: The Tom Mix-Zack Miller Lawsuits 1929-1934." The Chronicles of Oklahoma. Norman: The Oklahoma Historical Society, Vol. LV111, Number 1. Spring, 1980, p. 11.
45. Gossard, Jr., Wayne H. "Three Ring Circus: The Tom Mix-Zack Miller Lawsuits 1929-1934." The Chronicles of Oklahoma. Norman: The Oklahoma Historical Society, Vol. LV111, Number 1. Spring, 1980, p. 10, 11.
46. New York Police Gazette, 3/14/1931.
47. Collings, Ellsworth and Alma Miller England. The 101 Ranch. Norman: University of Oklahoma Press, 1937, p.218.
48. Anonymous. The Life of Tom Mix, Illustrated: Souvenir Program Sells Floto Circus, 1931.
49. "Two Gun Actor's Valet Held" Oakland (CA) Enquirer, 6/20/1929.

End Notes
Chapter Eighteen

1. Mix, Paul E. Tom Mix: A Heavily Illustrated Biography with a Filmography. Jefferson: McFarland, 1995, p. 173.
2. Birchard, Robert S. King Cowboy: Tom Mix and the Movies. Burbank: Riverwood Press, 1993, p. 232.
3. Ibid, p. 232.
4. Autry, Gene and Mickey Herskowitz. Back In The Saddle Again. Garden City: Doubleday & Co., 1978. p. 42, 43.

5. Birchard, Robert S. <u>King Cowboy: Tom Mix and the Movies</u>. Burbank: Riverwood Press, 1993, p. 232.
6. Ibid, p. 232, 233.
7. Telegram from Harold Lloyd to Tom Mix, 11/24/1931, Oklahoma Historical Society, Tom Mix Collection.
8. Telegram from Jack Dempsey to Tom Mix, 11/25/1931. Oklahoma Historical Society, Tom Mix Collection.
9. Telegram from Babe Ruth to Tom Mix, 11/25/1931, Oklahoma Historical Society, Tom Mix Collection.
10. Birchard, Robert S. <u>King Cowboy: Tom Mix and the Movies</u>. Burbank: Riverwood Press, 1993, p. 233.
11. Telegram from Mulhalls to Tom Mix, 11/27/1931, Oklahoma Historical Society, Tom Mix Collection.
12. Telegram from Betty Rogers to Tom Mix, 11/26/1931, Oklahoma Historical Society, Tom Mix Collection.
13. Telegram from George O'Brien to Tom Mix, 11/28/1931, Oklahoma Historical Society, Tom Mix Collection.
14. Telegrams from Leo Carillo to Tom Mix, 11/24, 27, 29/1931. Oklahoma Historical Society, Tom Mix Collection.
15. Telegram from John and Mary Ford to Tom Mix, 11/28/1931. Oklahoma Historical Society, Tom Mix Collection.
16. Telegram from Ruth Mix to Tom Mix, 11/29/1931, Oklahoma Historical Society, Tom Mix Collection.
17. Telegram from Elizabeth Mix, 11/28/1931, Oklahoma Historical Society, Tom Mix Collection.
18. Telegram from Leo Carillo to Tom Mix, 12/4/1931, Oklahoma Historical Society, Tom Mix Collection.
19. Telegram from Raoul Walsh to Tom Mix, 12/11/1931, Oklahoma Historical Society, Tom Mix Collection.
20. Parking ticket, Los Angeles Police Department to Tom Mix, 12/13/1931, Oklahoma Historical Society, Tom Mix Collection.
21. Birchard, Robert S. <u>King Cowboy: Tom Mix and the Movies</u>. Burbank: Riverwood Press, 1993, p. 234.
22. Ibid, p. 234, 235.
23. Ibid, p. 250.
24. Autry, Gene and Mickey Herskowitz. <u>Back In The Saddle Again</u>. Garden City: Doubleday & Co., 1978. p. 43.
25. Ibid, p. 43.

26. Wallis, Michael. <u>The Real Wild West: The 101 Ranch and the creation of the American West.</u> New York: St. Martin's Press, 1999, p. 511.
27. Birchard, Robert S. <u>King Cowboy: Tom Mix and the Movies</u>. Burbank: Riverwood Press, 1993, p. 250.
28. Ibid, p. 236.
29. Ibid, p. 250.
30. Ibid, p. 250.
31. Ibid, p. 253.
32. Ibid, p. 253.
33. Ibid, p. 239.
34. Ibid, p. 239.
35. Ibid, p. 258.
36. Ibid, p. 238.
37. Ibid, p. 258, 259.
38. Ibid, p. 258.
39. Ibid, p. 258.
40. Ibid, p. 259.
41. Mix, L, p. 141, 142.
42. Birchard, Robert S. <u>King Cowboy: Tom Mix and the Movies</u>. Burbank: Riverwood Press, 1993, p. 259.
43. "Tony spills Tom Mix," Oklahoma Times, 10/22/1932, p. 3; Mix, H, p. 179.
44. Gossard, Jr., Wayne H. "Three Ring Circus: The Tom Mix-Zack Miller Lawsuits 1929-1934." <u>The Chronicles of Oklahoma</u>. Norman: The Oklahoma Historical Society, Vol. LV111, Number 1. Spring, 1980, p.12.
45. "Mix daughter flays mother at trial," Erie, Pa. Daily Times, 3/27/1933.
46. Letter from Jack Webb to Eugene Walker, Esq. dated November 21, 1933, University of Oklahoma Library, Western History Collection, Box 69, Folder 69-2.
47. Gossard, Jr., Wayne H. "Three Ring Circus: The Tom Mix-Zack Miller Lawsuits 1929-1934." <u>The Chronicles of Oklahoma</u>. Norman: The Oklahoma Historical Society, Vol. LV111, Number 1. Spring, 1980, p. 12, 13.
48. Letter from Zack Miller to William Tubesing, 3/17/1933. University of Oklahoma Library, Western History Collection, MB File Box 69.
49. Norris, Merle. <u>The Tom Mix Book</u>. Waynesville: The World of Yesterday, 1989, p. 38.
50. Birchard, Robert S. <u>King Cowboy: Tom Mix and the Movies</u>. Burbank: Riverwood Press, 1993, p. 259.

51. Ibid, p. 263.
52. Ibid, p. 263.
53. Autry, Gene and Mickey Herskowitz. Back In The Saddle Again. Garden City: Doubleday & Co., 1978. p. 44.
54. Mix, Paul E. Tom Mix: A Heavily Illustrated Biography with a Filmography. Jefferson: McFarland, 1995, p. 180.
55. Ibid, p. 121, 122.

End Notes
Chapter Nineteen

1. Mix, Paul E. Tom Mix: A Heavily Illustrated Biography with a Filmography. Jefferson: McFarland, 1995, p. 180.
2. Ibid, p. 180.
3. Ibid, p. 182.
4. Ibid, p. 183.
5. Ibid, p. 182.
6. Ibid, p. 183.
7. Gossard, Jr., Wayne H. "Three Ring Circus: The Tom Mix-Zack Miller Lawsuits 1929-1934." The Chronicles of Oklahoma. Norman: The Oklahoma Historical Society, Vol. LV111, Number 1. Spring, 1980, p. 13.
8. Letter from E.G. Moseley to Zack Miller, April 12, 1934, University of Oklahoma Library, Western History Collection, MB File Box M-407.
9. Letter from Guy Weadick to Zack Miller, March 20, 1933, University of Oklahoma Library, Western History Collection, MB File Box 69.
10. Letter from Guy Weadick to Zack Miller, April 14, 1933, University of Oklahoma Library, Western History Collection, MB File Box 69.
11. Letter to Dale Tunney from Zack Miller, June 27, 1934, University of Oklahoma Library, Western History Collection.
12. Letter from Marshall Taylor, Esq. to Zack Miller, July 30, 1934, University of Oklahoma Library, Western History Collection.
13. Legal document memorializing settlement conference dated Sept. 21, 1934, University of Oklahoma Library, Western History Collection, MB, M-407, 88-6.
14. Mix, Paul E. Tom Mix: A Heavily Illustrated Biography with a Filmography. Jefferson: McFarland, 1995, p. 185.
15. Ibid, p. 183.
16. Ibid, p. 183.

End Notes
Chapter Twenty

1. Mix, Paul E. <u>Tom Mix: A Heavily Illustrated Biography with a Filmography</u>. Jefferson: McFarland, 1995, p. 185.
2. Birchard, p. 265.
3. Mix, Olive Stokes and Eric Heath. <u>The Fabulous Tom Mix</u>. Englewood Cliffs: Prentice-Hall, 1957, p. 148.
4. Collings, Ellsworth and Alma Miller England. <u>The 101 Ranch</u>. Norman: University of Oklahoma Press, 1937, p. 218.
5. Mix, Olive Stokes and Eric Heath. <u>The Fabulous Tom Mix</u>. Englewood Cliffs: Prentice-Hall, 1957, p. 149.
6. Birchard, Robert S. <u>King Cowboy: Tom Mix and the Movies</u>. Burbank: Riverwood Press, 1993, p. 266.
7. Mix, Paul E. <u>Tom Mix: A Heavily Illustrated Biography with a Filmography</u>. Jefferson: McFarland, 1995, p. 139.
8. Birchard, Robert S. <u>King Cowboy: Tom Mix and the Movies</u>. Burbank: Riverwood Press, 1993, p. 266.
9. Autry, Gene and Mickey Herskowitz. <u>Back In The Saddle Again</u>. Garden City: Doubleday & Co., 1978, p. 144.
10. Mix, Paul E. <u>Tom Mix: A Heavily Illustrated Biography with a Filmography</u>. Jefferson: McFarland, 1995, p. 186.
11. Ibid, p. 186.
12. Birchard, Robert S. <u>King Cowboy: Tom Mix and the Movies</u>. Burbank: Riverwood Press, 1993, p. 269.
13. Ibid, p. 267.
14. Ibid, p. 267.
15. Ibid, p. 269.

End Notes
Chapter Twenty-One

1. Mix, Paul E. <u>Tom Mix: A Heavily Illustrated Biography with a Filmography</u>. Jefferson: McFarland, 1995, p. 187.
2. Mix, Olive Stokes and Eric Heath. <u>The Fabulous Tom Mix</u>. Englewood Cliffs: Prentice-Hall, 1957 p. 153.
3. Mix, Olive Stokes and Eric Heath. <u>The Fabulous Tom Mix</u>. Englewood Cliffs: Prentice-Hall, 1957, p. 152.

4. Mix, Paul E. Tom Mix: A Heavily Illustrated Biography with a Filmography. Jefferson: McFarland, 1995, p. 187.
5. Ibid, p. 189.
6. Robinson, C.O. "Tom Mix Was My Boss." Frontier Times. Vol. 43, No. 4, New Series No. 60. Austin: Western Publications, Inc., June, 1969, p. 19.
7. Ibid, p. 20.
8. Carter, Joseph H. Never Met A Man I Didn't Like: The Life and Writings of Will Rogers. New York: Avon Books, 1991, p. 140.
9. Nicholas, John H. Tom Mix: Riding Up To Glory. Oklahoma City: National Cowboy Hall of Fame, 1980, p. 80.
10. Mix, Olive Stokes and Eric Heath. The Fabulous Tom Mix. Englewood Cliffs: Prentice-Hall, 1957, p. 158.
11. Mix, Paul E. The Life and Legend of Tom Mix. Cranbury: A.S. Barnes and Co., Inc., 1972., p. 143.
12. Mix, Paul E. Tom Mix: A Heavily Illustrated Biography with a Filmography. Jefferson: McFarland, 1995, p. 189.
13. Ibid, p. 190.
14. Ibid, p. 191.
15. Ibid, p. 191, 192.
16. Ibid, p. 192.
17. Mix, Olive Stokes and Eric Heath. The Fabulous Tom Mix. Englewood Cliffs: Prentice-Hall, 1957, p. 159.
18. Mix, Paul E. Tom Mix: A Heavily Illustrated Biography with a Filmography. Jefferson: McFarland, 1995, p. 192.
19. Ibid, p. 192.
20. Ibid, p. 192.
21. Ibid, p. 194.
22. Ibid, p. 194.
23. Ibid, p. 195.
24. Ibid, p. 194.
25. McCoy, Tim and Ronald McCoy. Tim McCoy Remembers the West. Lincoln: University of Nebraska Press, 1977, p. 251.
26. Mix, Paul E. Tom Mix: A Heavily Illustrated Biography with a Filmography. Jefferson: McFarland, 1995, p. 196.
27. Birchard, Robert S. King Cowboy: Tom Mix and the Movies. Burbank: Riverwood Press, 1993, p. 272.
28. Mix, Olive Stokes and Eric Heath. The Fabulous Tom Mix. Englewood Cliffs: Prentice-Hall, 1957, p. 159.

29. Ibid, p. 161.
30. Ibid, p. 161.
31. Ibid, p. 161.
32. Ibid, p. 168.
33. Ibid, p. 169.
34. Ibid, p. 170.
35. Ibid, p. 167.
36. Ibid, p. 170.
37. Ibid, p. 171.
38. Birchard, Robert S. King Cowboy: Tom Mix and the Movies. Burbank: Riverwood Press, 1993, p. 274.
39. Mix, Paul E. Tom Mix: A Heavily Illustrated Biography with a Filmography. Jefferson: McFarland, 1995, p. 196.
40. Ibid, p. 200.
41. Mix, Paul E. The Life and Legend of Tom Mix. Cranbury: A.S. Barnes and Co., Inc., 1972, p. 144.
42. Mix, Paul E. Tom Mix: A Heavily Illustrated Biography with a Filmography. Jefferson: McFarland, 1995, p. 197.
43. Mix, Olive Stokes and Eric Heath. The Fabulous Tom Mix. Englewood Cliffs: Prentice-Hall, 1957, p. 173.
44. Ibid, p. 173.
45. Mix, Paul E. Tom Mix: A Heavily Illustrated Biography with a Filmography. Jefferson: McFarland, 1995, p. 200.
46. Ibid, p. 200.
47. Ibid, p. 204.
48. Ibid, p. 204.
49. Ibid, p. 204
50. Ibid, p. 204.
51. Ibid, p. 204.

End Notes
Chapter Twenty-Two

1. Birchard, Robert S. King Cowboy: Tom Mix and the Movies. Burbank: Riverwood Press, 1993, p. 275.
2. Mix, Paul E. Tom Mix: A Heavily Illustrated Biography with a Filmography. Jefferson: McFarland, 1995, p. 122.
3. Ibid, p. 205.
4. Ibid, p. 205.

5. Birchard, Robert S. King Cowboy: Tom Mix and the Movies. Burbank: Riverwood Press, 1993, p. 275.
6. Ibid, p. 275.
7. Ibid, p. 275.
8. Birchard, Robert S. King Cowboy: Tom Mix and the Movies. Burbank: Riverwood Press, 1993, p. 275.
9. Mix, Olive Stokes and Eric Heath. The Fabulous Tom Mix. Englewood Cliffs: Prentice-Hall, 1957, p. 175.
10. Birchard, Robert S. King Cowboy: Tom Mix and the Movies. Burbank: Riverwood Press, 1993, p. 275.
11. Mix, Olive Stokes and Eric Heath. The Fabulous Tom Mix. Englewood Cliffs: Prentice-Hall, 1957, p. 174.
12. Ibid, p. 174
13. Garza, Alicia A. "El Sauz, Texas. The Handbook of Texas Online." www.tsha.Utexas.edu., p. 1.
14. Mix, Olive Stokes and Eric Heath. The Fabulous Tom Mix. Englewood Cliffs: Prentice-Hall, 1957, p. 174
15. Ibid, p. 174.
16. Mix, Paul E. Tom Mix: A Heavily Illustrated Biography with a Filmography. Jefferson: McFarland, 1995, p. 206.
17. Ibid, p. 206
18. Ibid, p. 206
19. Coburn, Walt. "Tom Mix's Last Sundown. Frontier Times. Vol. 42, No. 5, New Series No. 55. Austin: Western Publications, Inc., August, 1969, p. 7.
20. Ibid, p. 7.
21. Ibid, p. 7.
22. Ibid, p. 7.
23. Ibid, p. 8.
24. Ibid, p. 10.
25. Ibid, p. 10.
26. Ibid, p. 7.
27. Ibid, p. 9.
28. Ibid, p. 9.
29. Mix, Paul E. Tom Mix: A Heavily Illustrated Biography with a Filmography. Jefferson: McFarland, 1995, p. 209.
30. Ibid, p. 209.
31. Mix, Olive Stokes and Eric Heath. The Fabulous Tom Mix. Englewood Cliffs: Prentice-Hall, 1957, p. 174, 175.

32. Ibid, p. 175.
33. Mix, Paul E. Tom Mix: A Heavily Illustrated Biography with a Filmography. Jefferson: McFarland, 1995, p. 209.
34. Coburn, Walt. "Tom Mix's Last Sundown. Frontier Times. Vol. 42, No. 5, New Series No. 55. Austin: Western Publications, Inc., August, 1969, p. 9.
35. Rosebrook, p. 18.
36. Coburn, Walt. "Tom Mix's Last Sundown. Frontier Times. Vol. 42, No. 5, New Series No. 55. Austin: Western Publications, Inc., August, 1969, 11.
37. Mix, Paul E. Tom Mix: A Heavily Illustrated Biography with a Filmography. Jefferson: McFarland, 1995, p. 210.
38. Coburn, Walt. "Tom Mix's Last Sundown. Frontier Times. Vol. 42, No. 5, New Series No. 55. Austin: Western Publications, Inc., August, 1969, p. 11.
39. Ibid, p. 11.
40. Mix, Paul E. Tom Mix: A Heavily Illustrated Biography with a Filmography. Jefferson: McFarland, 1995, p. 210.
41. Mix, L, p. 151.
42. Mix, Olive Stokes and Eric Heath. The Fabulous Tom Mix. Englewood Cliffs: Prentice-Hall, 1957, p. 176.
43. Mix, Paul E. Tom Mix: A Heavily Illustrated Biography with a Filmography. Jefferson: McFarland, 1995, p. 211.
44. Ibid, p. 211.
45. Ibid, p. 211.
46. Ibid, p. 211.
47. Birchard, Robert S. King Cowboy: Tom Mix and the Movies. Burbank: Riverwood Press, 1993, p. 279.
48. Ibid, p. 278.
49. Mix, Paul E. Tom Mix: A Heavily Illustrated Biography with a Filmography. Jefferson: McFarland, 1995, p. 212, 213.
50. Birchard, Robert S. King Cowboy: Tom Mix and the Movies. Burbank: Riverwood Press, 1993, p. 124.
51. Mix, Paul E. Tom Mix: A Heavily Illustrated Biography with a Filmography. Jefferson: McFarland, 1995, p. 213.
52. Ibid, p. 214.
53. Ibid, p. 214.
54. Norris, Merle. The Tom Mix Book. Waynesville: The World of Yesterday, 1989 p. 25.
55. "Mulhall Ranch, The." www.jcs-group.com/oldwest/wildwestshow/mulhall.html., p.1.

Endnotes
Conclusion

1. Coburn, Walt. "Tom Mix's Last Sundown. <u>Frontier Times.</u> Vol. 42, No. 5, New Series No. 55. Austin: Western Publications, Inc., August, 1969, p. 48.
2. Collings, Ellsworth and Alma Miller England. <u>The 101 Ranch</u>. Norman: University of Oklahoma Press, 1937, p. 218

Bibliography

Anonymous. The Life of Tom Mix, Illustrated: Souvenir Program Sells Floto Circus, 1931.

Autry, Gene and Mickey Herskowitz. Back In The Saddle Again. Garden City: Doubleday & Co., 1978.

Barra, Allen. Inventing Wyatt Earp: His Life and Many Legends. New York: Caroll & Graf Publishers, 1998.

Bell, Gene. "Who the Hell is Tom Mix?" www.classicImages.com. Lee Enterprises, 1999.

Birchard, Robert S. King Cowboy: Tom Mix and the Movies. Burbank: Riverwood Press, 1993.

Carter, Joseph H. Never Met A Man I Didn't Like: The Life and Writings of Will Rogers. New York: Avon Books, 1991.

Coburn, Walt. "Tom Mix's Last Sundown. Frontier Times. Vol. 42, No. 5, New Series No. 55. Austin: Western Publications, Inc., August, 1969.

Cody, Iron Eyes and Collin Perry. Iron Eyes—My Life As A Hollywood Indian. New York: Everest House, 1982.

Collings, Ellsworth and Alma Miller England. The 101 Ranch. Norman: University of Oklahoma Press, 1937.

Davis, Ronald. Duke: The Life and Image of John Wayne. Norman, University of Oklahoma Press, 1998.

Emrich, David. Hollywood, Colorado. Lakewood: Post Modern Company, 1997.

Everson, William K. The Hollywood Western. New York: Citadel Press, 1992.

Eyles, Alan. John Wayne. Cranbury: A.S. Barnes and Co., Inc., 1976.

Garza, Alicia A. "El Sauz, Texas. The Handbook of Texas Online." www.tsha.Utexas.edu.

Gossard, Jr., Wayne H. "Three Ring Circus: The Tom Mix-Zack Miller Lawsuits 1929-1934." The Chronicles of Oklahoma. Norman: The Oklahoma Historical Society, Vol. LV111, Number 1. Spring, 1980.

"Guide to the Joe D. Young/Richard J. Flood Collection, circa 1860-1975." National Cowboy and Western Heritage Museum. www.nationalcowboymusem.org.

Horwitz, James. They Went Thataway. New York: E.P. Dutton, 1976.

Kahn, Roger. A Flame of Pure Fire: Jack Dempsey and the Roaring '20s. New York: Harcourt Brace & Co., 1999.

Kasson, Joy. Buffalo Bill's Wild West: Celebrity, Memory and Popular History. New York: Hill and Wang, 2000.

Lamar, Howard R. The Readers Encyclopedia of the American West. New York: Thomas Y. Crowell Co, 1977.

Loader, Jayne. "Flygirls."www.publicshelter.com. 1997.

Lynam, Bill. "Tom Mix History Intertwined with Yavapai Hills subdivision." Sharlot Hall Museum Days Past. www.sharlot.org. December 8, 2002.

Maltin, Leonard. Leonard Maltin's 2001 Movie and Video Guide. New York: New American Library, 2001.

Mast, Gerald. A Short History of the Movies—Fourth Edition. New York: McMillan Publishing Company, 1986.

McClure, Arthur F. and Ken D. Jones. Heroes, Heavies and Sagebrush. South Brunswick: A.S. Barnes and Co., 1972.

McCoy, Tim and Ronald McCoy. Tim McCoy Remembers the West. Lincoln: University of Nebraska Press, 1977.

McLynn, Frank. <u>Villa and Zapata: A History of the Mexican Revolution</u>. New York: Carroll & Graf Publishers, 2000.

Mix Family Genealogy. <u>freepages.genealogy.rootsweb.com.</u>

Mix, Olive Stokes and Eric Heath. <u>The Fabulous Tom Mix</u>. Englewood Cliffs: Prentice-Hall, 1957.

Mix, Paul E. <u>Tom Mix: A Heavily Illustrated Biography with a Filmography.</u> Jefferson: McFarland, 1995.

Mix, Paul E. <u>The Life and Legend of Tom Mix.</u> Cranbury: A.S. Barnes and Co., Inc., 1972.

Moore, Colleen. <u>Silent Star</u>. Garden City: Doubleday & Company, Inc., 1968.

Mosley, Leonard. <u>Zanuck: The Rise and Fall of Hollywood's Last Tycoon</u>. New York: McGraw Hill, 1984.

"Mulhall Ranch, The." <u>www.jcs-group.com/oldwest/wildwestshow/mulhall.html</u>.

Nicholas, John H. <u>Tom Mix: Riding Up To Glory</u>. Oklahoma City: National Cowboy Hall of Fame, 1980.

Norris, Merle. <u>The Tom Mix Book</u>. Waynesville: The World of Yesterday, 1989.

Pfening, Fred D., Jr. "Tom Mix: His Life, His Films, His Circus." <u>Bandwagon</u>, Vol.46, No. 6, (Nov.-Dec. 2002).

Roberts, Randy and James Olson. <u>John Wayne: American</u>. Lincoln: University of Nebraska Press, 1995.

Robinson, C.O. "Tom Mix Was My Boss." <u>Frontier Times.</u> Vol. 43, No. 4, New Series No. 60. Austin: Western Publications, Inc., June, 1969.

Rosebrook, Jeb J. and Jeb S. Rosebrook. "Arizona's Celluloid Cowboys." <u>Arizona Highways</u>. July 1997. Vol. 73, Number 7. Phoenix: 1997.

Strait, Raymond. <u>Star Babies</u>. New York: Berkley, 1979.

Streible, Dan. "Tom Mix meet Mr. Trotsky: Newsreels and Out-takes as Documentary." www. s.edu/park-row.html.

St. John, Adela Rogers. *The Honeycomb*. New York: Doubleday & Co., 1969.

Swindell, Larry. *The Last Hero: A Biography of Gary Cooper*. New York: Doubleday, 1980.

Tyler, Ron, ed., *The New Handbook of Texas, Vol. 5*. Austin, Texas: Texas State Historical Association, 1996.

Virgines, George. "The Guns of Tom Mix." *Guns Magazine*. February, 1970.

Waldo, Anna Lee. *Prairie: The Legend of Charles Burton Irwin and the Y6 Ranch*. New York: Charter Books, 1986.

Wallis, Michael. *The Real Wild West: The 101 Ranch and the creation of the American West*. New York: St. Martin's Press, 1999.

Wayne, Aissa and Steve Delsohn. *John Wayne, My Father*. New York: Random House, 1991.

Wyatt, Edgar H. *The Hoxie Boys: The Lives and Films of Jack and Al Hoxie*. Raleigh: Wyatt Classics, Inc., 1992.

About the Author

Drawing on his life in the saddle and a wealth of other life experiences, Richard D. Jensen and his off-beat western novels have garnered legions of fans. His first book, *Ride the Wild Trail*, and his second book, *When Curly Won A Cathouse*, were instant hits with readers and critics alike. *Tristeza*, his third novel, was submitted for the Pulitzer Prize. He is also the author of the non-fiction book *Trespass In Hazzard County: My Life As An Insider on the Dukes of Hazzard*, a tell-all memoir of his life in Hollywood.

The Amazing Tom Mix—The Most Famous Cowboy of the Movies is the culmination of more than 30 years of research into the life of the most famous cowboy of the movies.

Jensen's latest novel, *Lazarus, Man In Black #1: The Gates of Hell*, is scheduled for release this fall.

Visit www.cowboynovels.com for more information about Richard D. Jensen and his books.

Other Books by Richard D. Jensen from www.cowboynovels.com

Ride the Wild Trail

When silent movie cowboy stars Tom Mix and Hoot Gibson are fired by their movie studios as the era of sound movies approaches, they decide to go on a jaunt with real-life lawman Wyatt Earp, who is near death. Together they take one last wild ride through the rapidly disappearing old west.

When Curly Won A Cathouse

Curly and Pudge are two aging, broke cowboys who spend their summers working the range and their winters holed up in a brothel in Kansas. When Curly wins the brothel in a poker game, what follows is a hysterical example of the old adage "be careful what you wish for because you might get it."

Trespass In Hazzard County—My Life As An Insider on The Dukes of Hazzard

Richard D. Jensen spent two years working on the hit television series The Dukes of Hazzard. This is his scandalous, tell-all autobiography, a frank account of the sex, drugs, double-dealing, back-biting and intrigue that went on behind-the-scenes of the cult classic.

Tristeza

Richard D. Jensen's stirring and enchanting new novel of life, death, redemption and reincarnation set in sultry Mexico in the 1930s. Drifting cowboy Will Riley (son of Pudge Riley from Jensen's hit novel *When Curly Won A Cathouse*) travels to sultry Mexico seeking adventure. He meets iconic real-life Mexican painters Diego Rivera and Frida Kahlo and Communist Party leader Leon Trotsky. He also encounters Tristeza, a smouldering beauty with limitless black hair and sparkling eyes who bewitches Will and sets him on a collision course with destiny. Unbeknownst to Will, a dark secret threatens Tristeza's very soul.

The Amazing Tom Mix—The Most Famous Cowboy of the Movies

The most famous movie cowboy of them all died in 1940 and is all but forgotten today. Tom Mix was a town marshal, a real plains cowboy, a rodeo champion and a wild west show cowboy who went on to become the #1 movie cowboy of silent films. Famous the world over for his squeaky clean image, Tom Mix lived in fear that his deep, dark secrets would be discovered and his career and his cherished image would be destroyed.

978-0-595-35949-3
0-595-35949-3

Made in the USA
Lexington, KY
03 August 2011